QUANTITATIVE ECONOMICS OF SOCIALISM

INPUT-OUTPUT APPROACHES

QUANTITATIVE ECONOMICS OF SOCIALISM

INPUT-OUTPUT APPROACHES

BY

MASAAKI KUBONIWA

ECONOMIC RESEARCH SERIES
No. 27
THE INSTITUTE OF ECONOMIC RESEARCH
HITOTSUBASHI UNIVERSITY
KUNITACHI TOKYO 186

KINOKUNIYA COMPANY LTD.
OXFORD UNIVERSITY PRESS

Printed in 1989

Published by Kinokuniya Company Ltd.
17-7 Shinjuku 3-chome, Shinjuku-ku,
Tokyo 163-91, Japan

Distributed in Japan by Kinokuniya Company Ltd.
Distributed outside Japan by Oxford University Press,
Walton Street, Oxford, OX2 6DP, England
and 200 Madison Avenue, New York, NY 10016, USA

ISBN 4-314-10014-1

Printed by
Kokusaibunken Insatsusha
Tokyo, Japan

To Takanobu

Preface

This book is based on the author's papers previously published in Japanese, American and Russian academic journals. The common subject of the chapters in this book is input-output and optimization analyses as they apply to theoretical, numerical and empirical studies of the socialist economies, particularly the Soviet economy.

The book is based in part on the contributions of Soviet mathematical economists, including V.V. Novozhilov, L.V. Kantorovich, V.D. Belkin, V.A. Volkonsky, E.B. Ershov and I.Ia. Vakhutinsky who were instrumental in developing theoretical, numerical and empirical techniques for the application of input-output theory to socialist planning and pricing. For the past ten years the author has pursued promising areas of inquiry identified by the Soviet economists listed above in order to further develop a general mathematical, quantitative economic analysis of socialism.

The book is divided into three general parts. Chapters 2, 3 and 4 are devoted to theoretical analysis. Chapters 5, 6 and 7 provide an empirical analysis based on actual data. The final part of the book offers the author's observations on current Soviet reform efforts.

The first chapter presents a short historical description of Soviet mathematical economics from the Russian revolution to the present *Perestroika* (restructuring) era in order to provide motivation and to clarify the author's interests of inquiry. It should be noted that the terms, "mathematical economics" or "quantitative economics," which are interchangeably used in the book, include both pure mathematical economics in the western sense as well as operational and empirical studies. The author also employs the term "quantitative economics" in place of the more commonly used Soviet term "economic-mathematical methods," as it is understood in the Soviet academic context.

The second chapter provides a description of the basic theory of optimal planning and pricing which has played a prominent role in Soviet-bloc economic theory and practice. This chapter also focuses on providing a mathematical framework for studying the relationship between Marx's labor values and optimal prices.

Chapters 3 and 4 present planning processes with stepwise aggregation and disaggregation that appropriately coordinate an aggregated model in the Central Planning Board with more detailed models at lower levels in an iterative manner.

Chapters 5 and 6 are concerned with conventional static input-output analyses in order to investigate the basic input-output structures of the Soviet and East European economies from a comparative view. These chapters also include preliminary comparative analysis of the USSR and U.S. economies.

Chapter 7 attempts an application of two proto-types of a dynamic input-output model for optimal planning and presents turnpike and optimal paths for the Soviet economy.

In the last chapter we survey price reform proposals put forward by Soviet mathematical economists who have provided the theoretical foundation for the new Soviet policy. While Chapters 1 through 7 are based on the author's original research, the material in Chapter 8 was compiled from contemporary Soviet sources.

The author feels that an extensive understanding of Soviet economic theory and practice can be gained by bringing together pieces of analysis and viewpoints which are elsewhere rather disconnected. The book leaves open for further research many important subjects: e.g., descriptive input-output analysis to follow and develop Professor Kornai's *Economics of Shortage*; applications of dynamic multi-sectoral models with gestation lags, which have been developed by Soviet mathematical economists. The author hopes, however, that the materials contained in this book will provide, in part, a base which will allow a more comprehensive and synthesized study of the quantitative economics of socialism. The author shares the opinion of the late Professor Leif Johansen and Professor Andras Brody who have felt that studying the quantitative economics of socialism will also serve in the development of quantitative economics in general.

The author offers special thanks to his university Professor Shinzaburo Koshimura, graduate school Professors Tsuneyoshi Seki, Noboru Miyanabe and Yoshiaki Nishimura, and my colleagues for their efforts on his behalf as well as their constant support and encouragement; Professors Tsuneaki Sato and Kiichi Mochizuki for their support and encouragement; Director Valery L. Makarov, Deputy Directors Nikolai Ia. Petrakov and Aleksei Iu. Sheviakov, Professor Viktor V. Volkonsky and their colleagues at the Central Economic Mathematical Institute of the USSR Academy of Sciences, where, for seven months in 1987, I had the opportunity to study Soviet mathematical economics and experience first hand the changes and rapid developments which are taking place in the Soviet Union today; Deputy Director Emil' B. Ershov of the Institute of Economics and Prognosis of Scientific and Technical Progress of the USSR Academy of Sciences for his careful reading of an early Russian version of Chapter 4 of this book; Professor Iury N. Cheremnykh of the Moscow State University for his helpful comments on an early Russian version of Chapter 7 of this book; Professor Vladimir G. Treml of Duke University for supplying essential data and for being a constant source of support and encouragement; and to Dr. Lev M. Dudkin who also provided encouragement while in the Soviet Union and later in the United States.

The author also thanks Ms. Fumiko Arita and Ms. Yumiko Matsue for their assistance in developing the computerized simulations which appear in the book; Ms. Michiko Katsuta for her diligent assistance during the writing of the book; and Mr. Ronald Siani for checking the English grammar with much patience. Acknowledged also is the financial assistance from the Ministry of Education of Japan in fiscal year 1988 (Grant No. 63530003).

A final thanks to my wife Kuniko for her patience and understanding which were sorely taxed during the writing of this book.

This book could not have been written without the help of all the people listed here, but any mistakes remain the sole responsibility of the author.

July 1988

MASAAKI KUBONIWA

CONTENTS

CONTENTS

Chapter 1

A SHORT HISTORICAL DESCRIPTION

OF SOVIET MATHEMATICAL ECONOMICS

1. Introduction

In this introductory chapter we provide a brief description of Soviet mathematical economics and the use of quantitative methods in Soviet economics and practice in a historical context in order to clarify our interests of inquiry.[1] In this chapter we focus attention on the contribution of the Soviet school of mathematical economics to the development of quantitative economics in general, and to Soviet economics in particular. We will also describe some of the difficulties which Soviet mathematical economists have faced.

The historical course of Soviet mathematical economics can be divided into the following five stages:

The first stage (1920's):   The heroic period

The second stage (1929 to 1953):   The purge years

The third stage (1954 to 1968):   Economic renaissance

The fourth stage (1969 to 1985):   The attempt at computerization

The fifth stage (1985 to the present):   *Perestroika* (restructuring)

In the following material we will summarize Soviet mathematical economics at each stage of its development.

---

[1]   See the standard English language surveys of Soviet mathematical economics in Johansen (1966), Zauberman (1967; 1976), Ellman (1973), Katsenelinboigen (1978) and Cave (1980).

2. The Heroic Period

In the 1920's, shortly after the Russian Revolution, a trial and error process began for the development of long-term programs for rapid socialist industrialization and the compilation of a new statistical database for nation-wide planning. As a result of these efforts proto-types of a modern macro growth model and an early form of input-output analysis were developed. The most notable achievements of this period were Fel'dman's growth model for industrialization (Fel'dman (1928)) and the *Balance sheet of the national economy of the USSR for 1923–4* (Popov ed. (1926)).

The Fel'dman model, a pioneering work in the field of macro growth theory, was employed by Harrod, Domar and many economists in developed and developing countries from the end of the 1950's to the 1960's.[2] Surprisingly, the Fel'dman model also provided a clear exposition of technical progress, defined by a shift of the production possibility curve.

The Balance sheet of the national economy of the USSR for 1923–4, compiled by the Central Statistical Administration (TsSU) in 1926, includes a balance of the production and use of the social products and national income, "chessboard" balance sheets of productive consumption and an investment balance sheet.[3] The production and use of the social product is broken down into 4 sectors and 37 products. Construction and publishing are distinguished as independent sectors. Leontief's input-output table can be constructed by merging the balance of production and use of the social product and the balance of national income.

Therefore, we can state that the TsSU balance sheet serves as a proto-type for the contemporary input-output table. Further, the TsSU (1926) balance sheet also includes the proto-type table for the capital matrix and the employment matrix. In the balance sheet a distinction is made between transactions in producers' prices and purchasers' prices.

In the TsSU monograph we can discern the fundamental concept of input-output analysis: "it is also important to clarify the relationship and

---

[2] Domar (1957, Ch. 9) provided a faithful, compact description of the Fel'dman model.
[3] See Nemchinov ed. (1959, Ch. 1).

interdependence between individual industry groups of the national economy."

Following this pioneering effort by TsSU, Barengol'ts (1928) presented a chessboard balance sheet for 11 industry sectors over a three year period, 1922–3, 1923–4 and 1924–5. This paper also presented the concepts of intermediate demand ratios and input coefficients, the latter constituting the starting point for Leontief's input-output analysis.

In addition to these pioneering efforts a number of other significant works appeared.

Slutsky, who formulated the Slutsky equation for consumers' demand before the revolution, continued to develop his study of the utility function (Slutsky (1927)) until his death in 1948. Surprisingly, in his paper, published in 1926, on "a contribution to the formal-praxiological foundations of economics," Slutsky stated that only those who were familiar with "modern mathematical economics" could see the possibility of establishing a system of precise concepts for economic systems or processes (Johansen (1977)).

Shatunovsky and Lubny-Gertsyk began to study the mathematical formulation of the "full (direct and indirect)" labor input of each product, based on Dmitriev (1904). In his book, Dmitriev presented an algebraic equation system for Ricardian labor values, or full labor inputs embodied in each product, which Marx simply formulated as $p = c + v + m$. The concept of the feedback relationship in production implies that a product is utilized as the intermediate input required for producing the product as well as others. This concept constitutes the core of Leontief's input-output analysis. Therefore, we may be correct in assuming that Dmitriev and other Soviet economists of the period provided Leontief with the primary tool required for the development of input-output "analysis."

Lubny-Gertsyk (1922) developed an iterative method for solving the Dmitriev equation system which can be considered the prototype of a simple iterative method for static input-output systems.[4] Later, Boiarsky

---

[4] See Lur'e (1957).

(1957) applied this method to a description of a decentralized procedure for determining "labor-value-prices." Nemchinov (1957) applied this method for the measurement of labor productivity in agriculture. It should be noted that the iterative method can be applied for describing the material-balances process, which is considered in Chapter 3.

Novozhilov (1926), stressing the need to preserve marked equilibrium in planning, mathematically analyzed an economy characterized by a chronic shortage of commodities, which today constitutes the central problem confronting the Soviet and East European economies. Novozhilov's work can be compared to Kornai's studies on the economics of shortages.

Bazarov (1927) discussed the problems of balanced growth and the use of variation calculus to solve the problem of optimal growth which became fashionable in mathematical economics after the end of the 1950's (DOSSO (1958)).

Iushkov (1928) discussed ways to create an optimal planning process that appropriately coordinates optimal national economic development with optimal operational independence for each unit of the economy. The task proposed by Iushkov has challenged a succession of Soviet mathematical economists who followed.[5]

We can state from the above observation that the 1920's can be characterized as the "heroic" period of Soviet mathematical economics. It should be noted that during this period the NEP (New Economic Policy), the system incorporating active market activities, prevailed in the Soviet Union.[6]

3. The Purge Years

The "heroic" period came to an end in 1929 with Stalin's total assumption of social, political and economic power. Stalin attempted to end the NEP system and redirect the Soviet economy back to the "War

---

[5] Ellman (1973, p. 1) posed the contemporary significance of Iushkov's work.

[6] The similarity between NEP and *Perestroika* is a current topic for discussion in the Soviet Union; e.g., see Shmelev (1987).

Communism" system, which existed during the 1918-21 period, and is characterized by quantity-oriented planning, over-centralization, and reliance on administrative methods for economic management.[7]

Stalin pursued the goal of rapid industrialization and the collectivization of agriculture by means of a centralized management system. To achieve these aims he began a purge of many notable economists and non-Bolsheviks, including Fel'dman, Vainshtein, Kondratiev, Preobrazhensky, Chaianov, Groman and Bazarov. The result was an almost total elimination of the use of mathematical methods in Soviet economic theory and practice.

It is well known that in a speech at a conference of agricultural experts in December 1929, Stalin referred to the pioneering balance of the national economy developed by TsSU as a "game with figures."

In place of creative autonomy Stalin fostered the cult of personality and dogmatism, which severely restricted the activities of Soviet economists. However, even during this period some economists, the most prominent being Novozhilov and Kantorovich, retained the spirit of creativity. Novozhilov developed his theories in the 1920's and published the results in 1939, 1941 and 1946. Kantorovich, a notable mathematician, was the first to develop mathematically formulated linear programming (LP). Kantorovich's work on linear programming first appeared in 1939.[8] (Independent of Soviet mathematical economics, G. Dantzig invented the simplex method for linear programming in 1947). Novozhilov and Kantorovich were also pioneers in clarifying that Lagrange multipliers, or shadow prices, associated with the primal optimization problem of production, should serve as the basis of socialist price formation and decentralized planning.

By some stroke of good fortune Nemchinov survived the purges, but

---

[7] War Communism is the prototype of a Soviet-type centralized system. See also Shmelev (1987).

[8] Kantorovich's work published in 1939 is included in Nemchinov ed. (1959, pp. 251-309). Novozhilov's work at that time is also summarized in this book (Ch. 2). See also Kantorovich (1987), published after his death in 1986, where Kantorovich looked back upon his scientific activities, including his classical work of linear programming.

Stalin's prejudice toward the use of mathematical economic methods prevailed until his death in 1953.

4. Economic Renaissance

Soon after Stalin's death, Soviet economics and statistics began to be released from the confines imposed by the cult of personality and dogmatism. During the 1954 national congress of statisticians, advocates of mathematical methods who had been labeled as "mathematically-and-formalistically-biased" during the Stalinist era, had their tarnished reputations restored.[9] At the end of the 1950's, in order to allow economics to serve as a "flood light projector" for national economic planning, Soviet economists were given governmental approval to develop precise and strict quantitative tools. They were also empowered to incorporate mathematical methods into the study of economics and to use computers for economic calculations. Soviet authorities also approved the application of input-output analysis and the optimization theory to the centrally planned economies. In 1957 a preliminary version of the Soviet input-output table began to be compiled, and the first Soviet input-output table was published in 1961. Since 1956 TsSU has published the Soviet statistical yearbook (*Narkhoz*). Economists who were purged during the Stalin era, including Vainshtein, were allowed to return to Moscow and had their Soviet citizenships restored. In addition, important works of Kantorovich and Novozhilov, which had remained in obscurity, were collectively republished in a book edited by Nemchinov (Nemchinov (1959)). Slutsky's classical work was also republished (*Ekonomiko-matematicheskie* ..., 1963). (However, it was only due to the reforms of the *Perestroika* era that Kondratiev's classical work on the business cycle was authorized for republication in 1988).

The Laboratory of Economic Mathematical Methods, under the directorship of Nemchinov, was attached to the USSR Academy of Sciences in 1958. The laboratory was enlarged and re-established as the Central Economic Mathematical Institute (TsEMI) in 1963. In 1965 TsEMI

---

[9] *Uchenye zapiski po statistike*, Vol. III, 1957, p. 6.

began to publish a new journal, *Economics and Mathematical Methods* (*Ekonomika i matematicheskie metody*) under the editorship of N. P. Fedorenko. In 1961 a Scientific Council of the USSR Academy of Sciences on the Uses of Mathematics and Computers in Economic Studies and Planning was established. Prior to the establishment of this Council a Scientific Council of the USSR Academy of Sciences on Cybernetics under the direction of Berg was established, and cybernetics was approved as a field of science compatible with "dialectical materialism"(Cave (1980, Ch. 1)).

In 1961 the Laboratory of Economic Mathematical Studies, located in the Siberian city of Novosibirsk and under the direction of Aganbegian, was attached to the Institute of Economics and the Organization of Industrial Production (IEOPP) of the Siberian Branch of the USSR Academy of Sciences. In 1967 IEOPP was reorganized in order to study the application of statistical and mathematical methods to economic analysis, also under the direction of Aganbegian. Research on quantitative and mathematical economics in Siberia was also begun under the leadership of Kantorovich in the Department of Mathematical Economics of the Institute of Mathematics of the Siberian Branch of the USSR Academy of Sciences in 1960. This department was later headed by Makarov, who assumed the directorship of TsEMI in 1985. It should be noted that Aganbegian's and Kantorovich-Makarov's scientific activities were closely coordinated with the research taking place in the Computer Center of the Siberian Branch of the USSR Academy of Sciences, whose director was Marchuk (now the President of the USSR Academy of Sciences).[10]

During this period extremely active debates took place, attended by a large number of economists and mathematicians, on a series of problems regarding economic planning and calculations, including the law of value and price formation. This period can best be characterized as a *renaissance* of Soviet economics.

---

[10] See Shemetov (1983, Ch. 2). This book provides a detailed historical survey of the development of economic studies in Siberia.

During these debates Soviet mathematical economists played a leading role. The advocates of optimal planning and pricing theory clarified the close interrelationship between production planning, measurement of productivity, price formation, investment efficiency and the optimal allocation of scarce resources, and stressed the need to study these problems simultaneously and collectively. Traditional, neo-Stalinist political economists, such as Mstislavsky (1961), on the other hand, considered that these problems should be investigated separately rather than collectively.

Optimal pricing theory clarified that the Marx production price-type of price formation is necessary to rationally utilize capital stock and to eliminate inequity due to distinct technological conditions among sectors and/or enterprises. Optimal pricing theory also stresses the need for price formation based on marginal costs and for the introduction of payments for the use of resource stocks, including fixed capital stock, natural resources and labor resources. On the other hand, traditional political economists (e.g. Kats and Mstislavsky) and conservative mathematical economists (e.g. Boiarsky) labeled the reformers as advocates of "bourgeois marginalism" and insisted that the "factual value" provided by the Dmitriev value equation or price formation based on the Soviet prime cost concept (*Sebestoimost'*) reflects the core of Socialist price formation, based on Marx's labor theory of value.

In opposition to the conservative political and mathematical economists, the reformers clarified that the methodological errors inherent in the traditional approach were caused by the separate and isolated analysis of inter-related economic issues. Kantorovich and the notable mathematician Kolmogolov defended the use of the marginal principle in economic calculations, by insisting that "marginalism" contributed to progress in a wide range of scientific fields, and made possible the successful launching of the Sputnik satellite. Kantorovich also defended the optimal pricing theory by stating that it was impossible and also unnecessary to try to prove in a purely mathematical and formal way the nature of labor as the sole source of values (as an example of this argument it is mathematically impossible to prove whether a person pedaling a bicycle is moving the bicycle or whether the bicycle is moving the person)(*Obshchie...*, 1961, pp. 266–267). The advocates of "marginal" pricing and "average" pricing have conducted heated debates regarding the theoretical relationships and differences between these two pricing theories, but have not been able to reach any satisfactory conclusions. One reason is that conservative economists have yet to develop their theory of values from a quantitative mathematical point of view. Another reason is that optimal pricing theorists, Novozhilov, Kantorovich and Nemchinov have also been unable to reach a consensus among themselves. Therefore, we will attempt to clarify the relationship between optimal prices, based on the marginal principle, and labor values, based on the average principle, in Chapter 2. It should be noted that mathematical development of the theory of labor values beyond the level of the original Dmitriev equation has been carried out by scholars in the West, including Professors Okishio and Morishima, particularly in the 1970's.

Optimal planning theorists, including Novozhilov and Kantorovich, have also clarified the possibility and necessity of a transition from a centralized, quantity-guided economic management system to a decentralized price-guided system. Novozhilov proposed "indirect centralization," where enterprises are guided to socially optimal decisions by the establishment of appropriate rules of enterprise behavior [present cost (including capital charges and payments for natural resources) minimization or profit maximization] and appropriate economic parameters (prices, rental prices of capital stock and rents for natural resources). Novozhilov (1959, pp. 171–172) wrote:

"The centralized management of the economy can be realized in two basic forms: direct and indirect. For example, the demand for a scarce metal can be regulated either by limiting its cost or by fixing a higher price."

"Indirect centralization consists in establishing rules and economic parameters for the calculation of cost and benefits, with the help of which the 'peripheries' (sic, enterprises) can themselves find the best alternatives for the use of their efforts and means-the best from the point of view of the whole economy, corresponding to its optimal development plan."

"Planning includes both forms of centralization, the experience of the development of a socialist society having shown both to be necessary. Direct centralization is a basic form of planning; it is essential also to indirect centralization, since a scientifically established system of rules and economic parameters for the calculation of costs and benefits can be developed only from the plan as a whole. Thus, with indirect centralization each question (even the smallest) is answered jointly by the center and the 'peripheries.' The center works out the general rules and economic parameters for its solution, the 'periphery' applies these rules and economic parameters to each particular case."

"Only by the combination of these two forms of centralization can there be the greatest development of the planning principle and the widest democracy in economic development."

To demonstrate this theory, Novozhilov presented a mathematical formulation of his indirect centralization planning process, which is similar to, but preceded, the Arrow-Hurwicz process.

Kantorovich (1959) also clarified the possibility of market-oriented, decentralized decision-making by using the concept of the "relative stability" of optimal (shadow) prices, which is now considered an application of sensitivity analysis of linear programming. His main point is as follows. Optimal prices which are found by solving an optimization problem are logically associated only with the optimal production plans. The detailed decisions to be taken by the enterprises are concerned with questions such as whether certain new or modified production methods should be introduced, which were not fully taken into account in the *ex-ante* formalized plan calculations. To the extent that these circumstances are outside the *ex-ante* formalized plan calculations and are of a small order of magnitude, the shadow prices obtained will not deviate very much from the unknown "true" optimal prices which are to be computed by using all the detailed, complete information. Due to this the calculated shadow prices can be a basis for decisions regarding circumstances not formally covered by the model. It should be noted that this idea of Kantorovich's as well as Novozhilov's indirect centralization process assumes the prevalence of the full profit-and-loss accounting (*khozraschet*) of each economic unit.

The advocates of optimal planning and pricing theory were subjected to malevolent criticism by traditional conservative economists. While the debate, which began in the 1960's, continues to rage at the present time, it appears that the advocates for reform had their points of view accepted by some high governmental officials, including then Prime Minister Kosygin. Symbolic of the partial victory achieved by the reformers was the speech by Kosygin at the September 1965 Plenum of the CPSU Central Committee, in which he announced the adoption of the economic method of nationwide management in place of the former administrative method and the introduction of payments for fixed capital and the new material incentive funds for enterprises.

When we consider the background of the re-establishment and development of Soviet mathematical economics, we must consider two things, in addition to the cult of personality.

One is related to the stage of development of the Soviet economy. *Some* Soviet authorities strongly felt the need for a transitional policy to soften the switch from the traditional Soviet management system, based on centralized, quantity-oriented, administrative methods, to a new planning and management system based on decentralized, price-guided, economic methods. This was thought necessary, because even though the Soviet economy had attained the goal of industrialization, it required more widely balanced and efficient economic development. It was not the traditional political economist, but rather the mathematical economist or optimal planning theorist who provided the consistent theoretical foundation for the above requirement. The authorities planned to implement this change in the 1965 economic reform. Mathematical economics provided the economic backbone for this reform. However, it should be noted that this reflects only one aspect of the relationships between the authorities and the mathematical school of Soviet economics.

The second, which the author feels is more important, is that the concurrent advances in electronic computers in the 1950's and 60's caused some Soviet authorities to reconsider the use of mathematical models for planning since they eliminated the need for radical economic reforms. For example, in the publisher's preface of the above-cited work (Nemchinov ed. (1959)), which shows the re-establishment of Soviet mathematical economics, we find nothing to establish mathematical methods as the basic theory of economic management with decentralized economic methods. The logic contained in the preface is as follows: the nation-wide use of computers in planning is required to strengthen the technical planning base; the weakness of the study of mathematical methods hinders the use of computers; the study of mathematical methods must be actively pursued.

At first glance, it appears that the authorities accorded approval of the reform proposal put forward by Soviet mathematical economists. However, in actuality, the authorities intended only to make use of mathematical economists in order to develop the use of computers in planning, and did not, in fact, accept the active role of market and value relations at the expense of the state plan. This fact did not appear clearly until 1968 when Warsaw Treaty forces entered Czechoslovakia in response to that country's adoption of market-oriented policies and democratization of the political system.

Before moving on to the next stage, the author would like to summarize the main achievements of Soviet mathematical economists during the renaissance period.

1. the compilation and arrangement of an input-output database.

2. the application of an input-output database to central pricing and planning.

3. the clarification of the economic implications of optimal planning and pricing theory and the theory of decentralized optimal planning and their theoretical formulation.

4. the foundation of stepwise or iterative aggregation and disaggregation processes.

The first two achievements are related to the discussion in Chapters 5, 6, 7 and 8. The third achievement is discussed in Chapter 2. The last one is discussed in Chapters 3 and 4.

5. The Attempt at Computerization

The reform developed by Soviet mathematical economists, including Novozhilov, Kantorovich, Nemchinov, Aganbegian and Belkin, was based on two concepts which they felt must be adopted in toto: the creation of a computer network linking the central planning authorities and enterprises and the enterprises themselves; and the development of market relations ("autonomous feedback-control mechanism") and autonomy of each enterprise (see e.g. Novozhilov (1967)).

The authorities, including Brezhinev, viewed the use of computer networks as useful tools for the "rationalization" of a centralized economy. However, approval was not granted for the development of market relations. In point of fact, B. Stukalin, the Chairman of the Committee on the Press of the Council of Ministers, in an article in Pravda (Nov. 10, 1971) criticized the work of Petrakov (Petrakov (1970)), (who is well known as an advocate of the development of market relations), as an example of how economists sometimes fail to meet the requirements of the 21st Party Congress and are guilty of serious methodological errors and incorrect treatment of certain political and economic issues.[11] The lack of approval for the development of market relations seriously weakened the effectiveness of Soviet economic science and hindered the development and reform of the economic mechanism.

A stagnant, negative tone characterized Soviet economic thought, as well as other aspects of Soviet life, until the April 1985 Plenum of the CPSU Central Committee. The improvement and development of Soviet mathematical economics in this period was contradictory. On the one hand, the theoretical core of mathematical economics was subjected to malevolent criticism by the advocates of neo-Stalinist political economy, including many bureaucrats and economists such as Tsagolov and Cherkovets. On the other hand, Soviet authorities required the assistance of mathematical economists, since the neo-Stalinist economists could not provide concrete policy measures which required economic calculations.

In the 1970's the Soviet Union conducted a series of studies on the

---

[11]   See Ellman (1973, p. 204).

economic evaluation of natural resources, in which Soviet mathematical economists played a leading role. These economists proposed the introduction of payments for natural resources, but payments were not introduced for the use of land and water resources for agriculture because of the active opposition of the State Prices Commission (Goskomtsen). It should be noted, none-the-less, that the method developed by Soviet economists for the monetary evaluation of natural resources and products of the extractive industries have come to be widely used in local planning practice. In 1983, an authoritative interdepartmental commission prepared the Comprehensive Guidelines on Evaluating the Effectiveness of Social Production and Individual Economic Measures. In the course of preparation of this guideline, Soviet mathematical economists played a central role. However, these guidelines received a hostile reception since they attacked the traditional concept of pricing, investment efficiency indicators and current-oriented effectiveness. In the opinion of the leaders of the Central Planning Board the guidelines undermined the pillars of the centralized planning system.[12]

Mathematical economists also developed scientific methods for forecasting scientific-technical progress and formulated the principles of goal programming. This method became part of the practice, first and foremost, of the management of scientific-technical progress, not withstanding the resistance of some leaders of the central planning agencies.[13]

Even though Soviet mathematical economists were forced to abandon their position as advocates of economic reform, their efforts resulted in an improvement in Soviet mathematical economics. In the early 1970's economists on the staff of TsEMI developed a comprehensive, optimizing concept, namely, the optimal functioning of a socialist economy, SOFE (Fedorenko ed. (1972)). The central concept of "SOFE" is the possibility and necessity of developing and creating a step-by-step system for the optimal planning of the national economy, based on mathematical methods and computers.

---

[12] Academician Fedorenko's response to questions from *Kommunist* ("Ekonomicheskaia...", 1987). He was director of TsEMI for twenty years until 1985.
[13] *ibid.*

While neo-Stalinist economists, who executed control over Soviet economic theory, criticized the "SOFE" concept, it was supported by the Soviet authorities, since Soviet mathematical economists did not explicitly mention that "SOFE" assumes the development of nation-wide market relations.[14]

The main result of the "SOFE" concept in the 1970's was a system composed of multiple models developed at TsEMI (Baranov and Matlin (1976)).[15] A large-scale computerized simulation of this system was carried out at the Main Computer Center (GVTs) attached to Gosplan. The simulation covering ten-year period incorporated 98 products produced by 16 sector complexes, 78 categories of consumer goods, 33 categories of labor, seven natural resources and 24 regions. In the experimental solution of the system of models, it is assumed that the regional models maximizing regional income are first solved; consistency of the results is checked by the center (with regard to shortage producer goods they are assumed to be assigned by the center) ; sector-complex models maximizing profits are then solved; their solutions are fed back into the regional models and the next round iteration begins. Demand for consumer goods is estimated by using several types of econometric regression models, namely a central decision of demand schedule is not assumed. In the experimental iterative solution process many techniques of mathematical programming, including iterative aggregation and decomposition methods, are employed without assigning any particular economic meaning to them.

Construction of this type of nation-wide optimization system employing different optimal models can be regarded as the principal improvement in Soviet optimal planning theory in the 1970's. Unlike the "decomposition" method for solving an optimization problem with a single

[14] This aspect has not been clearly reflected in the Soviet literature up to date. Katsenelinboigen (1978) attempted to clarify the paradoxical role of the Soviet optimal planning concept in the 1970's. According to Professor Katsenelinboigen, the optimal planning concept serves the political purposes of the most reactionary members of the Soviet Politburo.

[15] An optimization system of multiple models was also constructed at IEOPP (Aganbegian et al. (1972a); (1972b)). See also Fedorenko et al. (1972).

objective function, the system developed by TsEMI did not assume a global optimization problem with a functional welfare function. In this system sectoral and regional optimization models were first set. Next, in the system composed of these models coordination of individual interests were pursued toward a "general equilibrium." The developers of this system called their method the "composition" method.[16] This is an interesting and important development for quantitative economics in general.

The coordination of the self-interests of different groups is one of the most important tasks for a socialist economy. The system of models served as a study for this aspect of the problem. While the developers of the simulation hailed the results as positive and the "composition" method provided a Soviet version of formulating "general equilibrium", the author feels that the results of the computerized simulation did not provide a positive means for economic reforms, since it did not provide any positive proposal for reforming price formation and extending autonomy for individual enterprises.

While decrees were adopted for the introduction of the above system, it was not implemented since most of the branch ministries stopped submitting the necessary data, fearing that Gosplan would cut their capital investment after making optimization calculations.[17] This was due in part to the prejudiced attitudes of the ministries toward mathematical economics. More importantly, the author feels that even minor improvements in economic performance which were brought about by the adoption of the simulation were not as effective as they could have been because of the low level of marketization, the restriction in the flow of information, and the general lack of openness and democratization which characterize the Soviet bureaucratic system. It should also be noted that in the past this system has been successful in thwarting any economic reforms which it opposed.

It should be further noted here that the attitudes of Soviet authorities

[16] See also *Matematika* ..., 1975, pp. 199–201.
[17] Fedorenko, *ibid*.

in accepting the need for computerization, while rejecting marketization and pluralism of the economic mechanism, resulted in the failure of the attempt at computerization. It should also be noted that while Soviet authorities emphasized the development of "high-technology" systems in the civilian area, it was clear by the end of the 1970's that their attempt had ended in failure. We characterize 1968 to 1985, the "third stage," as the attempt at computerization. Ironically, this attempt ended in total failure and caused the Soviet Union to fall even further behind the developed capitalist countries, especially in the field of high-technology.

Before completing this section we would like to describe the accomplishments of Soviet mathematical economists during this period.

1. The construction of a nation-wide optimization system composed of multiple models, by employing the "composition" (in contrast to the "decomposition") method and computerized simulations.

2. Studies of a variety of dynamic input-output models and computerized simulations.

3. Construction of stepwise aggregation and disaggregation processes for optimal planning.

4. Development of economic forecasting methods.[18]

5. Construction of the framework for a material-monetary balance and the Soviet system of national accounting, compatible with the United Nations SNA.

6. Development of the theory of economic efficiency in the use of economic resources.

7. Development of the theory of price formation, where prices satisfying the "self-financial" principle are determined during the process of compilation of the national economic plan.

Items 1 and 4, have been previously discussed. Item 2 is related to the discussion in Chapter 7. Item 3 is critically discussed in Chapter 4. Items 5, 6 and 7 form the basis for the new economic reforms discussed briefly in the following section and in detail in Chapter 8.

---

[18] Anchishkin (1973) also constitutes one of the accomplishments during this period.

6. *Perestroika*

As a result of the abandonment of economic reform in 1968 the Soviet Union faced the prospect of 'zero' economic growth and lacked the mechanisms required to redirect the economy to more intensive growth paths. Following the death of Brezhinev, Andropov, who deeply understood the actual extent of the social and economic crisis which was apparent in 1979 to 1982, began the reorganizing of the Soviet economy, but died before substantial efforts could be achieved. He was followed by Chernenko, a conservative protege of Brezhinev, who had sharply criticized TsEMI by claiming that it did not provide significant studies of actual economic problems (*Pravda*, June 15, 1983, p. 1). His efforts to turn back the clock of reform ended when he died in 1985.

In March of the same year, Gorbachev was named as the First Secretary of CPSU. While consolidating his power over the next two years, Gorbachev, in part, continued the policies developed under Andropov, i.e., on-going, large-scale economic experiments and an anti-alcohol program. He also claimed his intention to undertake the acceleration (*Uskorenie*) of modernization of Soviet industry, particularly the machine building industry. At first glance it appeared that Gorbachev had adopted a conservative approach toward economic reform, but in actuality, during this period he began to lay the foundation for the economic reform movement which has come to be known as *Perestroika*.

Soviet mathematical economists, including Aganbegian, Petrakov, Belkin, and Anchishkin (died in June of 1987), once again pressed for the economic reforms they advocated in the 1960's. Advocates of the development of market relations, who were subjected to malevolent criticism by neo-Stalinist economists during the Brezhinev era, began to mount an active attack on the neo-Stalinist political economy ("modernized Stalinist political economy"), where market relations are recognized as alien to planned economic development, as opposed to relations that are already "communistic" and as capitalist "birthmarks" surviving under socialism (Rakitsky (1987)).

An interesting development during this period was the transfer from Siberia to Moscow of leading economists, including Aganbegian (who was transferred from the IEOPP and assumed the position of Academic Secretary in charge of the Economics Department of the USSR Academy of Sciences), and Makarov (who was transferred from the Institute of Mathematics of the Siberian branch of the USSR Academy of Sciences and assumed the position of Director of TsEMI). The second development, which occurred in 1985, was the reorganization of TsEMI. This reorganization involved the dividing of TsEMI into two separate entities; two- thirds (approximately 800 researchers) of the original organization remained in TsEMI while the remaining one-third (approximately 350) were grouped in a new organization named the Institute of Economics and Prognosis of Scientific and Technical Progress (IEPNTP) of the USSR Academy of Sciences, under the directorship of Anchishkin. When this reorganization was announced many economists and political scientists in the West assumed that this represented an anti-reform movement on the part of the Soviet authorities and a reduction in the power of Soviet mathematical economists to effect reform. However, in the opinion of the author, this reorganization was rational, in that broke up what had heretofore been a "giant", inefficient, centralized organization into smaller entities which could be better managed and which could undertake clearer goals. If this reorganization had resulted in the adoption of conservative concepts, it would have meant the failure of the reform movement. This, however, is not the case. In point of fact both organizations are being directed by, and employ, advocates of radical economic reform. The author feels that much greater efforts must be made to further the process of decentralization of these scientific organizations in order to improve their efficiency and to expedite the progress of creative research.

Gorbachev's radical *Perestroika* plan was presented to the Central Committee Plenum in June of 1987 and the new Soviet "Law on the State Enterprise" was adopted by the Supreme Soviet at the same time. These radical reform plans are mainly based on proposals provided by Soviet mathematical economists in the 1960's, particularly those of the late Academician Nemchinov. The reforms for the nationalized sector include the radical development of autonomy for enterprises (socialist "commodity" producers), self-financing (full profit-and-loss accounting), market relations, radical changes in the price and finance system, "self-management" and the introduction of the election of managerial personnel. These measures, which were approved in 1987, go far beyond the concepts of the 1965 reform.

In 1986 and 1987, approval was also given to allow the development of pluralism in the economic mechanism, namely, development of the non-nationalized sectors, including cooperative and individual labor activities, but excluding private economic activities. This implies that a radical change has taken place in the fundamental ideological concept of the Soviet-type centralized system. The goal of convergence of multiple sectors to a single, monolithic nationalized sector has been rejected by Soviet authorities.

In tandem with the economic reforms, Soviet sociologists and economists also stressed the importance of the role of human factors in socio-economic activities, and their suggestions were accepted by the Soviet leadership (Aganbegian (1987)).

According to Makarov, the new director of TsEMI, by taking the interaction between production and the human factors and the pluralistic economic mechanism into consideration, it will be possible to develop the old SOFE concept, while at the same time developing a new concept, which he tentatively labeled SOFE-2. Makarov compares the relationship of SOFE and SOFE-2 to the relationship between Newtonian mechanics and Einstein's theory of relativity, i.e., the latter provides a more complete explanation for events than the former, but both concepts are complementary.[19] Since the SOFE-2 concept is still under development at this time, it has not yet been presented in a concrete form.

Scholars on the staff of TsEMI has begun to contribute to the preparation of the price and finance reforms. While their proposals for price revisions, based on input-output and marginal analysis, seem to the author to be a step in the right direction, Soviet mathematical economists

---

[19] Based on the author's record of an interview with V. L. Makarov (Kuboniwa (1987)). See also Makarov (1987).

are facing two difficulties. One is the "state commercial order system (*goszakaz*)," which Nemchinov proposed more than 20 years ago and which has been implemented in place of "obligatory target figures" (command) under the Gorbachev reforms. The second is the *Uskorenie* policy, drawn up by Soviet mathematical economists, and which was also implemented during the first two years under the Gorbachev regime. The large scale application of the "state commercial order system" can easily be bypassed by the traditional centralized resource allocation system.[20] The *Uskorenie* policy stresses rapid growth, but is in actuality a deterrent to true economic reform since the *Uskorenie* policy and economic reform cannot take place simultaneously. Also, the rush toward modernization of industry may lead to quantitative growth only in the heavy industry sector with no increase in the production of consumption goods.[21]

One striking difference between the 1965 and 1987 reforms is that the latter must address the problem of material-monetary imbalance, which is reflected in the extremely high level of personal savings. This high level of personal savings also results in a high level of excessive financial resources in enterprises, which in turn leads to economic distortions and accelerates the potential inflationary process. Excess financial resources and a shortage of goods represent different sides of the same coin. As was mentioned in the previous section, Soviet mathematical economists have sought to develop the theory of material-monetary balance. Isaev attempted to compile a synthesized material monetary balance which corresponds to the United Nations SNA (Isaev (1972) and Dadaian ed. (1973, Ch. 4)). In the 1970's, Belkin and Ivanter also made efforts to complete an extended input-output balance, including service activities and material-monetary balance, which they called the "income-commodity model." In 1983, they published the results of an analysis of the Soviet material-monetary imbalance (Belkin and Ivanter (1983)). Following this work, Belkin, Medovedev and Nit (1986) proposed a theory of marketization of the Soviet economy, in which the most important

[20] See Chapter 8 in the text.

[21] Along this line, Seliunin, an able economic journalist, criticized Aganbegian (Seliunin (1988)).

precondition of Soviet marketization is the absorption of excess financial resources. In order to absorb these financial resources they propose the extension of the market for light industry, followed by the extension of the market for heavy industry.

One of the recent developments of Soviet economics can be seen in the emphasis accorded to studies related to the problem of the chronic shortages of goods. Gorbachev, as well as prominent mathematical economists, have admitted that marketization is required in order to eliminate the shortages of goods (*Pravda*, June 10, 1987). It has previous been thought that marketization for a product would proceed once the shortage of that particular product was eliminated. It is now recognized that marketization must come first.

Recently, Soviet economists and sociologists[22] have shown keen interest in the work *Economics of Shortage* written by Professor Janos Kornai, although some conservative factions still remain entirely opposed to the theories developed by Kornai.[23] While work is presently in progress regarding disequilibrium factors,[24] efforts to create a Soviet analysis of shortages compatible with Kornai's work have still not been finalized.

Here, it is worth pointing out two controversial problems which are closely related to the dilemmas facing a socialist economy, as clarified by Kornai (1986).

One is the conflict between the need for efficiency and the socialist "ethical" requirement of full employment. Shmelev (1987), in cooperation with notable mathematical economists including Anchishkin and Shatalin, criticized the present state of the Soviet economy by pointing out two fundamental drawbacks of the system, namely the producer's monopoly in the face of general shortage and the lack of *entrepreneurship*

---

[22] Shubkin (1987) discussed the relationship between the Soviet bureaucrat system and shortages of goods, employing Kornai's work. Latsis (1987) and Aganbegian(1987) stressed the importance of assimilating Kornai's work.

[23] Smekhov, a conservative quantitative economist criticized Kornai's theory from the viewpoint of traditional socialism (Smekhov (1987)).

[24] For example, Matlin presented macro econometric growth models incorporating disequilibrium factors in Matlin and Bardina (1986, Ch. 1).

(the enterprise's lack of interest in pursuing innovation), and clarified the need to develop the market mechanism entirely throughout the Soviet economy. Shmelev's paper was rapidly popularized by the Soviet authorities. However, Gorbachev and leading reformists, including Aganbegian and Petrakov, did not concur with Shmelev's challenging attempt to present a Soviet "natural" rate of unemployment to raise the efficiency of the economy (Aganbegian (1987) and Petrakov (1987c)). The author feels that Aganbegian and Petrakov are too optimistic regarding the possibility of reconciling the need for efficiency and full employment requirements since full employment in the Soviet Union has been made possible by the simplistic policy of maintaining the generally low level of the workers' real income (Ellman (1979, p. 187)). This fact will make it difficult to streamline the bureaucracy and improve its efficiency.

Another point to be considered is the possibility of attaining social equilibrium which combines social security and economic efficiency. Petrakov (1987c) argued this problem as follows. When considering government subsidies for worker's security, price deviations from the equilibrium level are observed for a large set of goods and resources. Thus the system of social security comes up against the neo-classical equilibrium axioms and a narrow interpretation of production efficiency. However, since government is responsible for social security and for the fulfillment of adopted public priorities, we should admit that policy is oriented towards social multi-dimensional rationality. Deviation from the traditional equilibrium point results in the difference between producer and consumer prices for some basic goods. A low price stimulates higher consumer demand and, in order to meet this excess demand the producer incurs additional costs which cannot be recovered due to the low price. The difference is covered by subsidies. Without claiming any theoretical conditions, Petrakov concludes that this results in a new equilibrium point representing social priorities by deforming economically rational equilibrium conditions. Of course, he did not forget to stress that subsidies must be sufficient to ensure that the system passes into a new equilibrium, otherwise shortages and "gray" or "black" marketing may arise. However, Petrakov considered that this is far from being an inherent feature of a socialist economy, as Kornai suggests. In the author's opinion, the difference between the Petrakov and Kornai positions is that Petrakov is much more optimistic for the attaining of the social equilibrium or the harmonizing of social security and efficiency than Kornai.

Whether the Soviet economy is truly involved in the process of radical economic reform is debatable at this time. However, Gorbachev's policy of *Glosnost'* (openness) has radically enlarged the scope of Soviet intellectual criticism directed at a wide range of economic, political and social problems. The most important phenomena to date, in terms of the development of Soviet quantitative economics, has been the outspoken criticism of the level of quality of official Soviet statistical data and the bureaucratic tendency toward secrecy. For example, official Soviet statistics claim that national income increased 90 times from the period 1928 to 1985 (without publishing the national income deflators which reflect actual economic conditions). However, in their study of national income, Seliunin and Khanin (1987) found the growth rate to be only 6 to 7 times for the same period . The consensus of opinion of most Soviet economists who have "hungered" for reliable, adequate statistical data is that the bureaucratic system, which was developed during the Purge years, must be radically changed. In 1987 TsSU was reorganized as the State Statistics Commission (Goskomstat). The reorganization resulted in elevating the authority of the Central Statistical Administration to the level of a Commission. While the degree of openness practiced by this newly organized entity still leaves much to be desired, some changes are apparent. For example, in order to achieve growth in terms of quality, Goskomstat compiled GNP or GDP indicators which are commonly used in the West, and published the Soviet GNP growth rate for the first time on January 24, 1988 in *Pravda*. In order to improve the compilation methods[25] Goskomstat has sought the assistance of Soviet and American

---

[25] The present methodology for calculation of the Soviet GNP is described in Goskomstat and Gosplan (1988).

quantitative economists. This represents a radical change in Soviet attitude.

The signs of change in Soviet quantitative economics have been numerous since the start of the Gorbachev reform movement. However, concrete achievements in a mathematical context have yet to be produced, with the exception of the price revision proposal of TsEMI. This proposal is discussed in detail in Chapter 8.

Chapter 2

BASIC THEORY OF OPTIMAL PLANNING

AND PRICING

1. Introduction

After Stalin, as is now well known, the optimization approach to planning and pricing has played a constructive role in Soviet-block economic theory. During the last three decades a great deal of work has been carried out in the field of optimal planning and pricing; Novozhilov and Kantorovich being prominent as pioneers. It may be said that the optimization approach theory has been used to lay logical and computational foundations for an efficient and democratic planning system in general. Five main points can be distinguished in the concepts of the theory:

1. A large scale mathematical optimization model approximates an overall planning problem for a socialist system where associated producers are assumed to perform rational and coordinated control over reproduction processes with a minimum amount of labor input socially necessary for attaining a maximum satisfaction level of social needs under some initially endowed conditions.

2. A set of Lagrange multipliers associated with the model constitutes the most suitable social evaluation system of products and resources for the economy, i.e. optimal price-system, which helps the economy as a whole to reach an efficient production level and an equalization of distinct technical conditions (elimination of inequity due to distinct technical conditions) among enterprises, hence income distribution according to labor.

27

3. Some computational methods and algorithms for practical solution of optimization problems simulate an "indirectly centralized" procedure for planning where communications between a central planning bureau (CPB) and production units are carried out efficiently and democratically in terms of information flow, and where each production unit takes part in the planning process with a certain degree of autonomy regarding production decisions, based on economic regulators transmitted by the CPB.

4. The adoption of the optimization approach to socialist pricing does not in itself provide accurate computations of prices of all disaggregated products and the efficient development of a centralized pricing mechanism applied to all enterprises (which is apparent since the statistical information necessary for optimal price calculations can never be sufficiently perfect, cannot reach the CPB quickly enough to ensure that the computed prices are adequate for the day-to-day management of the economy, and even the most advanced computer cannot perform the calculations for millions of prices of fully disaggregated resources); it should therefore be apparent that the optimization approach does not assume an elimination of the market mechanism, but on the contrary, assumes the existence and development of the market mechanism and the coordination of planned prices and market prices responding sensitively and quickly to demand and supply; the significance of optimal price theory lies in that it yields basic points of reference for the formation and development of fundamental price proportions.

5. While dogmatic socialists and many scholars in the West view the optimization approach to socialist price formation as being in contradiction to Marx's labor theory of value, it does not necessarily contradict the principles of the theory and would pave the way for socialist pricing based on socialist principles; the economy (rational utilization) of labor, maximized satisfaction of needs and income distribution according to labor.

In regard to these five statements, we will explore in this chapter the basic theory of optimal planning and pricing and relationship between the optimal price-system and the labor theory of value, referring in part to the work of Novozhilov and Kantorovich.

The optimal price-system was critically debated from the late 1950's to the early 1960's, but in our opinion, a satisfactory solution has not yet been reached. The labor theory of value falls under a field of planning theory that has not been fully investigated in the economic literature in spite of its importance. In this chapter we will attempt to bring together analyses and view-points which are elsewhere rather disconnected.

In this chapter, we first describe a well-known linear programming model which allows for "polyhedral technology" and formulate the optimal price equation associated with the primal problem, discussing some implications of the optimal price-system with respect to management of the economy. Secondly, we provide the "(social) value" equation for a case with different technologies and the "individual value" equation based on these different technologies, and provide some mathematical representations to the relationship between optimal prices and (labor) values; we point out the similarity between the optimal prices and "production prices", and are concerned with the question of whether optimal prices are consistent with the labor theory of value. The model is closely related to the Novozhilov linear model for optimal pricing, and this relationship is also discussed. Thirdly, we consider relationship between Novozhilov and Kantorovich-type models and further present an indirectly centralized process for solving the Novozhilov-type model. In the following sections of this chapter our scope is confined to the consideration of a highly restricted linear economy over a single period which constitutes the plan period. It appears to the author that this approach will suffice for an elucidation of some of the basic problems associated with optimal planning and pricing.

2. A Novozhilov-Type Linear Model

Following Novozhilov's approach to problems, (Novozhilov (1972, pp. 298–312), we assume:

    (A1)   each and every production unit has a finite number of linearly homogeneous "processes" using all inputs in fixed proportions;

    (A2)   no joint-production takes place; each production unit, and therefore every process produces a single product;

(A3) labor is homogeneous;

(A4) the amount of net demand of each final product (capital or consumer goods desired) is fixed;

(A5) the net availability of each resource-stock (capital stock or natural resource initially endowed) is also fixed;

(A6) the single objective function ("minimand") in the model constructed in the present section concerns only the net availability of labor socially necessary for producing the final products.[1]

Let there be $i, j = 1, ..., n$ products, hence production units, and $k = 1, ..., m$ resource-stocks and $s_j = 1_j, ..., t_j$ processes available to the jth production unit. The economy as a whole has $s = 1_1, ..., t_n$; $\sum t_j = T$ processes. Let J, S_j and S denote the set of product (production unit) indexes, the set of the process indexes with respect to the jth unit and the set of process indexes for the whole economy, respectively. The non-negative numbers q_{js}, a_{is}, b_{ks} and c_s denote the output of the jth product, the direct input of the jth product required, the direct input of the kth resource-stock and the direct input of labor, respectively, per unit utilization of the process. The knowledge of the sth process can be completely described by these technical coefficients. We assume that the direct input coefficients of products include wear and tear on equipment. Further, let x_s be the production level by the sth process, y_i the net demand for the ith final product, b_k the net availability of the kth resource-stock and c the net availability of labor. These three types of numbers constitute the variables for the economy. By assumptions (A4) to (A6), however, y_i and b_k are written as y_i^o and b_k^o respectively, where superscript (o) designates exogenous variables, and the demand-supply

---

[1] As in the usual planning models, we assumed the society has a functional type of objective function. It is often said that this assumption results in a more or less undemocratic plan and is not desirable since freedom of consumption is constrained (Morishima (1976, Ch. 8; p. 338)). It is also said that such a social welfare function is inherently indefinable (Nove (1977)). The author agrees with the need for the relaxation of this assumption, but at the same time thinks that for many theoretical and practical purposes it is useful to construct such an objective function so long as we bear in mind the limited nature of the use of the assumption (see Johansen (1977)).

inequality condition for labor can be eliminated from the constraints. Hence only production levels x_s are endogenous variables, and by virtue of assumption (A2) we can define the output coefficients as the generalized Cronecker delta, i.e.

$$q_{js} = \begin{cases} 1 & \text{if } s \in S_j \\ 0 & \text{otherwise.} \end{cases}$$

We are now in a position to formulate the basic planning problem for our open economy which we refer to as a Novozhilov-type linear model: to minimize the total amount of direct labor input subject to

net output of each final product $\geq$ its net demand,

input of each resource-stock $\leq$ its net availability.

Symbolically,

$$[N] \qquad\qquad \min c = CX \qquad\qquad (1)$$

$$(Q - A)X \geq y^\circ, \qquad\qquad (2)$$

$$BX \leq b^\circ, \qquad\qquad (3)$$

$$X \geq o, \qquad\qquad (4)$$

where

$Q = (q_{js})$: an n by T matrix of output coefficients,

$A = (a_{is})$: an n by T matrix of direct product input coefficients.

$B = (b_{ks})$: an m by T matrix of direct resource-stock input coefficients,

$C = (c_s)$: a row T-vector of direct labor input coefficients,

$X = [x_s]$: a column T-vector of outputs,

$y^\circ = [y_i^\circ]$: a column n-vector of final outputs,

$b^\circ = [b_k^\circ]$: a column m-vector of resource-stock availability.

In the following we assume that there exists at least one solution to every programming problem including the problem [N]. As is common, optimized magnitudes are denoted by superscript ($*$), e.g. X^*.

Let p, or (p_j), be an n-dimensional row vector of the Lagrange multipliers associated with Eq. (2) and r, or (r_k), an m-dimensional row vector of those associated with Eq. (3). Then the Lagrangean associated with [N] is defined as follows:

$$L = -CX + p(QX - AX - y^\circ) + r(b^\circ - BX); \quad p \geq o, \quad r \geq o. \quad (5)$$

We can write Eq. (5) as

$$L = -(py^\circ - rb^\circ) + (pQ - pA - rB - C)X; \quad X \geq o, \ p \geq o, \ y \geq o. \quad (6)$$

Thus we obtain the dual problem of the primal problem [N]:

[NN] $$\max \ py^\circ - rb^\circ \quad (7)$$

$$pQ \leq pA + rB + C, \quad (8)$$

$$p \geq o, \quad r \geq o. \quad (9)$$

Assume that the unit cost of labor is defined to be unity. Then p and r can be interpreted as the price vector of products and the rental evaluation vector of resource-stocks, respectively, both of which are measured in terms of labor. When the price vector is augmented by the evaluation of labor, $P = (p, r, 1)$ defines the price-system of the economy. The dual problem [NN] states: To maximize the national income subject to the constraint that the price of each product is not greater than the cost of any process to the production unit.

By virtue of the fundamental theorems of linear programming, we obtain three results:

Rule of profitability

$$x_s^* = 0 \text{ if } [p^*Q - (p^*A + r^*B + C)]_s < 0, \quad (10)$$

Rule of free goods

$$p_i^* = 0 \text{ if } [(Q - A)X^* - y^\circ]_i > 0, \quad (11)$$

$$r_k^* = 0 \text{ if } [(b^\circ - B)X^*]_k > 0, \quad (12)$$

Duality equality

$$CX^* = p^*y^\circ - r^*b^\circ, \quad (13)$$

where $[\ ]_j$ denotes the jth element of the vector. The rule of profitability states that the sth process should not be utilized if the process does not reach its cost of required inputs. The rule of free goods makes the jth product free if there is over-production of the product, and it makes the kth resource-stock free if there is over-availability of the stock. The equality (13) states that the maximized national income equals the minimized labor input socially necessary to produce the final products.

We now arrive at a "reproduction-oriented" formula for the optimal price formation:

$$p_j^* = \sum_i a_{is} p_i^* + c_s + \sum_k b_{ks} r_k^* \quad (s \in S_j^*; j \in J), \qquad (14)$$

here S_j^* denotes the set of the optimal processes to be chosen by the jth production unit, i.e. $S_j^* = \{s \mid x_s^* > 0, s \in S_j\}$. On the other hand, we are familiar with the "marginal" formula:

$$p_j^* = \partial c^* / \partial y_j^\circ, \qquad (15)$$

$$r_k^* = -\partial c^* / \partial b_k^\circ, \qquad (16)$$

where c^* stands for CX^*.

The economic significance of these formulas can be stated briefly. Equation (14) informs us that the optimal price of a unit of a product is defined recursively as the production cost of product inputs required, plus the cost of labor used, plus the rental cost("feedback" cost) of the resource-stocks tied up, for any process operated at a positive level by the production unit. It should be noted that the production cost of intermediate product inputs are calculated in terms of optimal prices. The marginal formula (15) states that the price of the jth product is defined as the increment in the minimum amount of the overall labor input associated with the increment in the jth final output, while Eq. (16) states that the rental evaluation of a unit of the kth resource-stock is defined as the negative increment in the minimum labor input with respect to the given amount of resource-stock. Of course, in the marginal case, the optimal price-system is also independent of the operated processes. Consequently, the system p^* represents the relative scarcity of the factors of production, balancing supply and demand.

Let us now examine some implications of the model (Eqs. (1) to (16)), in regard to socialist management of the economy. For this purpose, we assume:

- (A-m1) the transaction price of each product is set equal to the optimal price;
- (A-m2) each production unit has certain autonomy with respect to the choice of its own processes, under a full profit-and-loss accounting system;
- (A-m3) every production unit and each process are regarded, respectively, as an industry (sector) and an enterprise;
- (A-m4) the resource-stock cost is entirely received into the state budget as payment for the utilization of the resource-stocks;
- (A-m5) the better quality of the knowledge of the techniques is indifferent to the past performance of industries and enterprises.

Then, by virtue of the rule of profitability (10), we can state that the use of price-system p^* would result in the adoption of optimal production techniques by enterprises, since the non-optimal processes can result in losses to the enterprises. Secondly, the prices may fulfill a socialist principle of income distribution according to socially useful labor input. This is easily verified. By assumptions (A-m2) to (A-m4), we can define the sth enterprise's income per unit of the jth product as follows:

$$u_s = p_j - (\sum_i a_{is} p_i + \sum_k b_{ks} r_k) \quad (s \in S_j; j \in J) . \tag{17}$$

Considering (Eq. 15), it follows that under the optimal state

$$u_s = c_s \quad (s \in S_j; j \in J) , \tag{18}$$

that is, the producers' income is always equal to their labor expenditure. (Note that, by assumption (A3), labor is homogeneous.) This fact also infers that the price-system tends to eliminate inequity due to distinct technological conditions among enterprises, through the stock evaluation vector r^*. In other words, there is little chance of problems arising from deviations between the "individual values" of a product and its "social value". Thirdly, the law of indifferences under the price-system prevails, so that management by means of the price-system may be more efficient than management with "differentiated prices", in terms of information processing costs.

3. Optimal Prices and the Labor Theory of Value

What is the relationship between optimal prices and "values"? This problem has been one of the fundamental problems for socialist economists. We would like to investigate this problem by making use of the model constructed in the previous section. For this purpose, let us first define the "value" (social value) of a unit of a product recursively as the average flow cost of required products plus the average cost of labor directly used. Symbolically, for $s \in S_j$

$$\nu_j = \sum_i h_s a_{is} \nu_i + \sum_s h_s c_s \quad (j \in J) , \tag{19}$$

where ν_j and h_s ($s \in S_j$) denote the value of the jth product and the fraction of the jth product by the sth process, respectively. Here, let $\bar{A}$ be an n by n matrix (matrix of average direct product input coefficients) whose elements $\bar{a}_{ij}$ denote $\sum_s h_s a_{is}$ ($s \in S_j$) and $\bar{C}$ an n-dimensional row vector (vector of average direct labor input coefficients) whose elements $\bar{c}_j$ denote $\sum_s h_s c_s$ ($s \in S_j$):

$$\bar{A} = A\hat{H}Q' , \quad \bar{C} = C\hat{H}Q' , \tag{20}$$

where $\hat{H}$ is the diagonal matrix with $h_{1_1}, ..., h_{t_n}$ on the diagonal and Q' is the transpose of matrix Q. Then, Eq. (19) implies

$$\nu = \nu\bar{A} + \bar{C}, \tag{21}$$

where ν is an n-dimensional row vector (value vector) whose elements are ν_j. The value vector which solves equation (21) is called the value vector associated with the production pattern $\hat{H}$. It should be noted that by definition we have

$$\hat{H}Q' = \hat{X}Q'\hat{Z}, \tag{22}$$

$$Q\hat{H}Q' = Q\hat{X}Q'\hat{Z} = I, \tag{23}$$

where $\hat{X}$ and $\hat{Z}$ are the diagonal matrix with $x_{1_t}, ..., x_{t_n}$ on the diagonal and the diagonal matrix with $1/\sum x_{s_1}, ..., 1/\sum x_{s_n}$, respectively, and I is the n by n identical matrix. Given the value vector ν associated with some production pattern, we can define the "individual value" of the jth product referring to the sth process as

$$\nu_s = \sum_i a_{is} \nu_i + c_s \quad (s \in S_j; j \in J) . \tag{24}$$

If we allow V to denote the T-dimensional row vector whose elements are ν_s, this implies

$$V = \nu A + C. \tag{25}$$

For the moment, consider an economy without resource-stocks and assume that many processes for producing the same product are to operate simultaneously in some convex combination. Even in such a restricted economy a transaction price set equal to the labor value defined by Eq. (21) does not fulfill the equalization of distinct technical conditions among enterprises, hence the income distribution according to labor, under assumptions (A-m2), (A-m3) and (A-m5) except for trivial cases. This is seen as follows. Let e_s denote the extra-income per unit of production of the jth product earned by the sth enterprise, i.e.

$$e_s = \nu_j - \nu_s \quad (s \in \bar{S}_j; j \in J) , \tag{26}$$

where $\bar{S}_j = \{s \mid x_s > 0, s \in S_j\}$. Then the extra-income plus the direct labor input defines the sth enterprise's income, i.e.

$$u_s = e_s + c_s \quad (s \in \bar{S}_j; j \in J) . \tag{27}$$

Considering Eqs. (26) and (27), we immediately obtain:

Proposition 1. *In an economy without resource-stocks and with assumptions* (A1) *to* (A3), (A-m2) *and* (A-m3)
(1) *the income earned by the enterprise producing a single product is higher than its actual direct labor input if the value of the product is greater than the individual value with respect to the enterprise and lower if the value of the product is less than the individual value;*

(2) *the income earned by the enterprise is equal to its actual direct labor input in the case where the value equals the individual value: for $s \in S_j$ and $j \in J$*

$$
\begin{aligned}
u_s > c_s & \quad if \quad \nu_j > \nu_s, \\
u_s < c_s & \quad if \quad \nu_j < \nu_s, \\
u_s = c_s & \quad if \quad \nu_j = \nu_s.
\end{aligned}
\tag{28}
$$

By assumption (A-m5) the value of a product and each individual value of the product depend upon technical conditions for which the sector and each enterprise producing the product are not responsible, so that the above proposition implies that the socialist principle of income distribution according to labor is violated. Therefore, we can not recommend the use of value-prices as a principle of socialist price formation. Efficient allocation of scarce resource-stocks is also one of the most important economic problems in a socialist economy as well as a capitalist economy. This problem can not be solved by the use of value-prices or its Soviet version (price formation based on prime cost) since value-prices never reflect any factor for economizing resource-stocks. (Only in an abstract theoretical world; a "flow-capital economy" can we claim the "rationality" of value-prices. See also Manove (1976).)

We now turn to an economy with resource-stocks. We confine ourselves to the optimal state associated with the model in the previous section and assume for the sake of simplicity that the vector of fixed final outputs and the vector of direct labor input coefficients are both strictly positive, i.e.

$$
y^\circ > o, \quad C > o.
\tag{29}
$$

Then, considering the rules (10) and (11), we have

$$
x^* = AX^* + y^\circ, \quad x^* > o
\tag{30}
$$

from the first constraint of [N], where x^* stands for QX^*. As is easily verified,

$$
X^* = \hat{H}Q'QX^*.
\tag{31}
$$

Therefore, Eq. (30) is written as

$$x^* = A\hat{H}Q'QX^* + y^\circ, \quad x^* > o.$$

In view of the definition of Eq. (20), this can be re-written as

$$x^* = \bar{A}^* x^* + y^\circ, \quad x^* > o. \tag{32}$$

It follows, by assumption (29), that the matrix of the average product input coefficients $\bar{A}^*$ is productive, so that $(I - \bar{A}^*)^{-1}$ with non-negative and non-zero rows exists.

Since $\bar{A}^*$ is productive and $\bar{C}^*$ is strictly positive by Eqs. (29) and (32), we obtain:

Proposition 2. *The value vector associated with optimal output vector* X^* *(optimal value vector) is given by*

$$\nu^* = \nu^* \bar{A}^* + \bar{C}^*; \tag{33}$$

$$\nu^* = \bar{C}^* (I - \bar{A}^*)^{-1}. \tag{34}$$

ν^* *is unique and strictly positive given* X^*.

Concerning the amount of final products in terms of optimal values $\nu_1^*, ..., \nu_n^*$, we can write it as follows:

$$\begin{aligned}
\nu^* y^\circ &= \nu^* (I - \bar{A}^*) x^* \quad &\text{(by (32))} \\
&= \bar{C}^* x^* \quad &\text{(by (33))} \\
&= C\hat{H}Q'QX^* \quad &\text{(by (20))} \\
&= CX^* \quad &\text{(by (31)).}
\end{aligned}$$

Hence we obtain:

Proposition 3. *The amount of final products in terms of optimal values is equal to the total amount of direct labor input, i.e.*

$$\nu^* y^\circ = CX^*, \tag{35}$$

and it follows from (13) that

$$p^* y^\circ = \nu^* y^\circ + r^* b^\circ, \tag{36}$$

namely, the amount of final products in terms of optimal prices is greater than the amount of final products in terms of the associated values by the sum of resource-stock costs necessary for optimal resource-stock allocation.

In the same manner as Eq. (20), define the matrix of the average direct resource-stock input coefficients as

$$\bar{B} = B\hat{H}Q' = B\hat{X}Q'\hat{Z}. \tag{37}$$

Postmultiplying the constraint of [NN] by X^*, we have

$$p^*Q\hat{X}^* = (p^*A + r^*B + C)\hat{X}^*$$

from the rule of profitability. Postmultiply this by $Q'Z^*$, and considering Eqs. (20), (22), (23) and (37), we obtain

$$p^* = p^*\bar{A}^* + r^*\bar{B}^* + \bar{C}^*. \tag{38}$$

Therefore, by virtue of the productiveness of $\bar{A}^*$, the optimal price vector p^* is given by

$$p^* = \bar{C}^*(I - \bar{A}^*)^{-1} + r^*\bar{B}^*(I - \bar{A}^*)^{-1}. \tag{39}$$

Hence, taking Proposition 2 into account, we obtain:

Proposition 4. *The optimal price of each product is also defined recursively as the optimal value of the product plus the average "full" (direct and indirect) cost of required resource-stocks, i.e.*

$$p^* = \nu^* + r^*\bar{D}^*; \tag{40}$$

$$p_j^* = \nu_j^* + \sum_k \bar{d}_{kj}^* r_k^* \quad (j \in J), \tag{41}$$

where $\bar{D}^*$, or $(\bar{d}_{kj}^*)$, which is defined by $\bar{B}^*(I - \bar{A}^*)^{-1}$, denotes the matrix of average full input coefficients $\bar{d}_{11}^*, ..., \bar{d}_{mn}^*$ of resource-stocks. By virtue of Proposition 2, p^* is strictly positive and unique, given output vector X^*.

The equalities (36) and (40) yields explicit representations to the relationship between the optimal price-system and the associated value-system.[2] So, we are now in a position to ask whether Propositions 3 and 4 are consistent with the labor theory of value. Obviously, (36) does not correspond to the fundamental requirement of the labor theory of value in Marx's *Capital* which states that the total amount of net outputs in terms of prices (expressed in units of labor) must be equal to the labor values of production of the whole, i.e.

$$py = \nu y, \tag{42}$$

where p is an n-dimensional row vector of prices expressed in units of labor. This is due to the resource-stock cost, which at first glance appears not to embody actual labor input into itself, but which is necessary for attaining socialist principles in regard to the successful performances of the economy. However, it should be noted that only the relative relations between optimal prices are important for their useful functions. Taking this fact into consideration, the difference between the sum of optimal prices and the sum of the associated values can be eliminated by an appropriate change in the units of measurement of optimal prices in the following way, as developed by Novozhilov (1972, pp. 307–308) and Kantorovich (1959, pp. 341–346).

Let us define the following numbers:

$$\zeta^* = r^* b^\circ / \nu^* y^\circ, \tag{43}$$

$$w^* = (1 + \zeta^*)^{-1}. \tag{44}$$

Multiply (36) by w^*, and considering the above definitions, we obtain

$$\begin{aligned}
w^* p^* y^\circ &= w^* (\nu^* y^\circ + r^* b^\circ) \\
&= \nu^* y^\circ (\nu^* y^\circ + r^* b^\circ) / (\nu^* y^\circ + r^* b^\circ) \\
&= \nu^* y^\circ,
\end{aligned}$$

---

[2] Equations (38) to (41) were first formulated in my "An Essay on the Function-Oriented Approach to a Planned Economy (in Japanese), *"Keizai Hyoron*, October 1976 and "On the Optimization Approach to Socialist Planning and Pricing," *Discussion Paper* (The Institute of Economic Research, Hitotsubashi University), March 1979. It was recently discovered that Tochilin (1979, pp. 37–44) presented results similar to those of the author's.

namely,

$$p_* y^\circ = \nu^* y^\circ , \qquad (45)$$

where p_* stands for $w^* p^*$. p_* is the vector of optimal prices adjusted to overall equality with the sum of values. Hence equality (45) states that the adjusted prices fulfill the fundamental requirement (42) and that the optimal prices are a transformed form of values. The adjusted optimal prices are obtained *via* a normalization in which each man-hour of optimal prices is equated to $w^*(\leq 1)$ man-hour of values. Thus w^* may be defined as a wage rate; wages are less than the value of the created product by $w^* \cdot 100\%$. Since ζ^* represents the degree of utilization of better resource-stocks as a social average, we may define ζ^* as the social average "organic composition of production" in a generalized form. Likewise, we may define ζ_j^* as the generalized organic composition of production of the jth product, where

$$\zeta_j^* = \Sigma_k d_{kj}^* r_k^* / \nu_j^* . \qquad (46)$$

As is easily seen, the proportions $p_1^*: \dots : p_n^*$ are equal to the proportions $p_{1*}: \dots : p_{n*}$, which do not equate the proportions $\nu_1^*: \dots : \nu_n^*$ except for trivial cases. Hence the adjusted prices of individual products may deviate for the most part from the associated values. What may cause these deviations? We can perform a solution to this problem as follows. Assume that:

$$\zeta_j^* > \zeta^* .$$

Then, obviously, $1 + \zeta_j^* > 1 + \zeta^*$, that is,

$$(\nu_j^* + \Sigma_k d_{kj}^* r_k^*)/\nu_j^* > (\nu^* y^\circ + r^* b^\circ)/\nu^* y^\circ .$$

It follows from Proposition 2 that

$$(\nu_j^* + \Sigma_k d_{kj}^* r_k^*)\nu^* y^\circ/(\nu^* y^\circ + r^* b^\circ) > \nu_j^* .$$

In view of the definitions of (41), (43) and (44) we obtain

$$p_{j*} > \nu_j^* \quad \text{if } \zeta_j^* > \zeta^* .$$

41

Conversely, if $p_{j*} > \nu_j^*$, it obviously follows that $\zeta_j^* > \zeta^*$. Likewise, we can obtain

$$p_{j*} < \nu_j^* \quad \text{iff} \quad \zeta_j^* < \zeta^*,$$
$$p_{j*} = \nu_j^* \quad \text{iff} \quad \zeta_j^* = \zeta^*.$$

Thus we obtain:

Proposition 5.

(1) *The adjusted optimal price of a product is evaluated higher than the value, if, and only if, the generalized organic composition of production of the product is greater than the social average for the economy as a whole, and lower, if, and only if, the generalized organic composition is less than the social average;*

(2) *The adjusted optimal price of a product is evaluated equal to the value, if, and only if, the generalized organic composition of production of the product is equal to the social average;*

(3) *The adjusted optimal price of each product is equal to the value, if, and only if, the generalized organic composition of production is the same for all products.*

This proposition shows that the optimal price-system has a macroeconomic feature similar to that of "production prices." Under production prices the price for a sector is higher [lower] than the value when the organic composition of capital in that sector is higher [lower] than the average, and the price is higher, the higher the organic composition of capital calculated by using both the price structure and pure technical conditions. Marx's labor theory of value does not imply that the "(market)value" of a product can be determined by "pure" technical conditions. It should also be noted that the labor theory of value does not exclude the existence of a price system (e.g. production price system) , different from the value prices, and rents for natural resources. It seems to the author that "scarcity" also constitutes a source of the "value" (social evaluation) of a product in the sense that the concept of "opportunity labor-cost" due to scarcity of resources should be considered in any society.

There is another approach to the adjusted price of each product. The total rating of the final outputs, in units of optimal prices, amounts to p^*y^o, while the whole final output should be produced by CX^* units of actual labor. It follows that one price-unit of this output requires an input of CX^*/p^*y units of actual labor. Therefore a unit of the jth product rated at p_j^* price-units requires an expenditure in units of actual labor that amounts to

$$\frac{CX^*}{p^*y^o} p_j^* \,.$$

Considering Eqs. (35), (43) and (44), it is easily seen that this amount is equal to the adjusted price of the jth product, p_{j*}. Thus the adjusted price of each product represents the socially necessary expenditure of actual labor on a unit of the product.

In turn, we would like to comment upon the relationship between the rule of free goods (11) and the Marxian theory of value. The rule with strict inequality states that if the net supply of the jth product exceeds the net demand for it, its optimal price must be set at zero in spite of the fact that a strictly positive amount of direct labor is expended on it. As is shown by Novozhilov (1972, p. 303), this could be consistent with Marx's qualification concerning the values in his *Capital* that if the product produced is useless, so is the labor embodied in it. It should be noted that the above argument does not take into account any possibility for the use of the excess product for other purposes within the plan period or beyond the time-horizon, and does not allow for the possibility of changes in the fixed final output, which is the weakness of this model.

It is worth making an additional comment in regard to this point. We have arrived at the adjusted prices and the rule of free goods, both of which are compatible with the labor theory of value, *via* the "Soviet Renaissance". It should also be recognized that similar results are reached by Morishima (1974, Ch. 14) in light of modern economics, although our assertions differ from those of Morishima, particularly in regard to resource-stocks.

4. A Critique of the Original Novozhilov Model

The model explored in section 1 of this chapter is a restructuring of the Novozhilov linear model for optimal pricing (Novozhilov (1972, pp. 298–312)) although our model belongs to a well-known class of models.

With regard to basic assumptions the present model is similar to the one developed by Novozhilov. However, unlike the model presented here, the Novozhilov model is described on the basis of final (net) outputs at the level of the national economy which are distinguished by the processes. The planning problem in the Novozhilov model is:

[No]
$$\min \tilde{V}Y$$

$$QY \geqq y^{\circ},$$
$$\tilde{D}Y \leqq b^{\circ},$$
$$Y \geqq o,$$

where

$\tilde{V} = (\tilde{\nu}_s)$: a row T-vector of "individual values" ("full" labor input coefficients) by processes whose sth element $\tilde{\nu}_s(s \in S_j)$ denotes the individual value (full labor input) of a unit of the jth product by the sth process,

$\tilde{D} = (\tilde{d}_{ks})$: an m by T matrix of "full resource-stock input coefficients whose k-sth element $\tilde{d}_{ks}$ denotes the full input of the kth resource-stock per unit utilization of the sth process,

$Y = [y_s]$: a column T-vector of final outputs by processes whose sth element y_s $(s \in S_j)$ denotes the amount of the jth final output produced by the sth process.

The dual problem of (N) is:

[NNo]
$$\max \tilde{p}y^{\circ} - \tilde{r}b^{\circ}$$

$$\tilde{p}Q \leqq \tilde{V} + \tilde{r}\tilde{D},$$
$$\tilde{p} \geqq o, \quad \tilde{r} \geqq o,$$

where $\tilde{p}$ and $\tilde{r}$ are the price vector and the rental evaluation vector respectively, both of which are similar to those of our Novozhilov-type model.

There follow the fundamental duality equality and "reproduction theoretic" optimal price formula associated with the problems [No] and [NNo]:

$$\tilde{V}Y^* = \tilde{p}^* y^\circ - \tilde{r}^* b^\circ , \qquad (47)$$

$$\tilde{p}_j^* = \tilde{v}_s + \sum_k \tilde{d}_{ks} \tilde{r}_k^* \quad (s \in \tilde{S}_j^*; j \in J) , \qquad (48)$$

$$\text{where } \tilde{S}_j^* = \{ s \,|\, y_s^* > 0 , \ s \in S_j \} .$$

As is easily seen, in the original Novozhilov model the technical coefficient matrixes $\tilde{V}$ and $\tilde{D}$, hence $\tilde{v}_s$ and $\tilde{d}_{ks}$ in (48) are all given at the beginning of the plan period. However, according to our framework $\tilde{V}$ and $\tilde{D}$ should be obtained *via* the inverse of $(Q-A)$ or the inverse of $(I-\bar{A}^*)$. Since the matrix $(Q-A)$ is in general rectangular, the inverse is not defined *a priori* (even if we consider a generalized inverse). The matrix $(I-\bar{A}^*)$ is also not defined *a priori* simply because it can be calculated only after the planning problem has been solved. Therefore, the full input coefficients; $\tilde{V}$ and $\tilde{D}$ cannot be given at the beginning of planning, so that we cannot theoretically support the Novozhilov model for optimal pricing. Here, it should be noted that in the formula (48) the price of each intermediate product is not given, while in our formula (14) it is explicitly included. Kantorovich (1959, p. 261) and Dadaian (1972, p. 245) seem to be aware of this failure on the part of Novozhilov's model. The fact that most economists in the West have made light of the Novozhilov model is also due to this failure in our opinion. On the other hand, in formula (48) the relationship between the (individual) values and the optimal prices is straight-forwardly expressed without the need for analysis. This may be one reason why some socialist Marxians in the Soviet bloc countries and Japan have paid respect to the Novozhilov model. In this context we can say that the Novozhilov model contributes its share to the theory of socialist pricing from the Marxian point of view. (In this aspect, Oka (1963) is prominent.)

Novozhilov erred in the formulation of his mathematical model. Nevertheless, as is shown in our analysis, particularly in Propositions 3, 4 and 5, the fundamental implications of the Novozhilov model can be retained in our restructured model.

5. The Kantorovich and Novozhilov-Type Linear Models

Assuming (A1) to (A3) and (A5), the Kantorovich-type model, where the final consumption composition is fixed and the level of such consumption is maximized, can be written as follows:

$$[K] \qquad \max \theta$$
$$y = (Q-A)X \geq \theta a ,$$
$$BX \leq b^{\circ} ,$$
$$CX \leq c^{\circ} ,$$
$$X \geq o ,$$

where

$a = [a_i]$: a column n-vector of final output composition;

θ: the level of final output$(\theta = \min (y_i/a_i))$;

c°: the labor availability.

The dual problem associated with the above primal problem can be written as the following primary-factor-cost minimization problem subject to the full profit-and-loss condition:

$$[KK] \qquad \min \gamma b^{\circ} + \omega c^{\circ}$$
$$\pi Q \leq \pi A + \gamma B + \omega C ,$$
$$\pi a \geq 1 ,$$
$$\pi \geq o , \quad \gamma \geq o , \quad \omega \geq 0 ,$$

where

π: a row n-vector of product prices;

γ: a row m-vector of resource-stock rental prices;

ω: an evaluation of labor.

With regard to the rule of profitability the Kantorovich and Novozhilov-type models are similar. However, the Kantorovich-type model also assumes the rule of free goods regarding labor, in addition to resource-stocks:

$$\omega^* = 0 \text{ if } \textstyle\sum_s c_s x_s^* < c^{\circ} . \tag{49}$$

It should be noted that the labor evaluation ω^* should be positive, since we can assume that direct labor has a positive, marginal productivity effect, and there is no difficulty in reducing the limit of labor availability.

The "reproduction-oriented" formula for the optimal price formation in the Kantorovich-type model is written as

$$\pi_j^* = \sum_i a_{is}\pi_i^* + \sum_k b_{ks}\gamma_k^* + \omega^* c_s \quad (s \in S_j^*; j \in J) ,$$

$$\sum \pi_i^* a_i = 1 . \tag{50}$$

The second equation of (50) can be regarded as a normalization condition. The duality equality is written as

$$\max \theta = \gamma^* b^0 + \omega^* c^0 (= \pi^* y^*) . \tag{51}$$

The "marginal" formula is as follows:

$$\gamma_k^* = \partial \max \theta / \partial b_k^0 , \quad \omega^* = \partial \max \theta / \partial c^0 . \tag{52}$$

Therefore, the resource-stock rental prices [the labor evaluation] shows the possibility of the increase of optimal final output level by one unit relaxation of the resource-stock availability [labor availability].

When we set the evaluation of labor as unity, the Kantorovich-type reproduction-oriented formula can be written as

$$\pi_j^*/\omega^* = \sum_i a_{is}(\pi_i^*/\omega^*) + \sum_k b_{ks}(\gamma_k^*/\omega^*) + c_s$$
$$(s \in S_j^*; j \in J) . \tag{53}$$

This shows the similarity between the Novozhilov and Kantorovich-type price formulas. Taking into consideration the fact that only relative evaluation is important for the optimal price system, we can state that the points made in regard to the Novozhilov-type model also hold for the Kantorovich-type model.

Let us apply the "Reciprocity Theorem" (*teorema vzaimnosti*) developed by Aganbegian and Bagrinovsky (1968) in order to clarify the close relationship between the Kantorovich and Novozhilov-type models.

Let

Primal problem: the primal problem [K] of the above Kantorovich-type model;

(the optimal value of the objective function and the optimal plan are denoted by $\theta^*_{(K)}$ and $X^*_{(K)}$, respectively.)

Reciprocal problem: a modified version of Novozhilov-type model with a utility level variable which should not be less than the optimal level of the above primal problem;

[R-K]
$$\min CX$$
$$y = (Q - A)X \geq \theta a ,$$
$$BX \leq b^\circ ,$$
$$\theta \geq \theta^*_{(K)} ,$$
$$X \geq o .$$

(the optimal value of the objective function and the optimal plan are denoted by $c^*_{(N)}$ and $X^*_{(N)}$, respectively.)

The Lagrangean for the primal problem [K] can be written as

$$L_{(K)}(\underset{\sim}{X};\ \underset{\sim}{\Pi}) = \theta + \pi g_1(\underset{\sim}{X}) + \gamma g_2(X) + \omega(c^\circ - CX);$$
$$\pi \geq o ,\ \gamma \geq o ,\ \omega \leq 0 .$$

where

$$\underset{\sim}{X} = (X,\ \theta);$$
$$\underset{\sim}{\Pi} = (\pi,\ \gamma,\ \omega);$$
$$g_1(\underset{\sim}{X}) = (Q - A)X - \theta a;$$
$$g_2(X) = b^\circ - BX .$$

The Lagrangean for the reciprocal problem [R-K] can be written as

$$L_{(N)}(\underset{\sim}{X};\ \underset{\sim}{P}) = -CX + p g_1(\underset{\sim}{X}) + r g_2(X) + u(\theta - \theta^*_{(K)});$$
$$p \geq o ,\ r \geq o ,\ u \geq 0 .$$

where

$$\underset{\sim}{P} = (p,\ r,\ u) .$$

By definition of the saddle point, we have

$$L_{(K)}(\underset{\sim}{X};\ \underset{\sim}{\Pi}^*) \leq L_{(K)}(\underset{\sim}{X}^*_{(K)};\ \underset{\sim}{\Pi}^*) .$$

Noting the positiveness of $\theta^*_{(K)}$ and ω^*, we have

$$[L_{(K)}(\underset{\sim}{X};\ \underset{\sim}{I\!\!P}^*) - \theta^*_{(K)}]/\omega^* \leqq [L_{(K)}(\underset{\sim}{X}^*_{(K)};\ \underset{\sim}{I\!\!P}^*) - \theta^*_{(K)}]/\omega^* \ .$$

This inequality can be written as

$$-CX + (\pi^*/\omega^*)g_1(\underset{\sim}{X}) + (\gamma^*/\omega^*)g_2(X) + (1/\omega^*)(\theta - \theta^*_{(K)})$$
$$\leqq -CX^*_{(K)} + (\pi^*/\omega^*)g_1(\underset{\sim}{X}^*_{(K)}) + (\pi^*/\omega^*)g_2(X^*_{(K)}) + (1/\omega^*)(\theta^*_{(K)} - \theta^*_{(K)})\ ,$$

namely

$$L_{(N)}(\underset{\sim}{X}_{(K)};\ \underset{\sim}{I\!\!P}^*/\omega^*) \leqq L_{(N)}(\underset{\sim}{X}^*_{(K)};\ \underset{\sim}{I\!\!P}^*/\omega^*) \ .$$

Noting that at the saddle point

$$\pi^*g_1(\underset{\sim}{X}^*_{(K)}) = \gamma^*g_2(X^*_{(K)}) = 0\ ,$$

and

$$g_1(\underset{\sim}{X}^*_{(K)}) \geqq o\ , \quad g_2(X^*_{(K)}) \geqq o\ ,$$

we have

$$p g_1(\underset{\sim}{X}^*_{(K)}) \geqq (\pi^*/\omega^*)g_1(\underset{\sim}{X}^*_{(K)}) = 0\ ;$$
$$r g_2(X^*_{(K)}) \geqq (\gamma^*/\omega^*)g_2(X^*_{(K)}) = 0\ ,$$

namely for any positive p

$$-CX^* + (\pi^*/\omega^*)g_1(\underset{\sim}{X}^*_{(K)}) + (\gamma^*/\omega^*)g_2(X^*_{(K)}) + (1/\omega^*)(\theta^*_{(K)} - \theta^*_{(K)})$$
$$\leqq -CX^* + p g_1(X^*_{(K)}) + r g_2(X^*_{(K)}) + u(\theta^*_{(K)} - \theta^*_{(K)})\ .$$

Collectively, we have

$$L_{(N)}(\underset{\sim}{X};\ \underset{\sim}{I\!\!P}^*/\omega^*) \leqq L_{(N)}(\underset{\sim}{X}^*_{(K)};\ \underset{\sim}{I\!\!P}^*/\omega^*) \leqq L_{(N)}(\underset{\sim}{X}^*_{(K)};\ \underset{\sim}{P}) \ .$$

This implies that $(\underset{\sim}{X}^*_{(K)};\ \underset{\sim}{I\!\!P}^*/\omega^*)$ i.e. $(X^*_{(K)}, \theta^*_{(K)};\ \pi^*/\omega^*, \gamma^*/\omega^*, 1/\omega^*)$ is the saddle point for the reciprocal problem [R-K].

Thus we obtain the following proposition:

Proposition 6. *The optimal plan solution of both the primal and reciprocal problems are the same, and the optimal prices of the above primal problem are proportional to those of the reciprocal problem: if the Lagrangean $L_{(K)}$ of the primal problem has the non-negative saddle point $(X^*_{(K)}, \theta^*_{(K)};\ \pi^*, \gamma^*, \omega^*)$ and $\omega^* > 0$, then the Lagrangean $L_{(N)}$ has the* *saddle point* $(X_{(K)}^*, \theta_{(K)}^*; \pi^*/\omega^*, \gamma^*/\omega^*, 1/\omega^*)$.

Next, let

Primal problem: the primal problem [N] of the above Novozhilov-type model with $\theta \geqq \theta^\circ(y^\circ = \theta^\circ a)$;

(the optimal value of the objective function and the optimal plan are denoted by $c_{(N)}^*$ and $X_{(N)}^*$, respectively. θ of g_1 and $\theta_{(K)}^*$ of $L_{(N)}$ are replaced by θ°.)

Reciprocal problem: a modified version of a Kantorovich-type model where a total sum of labor input should not be greater than the optimal value of the objective function of the above primal problem;

[R-N]
$$\max \theta$$
$$y = (Q - A)X \geqq \theta a,$$
$$BX \leqq b^\circ,$$
$$CX \leqq c_{(N)}^*,$$
$$X \geqq o, \quad \theta \geqq 0.$$

(the optimal plan is denoted by $X_{(N)}^*$.)

Using a method similar to that employed for the proof of Proposition 6, we obtain the following proposition:

Proposition 7. *The optimal plan solution of both the primal and reciprocal problems are the same and the optimal prices of the above primal problem are proportional to those of the reciprocal problem: if the Lagrangean $L_{(N)}$ of the primal problem has a non-negative saddle point $(X_{(N)}^*, \theta^*; p^*, r^*, u^*)$ and $u > 0$, then the Lagrangean $L_{(K)}$ has a saddle point $(X_{(N)}^*, \theta^*; p^*/u^*, r^*/u^*, 1/u^*)$.*

6. An Indirectly Centralized Planning Process

When the initial large-scale planning problem is formulated as an optimization problem with a single objective function (a sole social welfare function), the iterative methods for solving the problem by employing the "decomposition" principle can be interpreted as a decentralized planning process, where "dialogue" takes place between the

CPB and the production units. This application of the decomposition principle was already performed by Novozhilov (1959) for non-linear convex programming, which he referred to as "indirect centralization," although Arrow and Hurwicz (1960) were the first to give a rigorous, formal presentation and proof of convergence of the process for a strictly convex environment. Dantzig and Wolfe (1961) were the first to rigorously develop this principle for linear programming.

Following Novozhilov, Arrow-Hurwicz and Dantzig-Wolfe, a number of decentralized planning procedures, based on the decomposition method, were developed. These procedures can be classified by the differences in the characteristics of the initial overall optimization model (the shape of the production possibility set and the objective function), the methods used to decompose the initial externally-given information, the types of informational input and output codes of each sub-system and the adjustment rule of informational output.

For example, when we look at the types of informational outputs from the CPB and production units in the course of solving the initial problem, we can find at least four types:

1. evaluation (price)—quantity [Novozhilov (1959); Arrow and Hurwicz (1960); Dantzig and Wolfe (1961); Malinvaud (1967)];

2. quantity—evaluation [Kornai and Liptak (1965); Heal (1976)];

3. quantity—quantity; [Polterovich (1969)];

4. evaluation & quantity—evaluation & quantity [Volkonsky (1973)].

Further, when we look at the adjustment methods in the case of evaluation coefficients that the CPB sends to the production units, we can distinguish at least four types of adjustment methods:

1. directly solving the dual-problem of the "master program" [Dantzig and Wolfe (1961); Malinvaud (1967, Section 5)]

2. revising the prices by *tâtonnement* (the law of supply and demand) [Novozhilov (1959); Arrow and Hurwicz (1960)];

3. the solution of linear algebraic equations [Malinvaud (1967, Section 4)];

4. the mixed strategy based on the fictitious game theory [Volkonsky

(1973); Velen'ky and Volkonsky ed. (1974)].

Novozhilov (1959) presented an indirect centralized planning process for the initial problem with a strict convexity, where the type of informational output of the CPB and production units is evaluation—quantity, the evaluation is revised according to the law of supply and demand and an autonomous technological choice criteria of each production unit is to minimize the cost, including capital charges and payments for natural resources. However, Novozhilov did not provide the two-level planning process for his linear model as Dadaian (1970, p. 245) claimed. Therefore, the author will present a two-level planning process for the Novozhilov-type linear model by using techniques developed by Granberg (1969) and Malinvaud (1967).

Let us now clarify the assumptions regarding the initial information structure. We assume that (A-p1) each production unit has perfect knowledge of its technological activities and that (A-p2) the CPB has detailed information of the final outputs and initially-endowed resource-stocks. The former assumption is based on the fact that no planning organization can have a better understanding of the production conditions within an enterprise than the enterprise itself (Nemchinov (1964)).

Noting that the constraint matrix of the primal problem of the Novozhilov-type model is decomposed into two blocks ($Q-A$; B), we first apply the original Dantzig-Wolfe decomposition principle to the primal problem [N] of the Novozhilov-type model (Granberg (1969)).

The "master program" equivalent to the primal program, where a total sum of direct labor inputs is to be minimized under resource-stock constraints, can be written as follows:

$$\min \sum_{\sigma} c^{(\sigma)} \xi_{\sigma}$$
$$\sum_{\sigma} Z^{(\sigma)} \xi_{\sigma} = b^{\circ}, \quad \sum_{\sigma} \xi_{\sigma} = 1, \quad (\xi_{\sigma}) \geq o,$$

where

$Z^{(\sigma)} = BX^{(\sigma)}$;

$c^{(\sigma)} = CX^{(\sigma)}$;

$X^{(\sigma)}$: an extreme point of the set $\{X \mid (Q-A)X = y^{\circ}, X \geq o\}$.

The subprogram equivalent to the simplex criteria of the master program, where a total sum of direct labor inputs and resource-stock costs is to be minimized under final output constraints, can be written as follows:

$$\min\ (C+rB)X$$
$$(Q-A)X=y^{\circ},\ X\geqq o\,.$$

These two programs are the internal programs within the CPB. However, when we look at the structure of the subprogram we can apply the "non-substitution theorem" to the subprogram, since this does not include constraints on resource stocks; namely, we can separate technological choice from the determination of production levels (Malinvaud (1967, Section 4)). Therefore, when we consider our "master" iteration, which includes two sub-iterations, and apply the original decomposition method and a modified decomposition version, we can obtain the following indirectly centralized planning process:

"Master" iteration at round σ:

"the Master Program Management Commission (MMC) of the CPB" solves the dual program of the master program by using the information $[\mathbf{Z}^{(2)}, ..., \mathbf{Z}^{(\sigma-1)}]$ and $[c^{(1)}, ..., c^{(\sigma-1)}]$ and sends the solution; $r^{(\sigma)}$ the rental prices of resource stocks to each production unit to "the Subprogram Management Commission (SMC) of the CPB."

The SMC solves the subprogram by using the approximate optimal technological coefficients derived from the sub-iteration and sends the solution to the MMC.

[When the optimality condition is attained, the MMC computes the "true" optimal plan solution by solving the master program and provides the optimal production plan to each production unit as "orders."]

Sub-iteration at round t:

The SMC solves the equation

$$p=p\tilde{A}_{t-1}+r^{(\sigma)}\tilde{B}_{t-1}+\tilde{C}_{t-1}\,,$$

where $\tilde{A}(n$ by $n)$, $\tilde{B}(m$ by $n)$, $\tilde{C}(n$ by $1)$ denote the reduced matrixes and vector corresponding to A, B and C when a single activity is chosen for

53

producing each product. The SMC sends the solution p_t to production units.

The jth production unit sends to the SMC such an activity (a_{is}, b_{ks}, c_s) $(i=1, 2, ..., n)$ as to minimize the cost, including capital charges and payment for natural resources (In Novozhilov's terminology "differential" cost), namely

$$\min(\textstyle\sum_i a_{is} p_{it} + \sum_k b_{ks} r_k^{(\sigma)} + c_s) \quad (s \in S_j).$$

[When the optimality condition $p_t = p_{t-1}$ is attained, the SMC solves the subprogram and sends $B_t X^{(\sigma)}$, $C_t X^{(\sigma)}$ to the MMC.]

Employing the results of Dantzig and Wolfe(1961) and Malinvaud (1967, Section 4), we can easily verify the following proposition:

Proposition 8. *The indirectly centralized process presented in this section is convergent in finite iterations.*

It should be noted that the above process has a serious drawback. Regarding the final allocation, it will not necessarily correspond to the final technological programs of the production units. Rather, the CPB will order each production unit to undertake a program mixing several activities for producing each product; autonomy of each production unit is indeed strongly restricted in the above process.

7. Concluding Remarks

These observations on some fundamental aspects of the optimization approach to socialist planning and pricing are based on assumptions (A1) to (A6), (A-m1) to (A-m5) and (A-p1) to (A-p3). It would therefore be helpful to generalize our analysis by relaxing some of these assumptions. We have presented only an outline here.

If we relax assumption (A2) and introduce joint-production processes, a simple redefinition of output coefficients allows us to retain the planning and pricing problems, the discussions in section 2 and the argument related to the adjusted prices, in accordance with fundamental Marxian requirements. Then, Propositions 1 to 5 do not have to be retained in the same forms. These assertions may apply to a case which allows for joint-production and heterogeneous labor, if we consider Lagrange multipliers with respect to various categories of labor as coefficients which reduce heterogeneous labor to some form of homogeneous labor and assume these ratios to be compatible with the labor theory of value.

In a dynamic environment assumption (A-m5) may be unrealistic, since in practice the principle of income distribution according to labor implies income distribution according to present and "past" labor. An analysis of this aspect is important to assure the accuracy of the optimization approach, but it remains an issue that must be addressed. Further, assumption (A-m4) may be insufficient since some form of decentralization, with respect to profits, is required, in order to motivate producer's to improve the efficiency of their enterprises.

Lastly, we call attention to possible modifications of the procedure constructed in the previous section. There we assumed that the CPB is concerned with final outputs and resource-stocks. Instead, we can assume that some "final consumer goods agencies" and "final capital goods agencies" treat respective final outputs, and that some "resource-stock agencies" manage resource-stocks. Then, some type of decentralization with respect to the final output elements and resource-stock components would be realized without the need for changes in the mathematical reasoning employed in this chapter (see Johansen (1978, p. 112)). Further generalizations of the procedure, e.g., a planning process composed of two or more levels at different degrees of aggregation of goods, can be obtained using the stepwise aggregation or iterative aggregation methods (see Chs. 3 and 4).

Chapter 3

STEPWISE AGGREGATION FOR
MATERIAL BALANCES

1. Introduction

Montias (1959) and Levine (1959) presented an analytical model for the material-balances process in a Soviet-type economy by using the classical, simple, iterative method for a static input-output system. Their model is acceptable only at an extremely high level of abstraction because it does not allow for any aggregation of commodities. It abstracts from the natural, realistic features of daily-life planning and administration in a large-scale economy.

The introduction of aggregation in the material-balances process will generally be advantageous, but it has its own drawbacks. While it may relieve the Central Planning Bureau (CPB) of the need to make detailed calculations and will speed up the material-balances process, aggregation errors may arise that will bring about microplan imbalances in all but trivial cases.[1]

It would therefore be of considerable value if a well-defined process could be found that would incorporate aggregation in the material balances and thus take advantage of the aggregation factor, while avoiding the disadvantages that occur when this factor is introduced. One possible step toward this goal is to establish a process with stepwise aggregation and disaggregation that appropriately coordinates an aggregated model in the CPB with more detailed models at lower levels

---

[1] See Montias (1959, pp. 968–969); and Ellman (1972, p. 95).

(sectors or sector groups) in an iterative manner.

This point was first clearly posed by Soviet economists and mathematicians; Dudkin, Ershov, Vakhutinsky, and Shennikov being the most prominent. They have developed a new iterative method to solve this problem, which they call the iterative aggregation method. Their procedure seems to this author to be a most promising line in the development of, and contribution to, Soviet mathematical economics.[2] While this new method can be applied to a very wide class of mathematical programming problems, their exposition for the material-balances process is in most cases inadequate in that they start with an input-output system in value terms and only implicitly deal with the selection of a price-formation rule or aggregation weights.

Independently of the Soviet contribution, Manove and Weitzman (1978) studied an aggregation method for speeding up the material-balances process in an extreme case; aggregation into a single sector. They showed that the set of aggregation weights yielding the speediest convergence is the von Neumann price system. What makes this result particularly interesting is that the von Neumann price system belongs to the class of so-called "production prices" that has been proposed as a principle of socialist price formation by many mathematical economists in the Soviet-bloc countries since the death of Stalin.

This chapter first presents a process employing stepwise aggregation in which aggregation is limited to a single commodity, explicitly dealing with the price (aggregation-weight) formation rule.[3] It proves that the stepwise process in terms of any full-cost pricing system is well-defined, convergent, and speedier than the classical iterative process. It also shows that the Manove-Weitzman process is an important but very special

[2] Among others, see Dudkin and Ershov (1965); Vakhutinsky et al. (1979); and Dudkin (1979).

[3] An additional remark should be made on the relationship between the work of Dudkin et al. and the process presented in this chapter. The essential difference is a matter of the prices used in the aggregation process; our process may be more sophisticated. It should also be noted that our treatment makes use of their ideas in establishing Proposition 2 (see Dudkin (1979, p. 294)).

version of the stepwise aggregation process presented here. Second, this chapter sets forth a process employing stepwise aggregation in which a broad range of commodities are aggregated into a number of sector groups. It further shows that both processes have approximately the same properties, except for convergence. Third, numerical experiments, using the Soviet 15–and 76–sector input-output tables, are carried out to ascertain comparative degrees of convergence speed that can be achieved with various processes at different levels of aggregation. These experiments suggest that any process using stepwise aggregation is more effective than successive approximation methods carried out on the disaggregated data.

2. Classical Process

As far as possible, results are to be exploited for the simplest case of a static input-output model. For convenience we put down the equations and the classical, traditional iterative method for this model.

Let there be $h, k = 1, \ldots, n$ fully disaggregated commodities, and let $x = [x_h]$, $y = [y_h]$, and $A = (a_{hk})$ denote, respectively, the fully disaggregated output n-column vector, the final demand n-column vector, and the input-output n by n matrix. It should be noted that the vectors and matrix are all in physical terms. The economy-wide planning problem is written as

$$x = Ax + y. \tag{1}$$

It is assumed in the following that A is productive and that y is strictly positive. The Eq. (1) has a unique positive solution given by

$$x^* = (I - A)^{-1} y. \tag{2}$$

The classical iterative method to find a well-balanced output target approximating x^* is presented as follows: given that at round $t-1$ the target is x_t, at round t it is specified to be

$$x_{t+1} = Ax_t + y \ (t = 0, 1, 2, \ldots). \tag{3}$$

A natural closing rule of (3) is that the process is closed on the lowest round such that $t = T$, fulfilling the condition

$$||x_{t+1} - x_t|| = \sum_{h=1}^{n} |x_{h,t+1} - x_{h,t}| < \varepsilon , \qquad (4)$$

where ε is a sufficiently small, positive constant.

It is well-known that by virtue of the assumption of the input-output matrix the classical process (3) should converge for any initial target (control figures) x_0 with positive elements, and that its speed of convergence depends upon the distance between x_0 and x^*, in other words, upon a good specification of the initial target x_0. Also, it is known to be time-consuming to start with $x_0 = y$ which is often set for theoretical convenience. We can conclude that process (3) has no mechanism ensuring a speedy convergence. As will be shown in the following, one such mechanism that does offer speedy convergence is stepwise aggregation and disaggregation.

3. Stepwise Aggregation into a Single Commodity

We first study the case of aggregation of n sectors into a single macro-commodity. Referring to the specification of aggregation weights, or prices, it is assumed that prices fully cover costs and that they are fixed and known to all sectors. Each sector is assumed to produce one disaggregated commodity. The price system may be written

$$p = pA + v \quad (v > o) , \qquad (5)$$

where $p = (p_h)$ is the fully disaggregated price-row n vector and $v = (v_h)$ the value-added ratio-row n vector. Given the productiveness of the matrix A and a given positive v, Eq. (5) has a unique, positive solution.

We can describe the stepwise aggregation and disaggregation procedure as an incompletely centralized planning process in the following fashion.

(i)   On round t each sector k is given a target X_k; it determines its corresponding input requirements for commodity h, $a_{hk}x_k$, and calculates $p_k x_k$ and $p_h a_{hk} x_k$. Altogether, the sectors calculate px_t and pAx_t, and inform the CPB of these figures.

(ii)   The CPB compiles a "macrobalance" and solves it:

$$X_{t+1} = a_t X_{t+1} + Y, \qquad (6)$$

where $a_t = pAx_t/px_t$ is the macro input-output scalar, and $Y = py$ the aggregated value of final demand. Next, the CPB calculates the "macrobalancing multiplier"

$$z_{t+1} = X_{t+1}/X_t, \qquad (7)$$

where $X_t = px_t$. The CPB communicates to the sectors only the scalar z_{t+1} as a control figure.

(iii) Sector, k, taking into account z_{t+1}, calculates the sectoral input requirements in real terms, $z_{t+1} a_{hk} x_k$, and communicates these new input requirements to the appropriate supplier, sector h.

(iv) Sector h in turn revises its output target using its own "microbalance." Altogether, the sectors calculate

$$x_{t+1} = Az_{t+1}x_t + y. \qquad (8)$$

This completes the description of one iteration of the procedure. Let us next examine some properties of this stepwise aggregation process in the simplest case of aggregation.

First, unlike the classical process, the stepwise aggregation process introduces a macrobalance system (6), so that we have to consider whether (6) has a unique, positive solution on each round. If not, the new process is not meaningful. Within our framework this requirement is fulfilled:

Proposition 1. *The macrobalance system on any round has a unique, positive solution if the initial values of the production targets in vector x_0 are positive and prices fully cover costs as in Eq. (5).*

Proof. From (5) we have $pA < p$, and it follows that

$$a_t = pAx_t/px_t < px_t/px_t = 1.$$

Thus $a_t < 1$ for $t = 0, 1, 2, \ldots$, and Proposition 1 follows. Q.E.D.

It follows that in view of the definition, each macrobalancing multiplier z_t is positive and the disaggregated output targets on the next round

61

are also positive. It can also be easily seen that if the process reaches a stationary point $(x_{t+1} = x_t)$, the macrobalancing multiplier will be unity and the microbalance system will offer a solution to the initial planning problem.

Second, we would like to examine the convergence property:

Proposition 2. *The stepwise aggregation process* (6)–(8) *must converge to a positive solution* x^* *of the initial planning problem* (1) *by virtue of the assumption of the price-formation rule, Eq.* (5).

Proof. The process (6)–(8) can be reduced to an equation

$$x_{t+1} = A(px_{t+1}/px_t)x_t + y. \qquad (9)$$

Define

$P = \text{diag}\{p_1, ..., p_n\}$, an n by n matrix with prices p_1 to p_n on the diagonal;

$e = (1, ..., 1)$, an n-row vector;

$w_t = Px_t/px_t$.

Premultiplying (9) by P, we have

$$Px_{t+1} = PA(px_{t+1}/px_t)x_t + Py.$$

Dividing this equation by px_{t+1} yields

$$w_{t+1} = PAP^{-1}w_t + Py/px_{t+1}. \qquad (10)$$

On the other hand, premultiplying (9) by p and noting that $pP^{-1} = e$, we have

$$\begin{aligned}
px_{t+1} &= pA(px_{t+1}/px_t)x_t + py \\
&= px_{t+1} \cdot pP^{-1}PAP^{-1}(Px_t/px_t) + py \\
&= px_{t+1}e\bar{A}w_t + py,
\end{aligned}$$

where $\bar{A} = PAP^{-1}$.

Considering this equation and $ew_t = 1$, we can write (10) as

$$w_{t+1} = \bar{A}w_t(py)^{-1}Py \cdot (e - eA)w_t.$$

Define

$$M = \bar{A} + (py)^{-1} Py \cdot (e - e\bar{A}) ,$$

and it follows that

$$w_{t+1} = M w_t = \cdots = M^{t+1} w_o . \tag{11}$$

Since $p > o$ and $p > pA$, $\bar{A} \geq o$ and $e > e\bar{A}$. Thus we can state that M is a strictly positive matrix. Note that since $ePy = py$, we have

$$eM = e.$$

This implies that M is a positive Markov matrix. Therefore we can write

$$\lim_{t \to \infty} w_{t+1} = \lim_{t \to \infty} M^{t+1} w_o = w^*(>o) \quad \text{for any positive } w_o .$$

The positiveness of w_0 is derived from that of x_0. It follows that $x_t \to x^*$ ($t \to \infty$) for any positive x_0 and p. Q.E.D.

Third, speed of convergence should be explored. It is rather difficult to make a general comparison between the convergence speed of the classical process and of the stepwise aggregation process, but the relative merits of the latter may lie in the following:

Proposition 3. *The process (6)–(8) converges to x^* on the first round if the initial production targets in x_0 are equal to the elements of the solution vector x^* multiplied by the same scalar C, i.e., $x_1 = x^*$ if $x_0 = Cx^*$ (where C is a positive constant, not equal to unity). Then the stepwise aggregation process (6)–(8) converges more speedily than the classical process (3).*

Proof. Considering (6)–(8), we have

$$\begin{aligned} z_{t+1} &= Y/(1 - a_t)X_t \\ &= py/(px_t - pAx_t) . \end{aligned} \tag{12}$$

Premultiplying (1) by p, we have

$$px^* = pAx^* + py. \tag{13}$$

Since $x_0 = Cx^*$, in view of Eq. (13), Eq. (12) for $t = 0$ can be written as

$$z_1 = py/Cp(I - A)x^* = 1/C ,$$

63

and from (8) we then have

$$x_1 = AC^{-1}Cx^* + y$$
$$= Ax^* + y = x^*.$$

Thus $x_1 = x^*$.

If $C \neq 1$, it is obvious that

$$x_1 = CAx^* + y \neq x^*.$$

From this, Proposition 3 follows. Q.E.D.

Fourth, in the process stated above, the CPB is relieved of the need to make detailed calculations and has only to inform lower levels of the scalar, z. That is to say, the informational flow from the CPB is lessened in comparison with the traditional interpretation of the material-balances process.

It is worth making an additional comment on the process here described. We have up to now employed Eq. (5) as a price-formation rule. However, Eq. (5) covers many classes of the price system, so that a question arises as to how to specify the price system to reduce the intervention of the CPB in the allocation process and speed up the procedure. To answer this question we should first look at the so-called production-price system because it is known to work better than other classes of full-cost pricing in many respects.

Let the matrix A be an augmented input-output matrix. A production-price vector p^* for a uniform profit rate r^* is such that

$$p^* = (1+r^*)p^*A. \tag{14}$$

Assume that the augmented matrix A is productive and indecomposable. According to the Perron-Frobenius theorem, A must possess a unique, positive eigenvalue $g^* = 1/(1+r^*)$ less than unity, to which should be associated a unique, positive eigenvector p^* up to multiplication by scalars. Applying p^* as an aggregation vector to the stepwise aggregation process (6)–(8), we can state

Proposition 4. *The macrobalancing multiplier should be unity on any round other than the first round if the price system is of the production-price type:*

$$z_{t+1} = 1 \ (t = 1, 2, \ldots) \quad if \ p = p^*.$$

This implies that the CPB should participate in the process only in the first round.

Proof. Letting $p = p^*$ and $g^* = 1/(1 + r^*)$, we have $p^*A = g^*p^*$. Then

$$a_t = p^*A x_t / p^*x_t = g^* \quad (t = 0, 1, 2, \ldots).$$

Hence, from (12),

$$z_{t+1} = \frac{p^*y}{(1 - g^*)p^*x_t} \ (t = 0, 1, 2, \ldots). \tag{15}$$

Using the above and $p^*A = g^*p^*$, we have from the microbalance (8) premultiplied by p^*,

$$p^*x_t = z_t p^*A x_{t-1} + p^*y$$

$$= \frac{p^*y}{(1 - g^*)p^*x_{t-1}} g^*p^*x_{t-1} + p^*y$$

$$= p^*y/(1 - g^*) \ (t = 1, 2, \ldots).$$

Considering this relation, Eq. (15) yields

$$z_{t+1} = 1 \ (t = 1, 2, \ldots). \ Q.E.D.$$

Proposition 4 shows that process (6)–(9) is mathematically equivalent to the model presented by Manove and Weitzman. Thus their model is a special class of the stepwise aggregation process. However, by virtue of their theorem, we are able to state that the macro input-output coefficient a_t is equal to the Frobenius root g^* on any round t, and that the process with the aggregation-weight vector p^* is the speediest of the stepwise aggregation processes in the case of aggregation to one commodity. It should be noted that the Manove-Weitzman theorem makes the additional assumption that A is diagonalizable.

4. A Generalization

We next explore the possibilities of a generalization of the stepwise aggregation process. Let the basic primal-dual structure be as given by (1) and (5). In this section let us consider the lower level as a sector group $i, j = 1, \ldots, m$, which produces multiple commodities. Define the set H_j of commodities belonging to group j as

$$H_j = \{h_{j-1}+1, \ldots, h_j\}; \ h_o = 0, h_m = n \quad (j = 1, \ldots, m) .$$

Furthermore, denote an output vector, the input-output matrix, a final-demand vector, and a price vector for the group as, respectively,

$$x_j = [x_h \,|\, h \in H_j] \ ; \ A_{ij} = (a_{hk} \,|\, h \in H_i, k \in H_j) \ ;$$
$$y_j = [y_h \,|\, h \in H_j] \ ; \ p_j = (p_h \,|\, h \in H_j) \ , \quad i, j = 1, \ldots, m \ .$$

We are now in a position to describe a generalized stepwise aggregation process as follows:

(i)   Each group j calculates its aggregated output X_{jt} and input needs X_{ijt} using X_{jt} previously presented, and submits them to the CPB, where

$$X_{jt} = p_j x_{jt}, \ X_{ijt} = p_i A_{ij} x_{jt} \ (i, j = 1, \ldots, m) . \tag{16}$$

Note that group j has only to submit its output proposal to the CPB on the initial round.

(ii)   The CPB constructs the following input-output type of macrobalance:

$$X_{i,t+1} = \sum_{j=1}^{m} a_{ijt} X_{j,t+1} + Y_i \ (i = 1, \ldots, m) , \tag{17}$$

where

$$a_{ijt} = X_{ijt}/X_{jt}, \ Y_i = p_i y_i .$$

Using the solution for the balance equations, the CPB composes macrobalancing multipliers

$$z_{j,t+1} = X_{j,t+1}/X_{jt} \quad (j = 1, \ldots, m) , \tag{18}$$

and sends the corresponding multiplier to group j.

(iii)   Group j in turn calculates its disaggregated input needs $z_{j,t+1}$, taking into account the directed multiplier, and presents this to the appropriate supplier group i.

(iv) Group i determines its disaggregated output target $x_{i,t+1}$ on round $t+1$ through a simple calculation for the corresponding microbalance:

$$x_{i,t+1} = \sum_{j=1}^{m} A_{ij} z_{j,t+1} x_{jt} + y_i \quad (i=1, \ldots, m) . \tag{19}$$

This completes the description of the generalized procedure. It is easily seen that Propositions 1 and 3 can be generalized in a straightforward fashion. We are then able to obtain

Proposition 1*. *The input-output type of macrobalance* (17) *has a unique positive solution if the initial value of the production target x_0 is positive and the price system is based on Eq.* (5) (*full-cost pricing including a uniform profit rate*).

Proof. Denote

$$\hat{P} = \mathrm{diag}\{p_1, \ldots, p_m\}, \quad \hat{X} = \mathrm{diag}\{x_1, \ldots, x_m\},$$
$$\tilde{A} = (a_{ij}), \quad e_m = (\underset{(1)}{1}, \ldots, \underset{(m)}{1}), \text{ an } m\text{-row vector.}$$

We then have

$$\begin{aligned} e\tilde{A}_t &= e\hat{P}A\hat{X}_t(\hat{P}\hat{X}_t)^{-1} \\ &= pA\hat{X}_t(\hat{P}\hat{X}_t)^{-1} \\ &< p\hat{X}_t(\hat{P}\hat{X}_t)^{-1} = e_m . \end{aligned}$$

Therefore

$$||\tilde{A}_t|| = \max_j \sum_i a_{ijt} < 1 \quad (t=0, 1, 2, \ldots) .$$

From this, Proposition 1* follows. Q.E.D.

Proposition 3*. *The process* (16)–(19) *converges to x^* on the first round if the initial target level for each sector group is a multiplication by a scalar of the corresponding solution for the group. Assume that*

$$x_{j0} = C_j x_j^*; \; C_j > 0, \; C_j \neq 1 \quad \text{for } j=1, \ldots, m .$$

Then $x_1 = x^*$. *If it is furthermore assumed that* $C_i \neq C_j$ *when* $i \neq j$, *the process in Section 3 is less speedy than the generalized process.*

Proof. If $x_{j0} = C_j x_j$, the macrobalance system (17) can be written as

$$C_i z_{i1} X_i^* = \sum_j a_{ij}^* (C_j z_{j1}) X_j^* + Y_i \quad (i = 1, \ldots, m) ,$$

where $X_i^* = p_i x_i^*$, $X_{ij}^* = p_i A_{ij} x_j^*$, and $a_{ij}^* = X_{ij}^*/X_j^*$. Note that

$$X_i^* = \sum_j a_{ij}^* X_j^* + Y_i \quad (i = 1, \ldots, m) ,$$

and taking into account Proposition 1, we have

$$C_j z_{j1} = 1; \ z_{j1} = 1/C_j \quad (j = 1, \ldots, m) .$$

Considering these relations, we can write the microbalance system (19) as

$$x_{i1} = \sum_j A_{ij} C_j^{-1} C_j x_j^* + y_i \quad (i = 1, \ldots, m) ,$$

and it follows that $x_1 = x^*$. If $C_i \neq C_j$ $(i \neq j)$, we can easily verify that in both process (3) and process (6)–(8), x_1 does not yield x^*; we omit this proof. Q.E.D.

However, a general convergence result similar to Proposition 2 has not been found due to the difficulty of assigning an explicit mathematical formulation to consolidation of commodities into aggregated categories. Neither has the speed of relative convergence been fully investigated. However, we can expect that the generalized process with aggregation-weight system p^* should be speedier than the generalized process not employing p^*. One reason for this is that the range of values of group-aggregated output will more or less tend to be fixed since the total output remains constant over each round when $p = p^*$.

5. Numerical Experiments

Having investigated the properties of stepwise aggregation processes, we next examine their behavior by using real data. We use Treml's 15-sector and 76-sector versions of the 1966 Soviet A matrix in current purchasers' price terms[4] to evaluate the total supply-demand imbalance shift over each round in the classical iterative and stepwise-aggregation process with current Soviet prices and the production-price system, at various aggregation levels. In numerical experiments we relax the assumptions on A and y; A is not diagonalizable and y may have some negative elements. The experiments begin with the initial output targets x_0 generated randomly from a distribution over an interval of $\pm 10\%$ around the Soviet 1966 level. The total absolute plan imbalance is measured by the distance between x_{t+1} and x_t; $||x_{t+1} - x_t|| = \sum_h |x_{h,t+1} - x_{h,t}|$. The relative imbalance is measured by the ratio $||x_{t+1} - x_t|| / ||x_1 - x_0||$, and we index $||x_1 - x_0||$ by 100. Many results are possible, but we list only the typical cases.

Table 1 compares the total imbalance shift over seven rounds between the classical iterative process and stepwise aggregation processes in the case of the 15-sector version ($n = 15$). Line 1 is clearly understandable but lines 2, 3, 4, and 5 may need some explanation. Line 2 shows the plan imbalance remaining after each round in the case of aggregation into a single commodity with the Soviet purchase-price system p which is set as $p = (1, ..., 1)$. Line 3 shows the corresponding imbalance with production prices ($p = p^*$). Line 4 shows the plan imbalance in the case of aggregation into three commodity groups ($m = 3$) with purchaser prices and line 5 does the same with production prices. Table 2 gives corresponding results using the 76-sector input-output table ($n = 76$).

From Tables 1 and 2 we can state the following: first, every stepwise aggregation process leads to considerably smaller errors than its corresponding classical iterative process after only a few rounds, particularly after one round. Second, a stepwise aggregation employing production prices rather than current purchaser prices results in slightly smaller margins of error. Third, a stepwise aggregation process where the number of aggregated groups equals one is remarkably less speedy than the process when the number is greater than one. Other than the

---

[4] For the Soviet 15-sector I-O table, see Treml (1977, pp. 52–54); for the 76-sector version and associated input-output matrix A, see Treml et al. (1972, pp. 430–511).

Table 1. Plan Imbalance Remaining After Each Round Using the 15-Sector I-O Table[a]

Process	Aggregation level	Price type	Round number							
			0	1	2	3	4	5	6	7
Classical process		Purchasers prices	100	71	54	42	33	26	20	16
Stepwise aggregation process	Aggregation into a single commodity ($m=1$)	Purchasers prices	100	25	9	2.5	1.6	0.71	0.25	0.13
		Production prices	100	21	9	3.6	1.7	0.69	0.31	0.14
	Aggregation into 3 groups ($m=3$)	Purchasers prices	100	19	7.3	2.9	1.2	0.48	0.19	0.08
		Production prices	100	17	6.8	2.8	1.1	0.46	0.19	0.08

[a]$n=15$.

Table 2. Plan Imbalance Remaining After Each Round Using the 76-Sector I-O Table[a]

Process	Aggregation level	Price type	Round number							
			0	1	2	3	4	5	6	7
Classical process		Purchasers prices	100	33	19	9	4.4	2.2	1.1	0.52
Stepwise aggregation process	Aggregtion into a single commodity ($m=1$)	Purchasers prices	100	14	4.2	1.0	0.48	0.15	0.06	0.02
		Production prices	100	12	2.9	0.90	0.30	0.12	0.02	0.01
	Aggregation into 3 groups ($m=3$)	Purchasers prices	100	6	1.5	0.33	0.09	0.02	0.01	0.00
		Production prices	100	6	1.3	0.25	0.07	0.02	0.00	0.00

[a]$n=76$.

statements given above, we can conclude in all the experiments performed, every macrobalancing multiplier converges to unity after only a few rounds. Due to these properties the stepwise process is very speedy.

6. Concluding Remarks

We have up to now assumed that the price system (5) or (14) should be given and fixed *a priori*. We can easily present iterative methods for determining the price system that are dual to (8) or (19). We could also solve the production-price Eq. (14) employing the iterative method:

$$p_{t+1} = \frac{p_t x}{p_t A x} p_t A, \ p_0 > o, \tag{20}$$

where x is a given positive output vector. However, any price-calculation process including Eq. (20) is outside the framework of the output-calculation process. Therefore, we have not answered the question posed by Manove and Weitzman: If the CPB had the information and facilities necessary to calculate a full-cost price vector, why could it not also calculate a well-balanced output target directly? This problem always arises when we employ standard static and dynamic input-output models as an analytical framework. Thus we must further explore stepwise aggregation processes allowing for polyhedral technologies and primary resources, which are considered in the following chapter. In conclusion, we feel that the stepwise aggregation process using production prices constitutes a critical step towards a more generalized stepwise aggregation process associated with shadow prices.

NOTES: A COMPARISON OF CONVERGENCE SPEED OF OLD AND NEW ITERATIVE PROCESSES FOR AN INPUT-OUTPUT SYSTEM

1. Introduction

It has been pointed out in the text that the old, standard iterative process employing power series expansion for solving the standard linear input-output system has the disadvantage of generally slow convergence speed. To speed up this process, a new iterative process using stepwise aggregation has been developed. While it has been verified that numerical experiments guarantee the speedier convergence of this new process, the theoretical setting for the comparison of convergence speed was confined to very special cases in the text and Soviet literature.

This note makes a comparison of the convergence speed of the two processes in a more general setting. Two sufficient conditions, using upper bounds of non-maximal eigenvalues of a stochastic matrix, are presented showing that the new process might converge more speedily than the old, standard process. This note will present some implications of these conditions, which may appear to be somewhat paradoxical in that the new process may not be as effective in the adjustment of relative output ratios as in the adjustment of output scale. This note is limited to an investigation of the stepwise aggregation process in the simplest case, and deals exclusively with the standard input-output model in *value terms*.

2. The Old and New Iterative Processes

In order to make this note self-contained, we begin by putting down the standard static input-output model that is assumed to be the economy-wide planning problem. Let there be n fully disaggregated commodities ($i, j = 1, \ldots, n$) and let $x = [x_i]$, $y = [y_i]$ and $A = (a_{ij})$ denote respectively, a fully disaggregated output n-column vector, final demand n-column vector, and an input-output n by n matrix appropriate to the given economy. For convenience we assume in the sequel that the nonnegative matrix A is productive and indecomposable, and that y is semi-positive. The model is written as

$$x = Ax + y, \qquad (\text{n.1})$$

and the unique positive solution to this equation is given by

$$x^* = (I - A)^{-1}y. \qquad (\text{n.2})$$

The old iterative method for finding a well-balanced output near x^* is described as follows: at round t the target is specified to be

$$x_t = Ax_{t-1} + y \quad (t = 1, 2, \ldots). \qquad (\text{n.3})$$

In view of the assumptions of the input-output matrix the process (n.3) should converge for any initial output vector x_0 with nonnegative elements. It can also be stated that its convergence speed is generally determined by the magnitude of the Frobenius eigenvalue λ^* of matrix A, and by the distance between x_0 and x^*.

These statements may be clarified as follows.
Define $E_t = x_t - x^*$, and it follows from (n.1) and (n.3) that

$$E_t = A^t E_0 \quad (t = 1, 2, \ldots). \qquad (\text{n.4})$$

Since A is productive, we have $A^t \to 0$ ($t \to \infty$), and $E_t \to 0$ ($t \to \infty$) for any E_0; $x_t \to x^*$ ($t \to \infty$) for any x_0. Further, let P and Λ be the matrix of row eigenvectors of A and the diagonal matrix of the corresponding eigenvalues; let P_i and $\bar{P}_i$ denote the ith row of P and the ith column of P^{-1}, and let λ_i be the ith diagonal of $\Lambda(\lambda_1 = \lambda^*)$. If an additional assumption is made that A is diagonalizable, we then have $A = P^{-1}\Lambda P$.

Hence we can rewrite (n. 4) as

$$E_t = P^{-1} \Lambda^t P E_0 = \sum_{i=1}^{n} \lambda_i^t (P_i E_0) \bar{P}_i . \qquad (\text{n.5})$$

$\bar{P}_1$ is strictly positive since A is indecomposable. Assume that $P_1 E_0 \neq 0$, and the absolute value of the first term of (n.5) is also strictly positive. Since the magnitude of the eigenvalues λ's other than λ^* is less than λ^*, the geometrical decline factor of the slowest damping term is λ^*. Accordingly, we can evaluate the rate of convergence of (n.3) by the unique, positive Frobenius eigenvalue of A, λ^*.

We next turn to the new iterative process for solving (n.1). The simplest version of this process can be written as

$$x_t = A z_t x_{t-1} + y,$$

$$z_t = \frac{py}{p(x_{t-1} - A x_{t-1})} = \frac{px_t}{px_{t-1}} \quad (t = 1, 2, \ldots) . \qquad (\text{n.6})$$

where p denotes the n-row vector of aggregation weights. As Eq. (n.1) is defined in value terms, p may be specified as the n-row vector e whose elements are all unity. The advantage of Eq. (n.6) may lie in the fact that the convergence will be speedier if we go beyond the old method by using the single parameter z: if $z > 1$ we are 'over-correcting'; if $z < 1$ we are 'under-correcting'; if $z = 1$ the new process mirrors the old process (n.3). Hence, the new process may be more effective when the initial output x_0 is far from the solution x^*; $x_0 \gg x^*$ or $x_0 \ll x^*$. It should be noted that a similar idea is employed in the successive over-relaxation (SOR) method (see Berman (1979, ch. 7)).

We now proceed to the aspect of convergence speed of (n.6). Define

$$w_t = x_t / e x_t ,$$

and

$$M = A + (ey)^{-1} y \cdot (e - eA) . \qquad (\text{n.7})$$

Then the process (n. 6) can be written in the form

75

$$w_t = Mw_{t-1} = \cdots = M^t w_0 .$$

As A is nonnegative, $e \geq eA$. Considering the semi-positiveness of y and $eM = e$, we find that M is a column stochastic matrix. As A is indecomposable, M is also indecomposable. Therefore, we have $w_t \to w^*$ ($t \to \infty$) for any positive w_0, and $x_t \to x^*$ for any positive x_0. Since the Frobenius eigenvalue of M equals unity, we should evaluate the convergence speed of (n. 6) by the second largest magnitude of eigenvalues of M (see Howard (1960, ch. 1)). It should be noted that we are assuming that the speed of convergence of w_t in the new process is proportional to that of x_t in the new process. This assumption seems to be plausible, since it is difficult to find examples where x_t converges slowly and w_t converges quickly in the same process. For example, if x_t is a scalar, both x_t and w_t in the new process converge to x^* and w^*, respectively, on the first round.

3. A comparison of Convergence Speed of Two Processes

For nonnegative matrix A we have the inclusion (Nikaido (1986, Theorem 7.5)):

$$\min_j \sum_{i=1}^n a_{ij} \leq \lambda^* \leq \max_j \sum_{i=1}^n a_{ij} \quad (j = 1, \ldots, n) . \qquad (n.8)$$

It should be noted that if we define the norm of A as l_1-norm we have $\|A\| = \max_j \sum_{i=1}^n a_{ij}$. Conversely, we have at least two upper bounds for the magnitude of an eigenvalue $\rho \neq 1$ of a column stochastic matrix $M = (m_{ij})$ (see Seneta (1981, Theorem 2. 10)) and (Berman (1979, Theorem 5.10):

$$|\rho| \leq \frac{1}{2} \max_{i,j} \sum_{s=1}^n |m_{si} - m_{sj}|; \qquad (n.9)$$

$$|\rho| \leq \min \{1 - \sum_{i=1}^n \min_j (m_{ij}), \sum_{i=1}^n \max_j (m_{ij}) - 1\} . \quad (n.10)$$

Letting the right sides of (n.9) and (n.10) denote B_1 and B_2, we have $|\rho| \leq B_k$ ($k = 1, 2$). Hence, considering (n.8), it is sufficient for the speedier convergence of the new process (n.6) to state that $B_k < \min_j \sum_{i=1}^n a_{ij}$ for either $k = 1$ or 2. If we employ (n.9) and (n.10), in view of the definition of M, we will be able to show that sufficient conditions for the faster convergence of (n.6) can be presented only by the a_{ij} elements excluding the y_i elements. The results are summarized in the following:

Proposition [Rabinovich(1980); Kuboniwa(1983)]. *The new process* (n.6) *converges more speedily than the old process* (n.3) *if one of the following conditions is fulfilled*:

[a] $\max\limits_{j} \sum_{s=1}^{n} a_{sj} < 3 \min\limits_{i} \sum_{s=1}^{n} a_{si} - \max\limits_{i,j} \sum_{s=1}^{n} |a_{si} - a_{sj}|$;

[b] $\min\limits_{j} \{ \max\limits_{j} \sum_{i=1}^{n} a_{ij} - \sum_{i=1}^{n} \min\limits_{j} a_{ij},$

   $\sum_{i=1}^{n} \max\limits_{j} a_{ij} - \min\limits_{j} \sum_{i=1}^{n} a_{ij} \} < \min\limits_{j} \sum_{i=1}^{n} a_{ij}$.

Proof.   In view of the definition of M, we have

$$m_{ij} = a_{ij} + (\sum_{k} y_{k})^{-1} y_i \cdot (1 - \sum_{i=1}^{n} a_{ij}),$$

we then have:

$$B_1 = \frac{1}{2} \max\limits_{i,j} \sum_{s=1}^{n} |m_{si} - m_{sj}|$$

$$= \frac{1}{2} \max\limits_{i,j} \sum_{s=1}^{n} |a_{si} - a_{sj} + (\sum_{k} y_{k})^{-1} \cdot y_s (\sum_{s} a_{sj} - \sum_{s} a_{si})|$$

$$\leq \frac{1}{2} \max\limits_{i,j} \sum_{s=1}^{n} |a_{si} - a_{sj}| + \frac{1}{2} \max\limits_{i,j} (\sum_{s} a_{sj} - \sum_{s} a_{si})$$

$$= \frac{1}{2} \max\limits_{i,j} \sum_{s=1}^{n} |a_{si} - a_{sj}| + \frac{1}{2} (\max\limits_{j} \sum_{s} a_{sj} - \min\limits_{i} \sum_{s} a_{st})$$

$$< \frac{1}{2} (3 \min\limits_{i} \sum_{s} a_{si} - \max\limits_{j} \sum_{s} a_{sj})$$

$$+ \frac{1}{2} (\max\limits_{j} \sum_{s} a_{sj} - \min\limits_{i} \sum_{s} a_{si}) \text{ (using [a])}$$

$$< \min\limits_{i} \sum_{s=1}^{n} a_{si}.$$

Hence, $|\rho| \leq B_1 < \lambda^*(\rho \neq 1)$ if condition [a] holds. Let us now turn to

77

the case of condition [b]. As is easily verified, we can have

$$1 - \sum_{i=1}^{n} \min_{j} (m_{ij}) = 1 - \sum_{i} \min_{j} \{a_{ij} + (\sum_{k} y_{k})^{-1} y_{i} (1 - \sum_{i} a_{ij})\}$$

$$= 1 - \sum_{i} \min_{j} a_{ij} - (\sum_{k} y_{k})^{-1} \cdot \sum_{i} y_{i} \cdot \min (1 - \sum_{i} a_{ij})$$

$$= \max \sum_{i=1}^{n} a_{ij} - \sum_{i=1}^{n} \min a_{ij},$$

and in an analogous manner

$$\sum_{i=1}^{n} \max (m_{ij}) - 1 = \sum_{i=1}^{n} \max_{j} a_{ij} - \min_{j} \sum_{i=1}^{n} a_{ij}.$$

This shows that B_2 is equal to the left-hand side of condition [b]; $B_2 < \min_{j} \sum_{i=1}^{n} a_{ij}$. The proposition follows. Q.E.D.

We may assign clear economic meanings to these conditions. Let us begin with condition [b]. Basically every row of an input-output matrix has at least one very small component so that $\min_{j} a_{ij}$ is basically equal to zero, hence $\max_{j} \sum_{i=1}^{n} a_{ij} - \sum_{i=1}^{n} \min_{j} a_{ij} = \max_{j} \sum_{i=1}^{n} a_{ij}$, and is never smaller than $\min_{j} \sum_{i=1}^{n} a_{ij}$. The condition therefore reduces to

$$\sum_{i=1}^{n} \max_{j} a_{ij} < 2 \min_{j} \sum_{i=1}^{n} a_{ij}.$$

This appears to be a very strong condition.

Similarly, condition [a] is stronger than $\max_{j} \sum_{s=1}^{n} a_{sj} < 3 \min_{j} \sum_{s=1}^{n} a_{si}$, which implies that the value of the inputs of an industry which uses the most inputs is less than three times the value of the inputs to the industry which uses the smallest amount. This is indeed a very strong condition.

Speed of convergence of planning procedures consists of two factors: adjustment speed of output scale and that of relative output ratios. In terms of scale adjustment, the new process is very effective as was stated in the text. Further, if we employ the von Neumann aggregation weights, the new process is effective in both the scale and relative ratios adjustment. However, as the above conditions suggest, in the general setting of a theoretical framework, the new process may not be as effective in the adjustment of relative output ratios as in the adjustment of output scale.

4. Seneta's Counter-example

Responding to Kuboniwa(1983), Seneta(1984) attempted to show that A exists for which even Jacobi iteration, defined by (n.3), is faster than the stepwise aggregation process, defined by (n.6). According to Seneta, sufficient conditions on A, which were found to ensure that $|\rho| < \lambda^*$, will not necessarily ensure that λ^* is smaller than the convergence rate for the Gauss-Seidel procedure. He found the following counter-example:

Take.

$$A = \begin{bmatrix} 0 & 0 & b \\ a & 0 & 0 \\ 0 & a & 0 \end{bmatrix}, \quad 0 < a, b < 1.$$

This has all its eigenvalues of modulus $\lambda^* = (a^2 b)^{1/3}$. Taking $y' = (1, 0, 0)$, it follows from (n.7) that

$$M = \begin{bmatrix} 1-a & 1-a & 1 \\ a & 0 & 0 \\ 0 & a & 0 \end{bmatrix}.$$

This has the eigenvalues 1 and $a(-1 + i\sqrt{3})/2$. Hence $|\rho| = a$. Taking $b < a$ ensures that $\lambda^* < |\rho|$.

The convergence rate of the Gauss-Seidel scheme for A is $(a^2 b)^{1/2}$. Therefore, even if $b \geq a$, the Gauss-Seidel rate, $(a^2 b)^{1/2}$, $< |\rho| = a$.

In regard to the above counter-example, we would like to note that the convergence speed of the Jacobi and Gauss-Seidel methods also depends upon the distance between the initial output x^0 and x^*. In fact, Seneta's counter-example does not necessarily ensure the generality of the slower convergence of the new, stepwise aggregation method.

Take

$$A = \begin{bmatrix} 0 & 0 & 0.2 \\ 0.5 & 0 & 0 \\ 0 & 0.5 & 0 \end{bmatrix}, \quad y = \begin{bmatrix} 1 \\ 0 \\ 0 \end{bmatrix} \quad \text{and} \quad x_0 = \begin{bmatrix} 4 \\ 2 \\ 1 \end{bmatrix}.$$

Then we have the following computation results:

the Jacobi process:

$x_1 = (1.200 \ 2.000 \ 1.000)'$
$x_2 = (1.200 \ 0.600 \ 1.000)'$
$x_3 = (1.200 \ 0.600 \ 0.300)'$
$x_4 = (1.060 \ 0.600 \ 0.300)'$
$x_5 = (1.060 \ 0.530 \ 0.300)'$
$x_6 = (1.060 \ 0.530 \ 0.265)'$
$x_7 = (1.053 \ 0.530 \ 0.265)'$

the Gauss-Seidel process:

$x_1 = (1.200 \ 0.600 \ 0.300)'$
$x_2 = (1.060 \ 0.530 \ 0.265)'$
$x_3 = (1.053 \ 0.527 \ 0.263)'$
$x_4 = (1.053 \ 0.526 \ 0.263)'$

the stepwise aggregation process:

$x_1 = (1.053 \ 0.526 \ 0.263)'; \ z_1 = 0.263$
$x_2 = (1.053 \ 0.526 \ 0.263)'; \ z_2 = 1.000$

5. Concluding Remarks

We have obtained two sufficient conditions for the faster convergence of the new iterative process which we call the stepwise aggregation process. We have clarified that these conditions are very strong from an economic view point. This economic interpretation suggests that the new process may not be as efficient in the adjustment of relative output ratios as in the adjustment of output scale. Seneta's counter-example should be understood in this context. Let us conclude this note with the following additional remarks. First, unlike the SOR method, we can assign clear economic meaning to the stepwise aggregation process presented in the text. Secondly, this note shows that an iterative method for the solution of a linear system is closely related to the "probability algorithm" and the theory of eigenvalues of a stochastic matrix (see e.g., Seneta (1981, 2.2., 2.5 and 7.5).

Chapter 4

STEPWISE AGGREGATION FOR OPTIMAL

PLANNING

1. Introduction

Mathematical models for indirectly centralized planning processes can be classified into two types:

1. models for material-balances processes i.e., the Montias-Levine model for the material-balances process in a Soviet-type economy, and so on.

2. models for optimal planning, i.e., the Lange-Arrow-Hurwicz-Novozhilov model of price-guided planning, the Kornai-Liptak-Weitzman-Heal model of quantity-guided planning, and so on.

These models showed that the decomposition and iterative methods are useful for planning models in a large scale economy. However, they have two disadvantages. First, they do not allow for any aggregation of the variables and parameters in the initial nation-wide economic planning problem. Secondly, their convergence speed is generally very slow.

One possible way to avoid these disadvantages is to establish an optimal planning process with stepwise aggregation and disaggregation that appropriately coordinates an aggregated "macro-model" in the Central Planning Bureau (CPB) with more detailed "micro-models" at lower levels (sectors or sector groups) in an iterative manner, and thus accelerates its convergence to the solution.[1] As one step toward this goal, in the previous chapter we developed the Montias-Levine model for the material balances process, based on the Soviet contribution, and considered a stepwise aggregation process with full-cost price formation, for a static input-output system.

This chapter further develops this line, and presents an optimal step-wise aggregation process (K-process) for a convex programming problem, including the linear programming case, which provides for speedier convergence than the process (V-process) presented by Vakhutinsky (1979).

2. The Initial Model

Let us introduce the following notations:

$s \in S$: an index of a resource and its set; $k \in K$: an index of a macro-variable (activity level) and its set; $j \in J$: an index of a sector and its set; $k \in K_j$: an index of the micro-variables belonging to sector j and its set. For sets S, K, J, and K_j we assume:

$$|K| \geq |S|, \quad |K| \geq |J| \text{ and } |K| = \sum_{j \in J} |K_j|.$$

Define x_j: sector j's activity vector (a $|K_j|$ dimensional column vector, $x_j = (x_k | k \in K_j)'$); $f_{sj}(x_j)$: sector j's net output of resource s (a C^2 class concave function; $f_{sj}(o)=0$); $c_j(x_j)$: sector j's labor input (a C^2 class concave function; $c_j(o)=0$); and $y_s(s \in S)$: net final demand for resource s. The notation ($'$) shows the transpose of the corresponding vector or matrix.

We can now write the initial model as

(NLP) $\min \sum_{j \in J} c_j(x_j)$

$$\sum_{j \in J} f_{sj}(x_j) = y_s, \quad s \in S,$$

$$x_j \geq o, \quad j \in J.$$

The set of the optimal plans and prices is denoted as

---

[1]   Another method for avoiding the slow convergence of the Dantzig-Wolfe process was presented by Kornai (1969). A different approach to the problem of aggregation in optimal planning was employed by Hare (1981). However, the latter did not consider the problem of convergence speed. Further, his process does not give an optimal plan for the initial planning problem. The importance of the introduction of aggregation in optimal planning was also suggested by Koopmans (1951) and Malinvaud (1967).

$[x^*, p^*]$, where $x^* = (x_k^* \mid k \in K)'$ and $p^* = (p_s^* \mid s \in S)'$.

It should be noted that in this chapter all the vectors, including a vector of prices, are defined as a column vector.

For the initial model we assume:

(A1) f_{sj} and c_j are homogeneous functions of the first degree, namely for any scalar $Z_j \geqq 0$

$$f_{sj}(Z_j x_j) = Z_j f_{sj}(x_j) , \quad s \in S; j \in J \tag{1}$$

$$c_j(Z_j x_j) = Z_j c_j(x_j) , \quad j \in J .$$

Then, by virtue of the Euler theorem, we can write

$$f_{sj}(x_j) = \sum_{k \in K_j} a_{sk} x_k, \text{ where } a_{sk} = \partial f_{sj}(x_j)/\partial x_k \tag{2}$$

and

$$c_j(x_j) = \sum_{k \in K_j} c_k x_k, \text{ where } c_k := \partial c_j(x_j)/\partial x_k .$$

Therefore the initial model (NLP) can be written as

(NLP') $\min \sum_{k \in K} c_k x_k$

$$\sum_{k \in K} a_{sk} x_k = y_s , \quad s \in S ,$$

$$x_k \geqq 0 , \quad k \in K .$$

It also follows from assumption (A.1) that for any scalar $\theta_j \geqq 0$

$$a_{sk}(\theta_j x_j) = a_{sj}(x_j) . \tag{3}$$

3. Stepwise Aggregation in Optimal Planning

We assume that on round $t-1$ each sector j computes its net demand-supply of resources $f_{sj,t-1}$ and profit $\Pi_{j,t-1}$, and communicates this information to the CPB:

$$f_{sj,t-1} = f_{sj}(x_{j,t-1}) , \quad s \in S; j \in J ,$$

$$\Pi_{j,t-1} = \sum_{s \in S} f_{sj}(x_{j,t-1}) p_{s,t-1} - c_j(x_{j,t-1}) , \quad j \in J . \tag{4}$$

The steps of a stepwise aggregation process, the K-process for the solution of the initial model as a non-centralized planning procedure, are described in the following fashion:

Step 1.   The CPB solves the following profit maximization macro-model, and sends the corresponding macrobalancing multiplier $Z_{jt}(j \in J)$ to sector j.

(C) $\max \{ \sum_{j \in J} \Pi_{j,t-1} Z_j - 2^{-1} Q_o \sum_{s \in S} (y_s - \sum_{j \in J} f_{sj,t-1} Z_j)^2 \}$,

$$Z_j \geqq 0, \quad j \in J,$$

where Q_o is a positive parameter.

Step 2.   Each sector j $(j \in J)$ solves the following profit maximization micro-model.

(L_j) $\max \{ \sum_{s \in S} f_{sj}(x_j) P_{s,t-1} - c_j(x_j) - 2^{-1} Q \sum_{s \in S} (f_{sj}(x_{j,t-1}) Z_j - f_{sj}(x_j))^2 \}$,

$$x_j \geqq o,$$

where Q is a positive constant.   Using the solution x_{jt} and Eq. (4), each sector j calculates its net outputs $f_{sjt}(s \in S)$ and submits them to the CPB, where

$$f_{sjt} = f_{sj}(x_{jt}) . \tag{5}$$

Step 3.   The CPB (or "market") adjusts prices by

$$p_{st} = \max \{ 0, p_{s,t-1} + \alpha Q(y_s - \sum_{j \in J} f_{sjt}) \} , \quad s \in S , \tag{6}$$

where α is a positive parameter, and sends $p_t = (p_{st} | s \in S)'$ to each sector j.

Step 4.   Each sector j $(j \in J)$ calculates its profit Π_{jt}, and communicates it to the CPB, where

$$\Pi_{jt} = \sum_{s \in S} f_{sj}(x_{jt}) p_{st} - c_j(x_{jt}) , \quad j \in J . \tag{7}$$

It should be noted that in this process the dimension of the CPB macro-model is not the dimension of vector x, the number of activities

($|K|$), but that of vector Z ($Z=(Z_j|j{\in}J)'$), the number of sectors ($|J|$). Assuming that the number of activities are much greater than that of sectors ($|K|{\gg}|J|$), this process may relieve the CPB of the need to make detailed information processing.

4. Properties of the K-Process

We first prove the following proposition.

Proposition 1. *Assume*

(A2) $\qquad \Sigma_{s{\in}S}(f_{sj}(x_{jt}))^2>0$, $j{\in}J;\ t=0,\ 1,\ 2,\ ...$.

Under assumptions (A1) *and* (A2) *the stationary point of K-process* $[x^{\dagger},\ p^{\dagger}]$ *is the optimal solution* $[x^*,\ p^*]$ *of the initial problem* (NLP).

Proof Using Eq. (2), the Kuhn-Tucker condition for the macro-model, (C), and the micro-models, (L_j)s, can be written as

$$x'_{j,t-1}(A'_{j,t-1}p_{t-1}-c_{j,t-1})$$
$$-Q_0x'_{j,t-1}A'_{j,t-1}(\Sigma_{j{\in}J}A_{j,t-1}x_{j,t-1}Z_{tj}-y)\leqq0, \quad j{\in}J, \qquad (8)$$

and

$$A'_{jt}p_{t-1}-c_{jt}-QA'_{j,t-1}(A_{jt}x_{jt}-Z_{jt}A_{j,t-1}x_{j,t-1})\leqq o, \quad j{\in}J, \qquad (9)$$

where

$$c_j=(c_k|k{\in}K_j)', \text{ where } c_k={\partial}c_j(x_j)/{\partial}x_k,$$
$$A_j=(a_{sk}|s{\in}S,\ k{\in}K_j), \text{ where } a_{sk}={\partial}f_{sj}(x_j)/{\partial}x_k,$$
$$y=(y_s|s{\in}S)'.$$

By definition

$$x_{t-1}=x_t=x^{\dagger};\ p_{t-1}=p_t=p^{\dagger};\ Z_t=Z^{\dagger};$$
$$C_{j,t-1}=C_{jt}=C_j^{\dagger};\ A_{j,t-1}=A_{jt}=A_j^{\dagger}(j{\in}J).$$

In the following we consider only the stationary point and omit the superscript ($\dagger$).

On the stationary point we have by Eq. (6)

$$\Sigma_{j\in J} A_j x_j = y.$$ (10)

Using Eq. (10), compile $\Sigma_{j\in J}(1-Z_j)\times$ Eq. (8). We then have

$$\Sigma_{j\in J}(1-Z_j)x_j'(A_j'p-c_j)+Q\Sigma_{j\in J}(1-Z_j)^2 x_j' A_j' A_j x_j \leq 0.$$ (11)

Compiling $\Sigma_{j\in J}(1-Z_j)x_j'\times$ Eq. (9), we have

$$\Sigma_{j\in J}(1-Z_j)x_j'(A_j'p-c_j)-Q_0\Sigma_{j\in J}(1-Z_j)^2 x_j' A_j' A_j x_j = 0.$$ (12)

Subtracting Eq. (12) from (11), it follows from $(Q_0+Q)>0$ that

$$\Sigma_{j\in J}(1-Z_j)^2 x_j' A_j' x_j \leq 0.$$ (13)

By assumption (A2) we have

$$x_j' A_j' A_j x_j = \Sigma_{s\in S} f_{sj}^2 > 0.$$

Therefore we have

$$Z_j = 1, \quad j\in J.$$ (14)

Eq. (9) can then be written

$$A_j'p-c_j \leq o, \quad j\in J.$$ (15)

From Eqs. (10) and (15), Proposition 1 follows. Q.E.D.

For simplicity, let us assume

(A3) Any micro-model (L_j) has a unique solution on each round of iteration.

We have then an interesting proposition.

Proposition 2. *Assume* (A1) *to* (A3). *The K-process converges to* x^* *on the first round if the initial activity level for each sector is a multiplication of the corresponding solution for the sector and the initial prices are optimal. Assume*

$$x_{j_0} = \theta_j x_j^*; \; \theta_j > 0; j\in J, \text{ and } p_0 = p^*.$$

Then $x_1 = x^*$; i.e., $x_{k1} = x^*$, $k \in K$.

Proof. Assume $x_{j_0} = \theta_0 x_j^*$. We then have by Eqs. (1) to (3)

$$c_j(\theta_j x_j^*) = \sum_{k \in K_j} \frac{\partial c_j(\theta x_j^*)}{\partial x_k} \theta_j x_k^*$$

$$= \sum_{k \in K_j} \frac{\partial c_j(x_j^*)}{\partial x_k} \theta_j x_k^*$$

$$= \theta_j \sum_{k \in K_j} c_k^* x_k^* , \quad j \in J .$$

We also have

$$f_{sj}(\theta_j x_j^*) = \theta_j \sum_{k \in K_j} a_{sk}^* x_k^* , \quad s \in S; j \in J .$$

Hence, taking into consideration the relation

$$\theta_j x_j^{*\prime}(A_j^{*\prime} p^* - c_j^*) = 0 , \quad j \in J ,$$

Eq. (13) can be written as

$$\sum_{j \in J}(1 - \theta_j Z_j)^2 \theta_j^2 x_j^{*\prime} A_j^{*\prime} x_j^{*\prime} \leq 0 . \tag{16}$$

Considering the assumption (A2) and $\theta_j > 0$ $(j \in J)$, we have

$$Z_{j1} = 1/\theta_j \quad (j \in J) . \tag{17}$$

Then, it follows from Eq. (9) that

$$x_{j1}' A_j^{*\prime}(A_{j1} x_{j1} - \theta_j^{-1} A_j^*(\theta_j x_j^*)) = 0 , \quad j \in J . \tag{18}$$

Hence, from Eq. (18) and assumption (A3) we obtain

$$x_{j1} = x_j^* \quad (j \in J); \ x_1 = x^* . \qquad \text{Q.E.D.}$$

It should be noted that this proposition is an extension of Proposition 2 in Chapter 3, which is related to the assertion of Manove-Weitzman (1978).

As is easily verified, Propositon (P2) has the following corollaries.

Corollary. *Assume* (A1) *to* (A3). *Then*

(1) $x_{t+1} = x^*$ if $x_{jt} = \theta_j x_j^*$ $(\theta_j > 0; j \in J)$ and $p_t = p^*$.

(2) $x_{t+1} = x^*$; $p_{t+1} = p^*$ if $x_t = x^*$ and $p_t = p^*$.

If we employ the method used by Vakhutinsky et al. (1979) and Vakhutinsky (1979), we can easily obtain:

Propositon 3. *Assume that the non-degeneracy conditions hold at the optimal solution of the initial model (NLP) and that*

$$0 < \alpha < \frac{2}{Q/Q_0 + |J|} .$$ (19)

Then the K-process locally converges to the solution.

Considering Propositions 1 and 3, we may state that for any $j \in J$

(I) $\begin{cases} x_{j0} \approx \theta_j x_j^*; \to \text{(II)} \\ p_0 \approx p^* \end{cases}$ $\begin{cases} x_{j1} \approx x_j^* \to \text{(III)} \\ p_1 \approx p^* \end{cases}$ $\begin{cases} x_{j2} = x_j^*; \\ p_2 = p^*. \end{cases}$

Namely, if the initial activity level for each sector is approximately a multiplication of the corresponding optimal plan for the sector and the initial prices are approximately optimal (stage (I)), then the activity level for each sector approaches close to the corresponding approximate optimal plan on the first round (stage (II)), and thus the K-process converges to the optimal plans and prices on the second round (stage (III)).

As is well known, the convergence speed of the Dantzig-Wolfe process (DW-process), based on a decomposition principle, depends upon how near its initial plan x_0 is to the optimal plan x^*. While the DW-process does not incorporate any mechanism for speeding up the iterative process, Proposition 2 shows that the K-process provides one such mechanism which does offer speedy convergence if the sectoral initial plans are uniformly far from the optimal plans. By virtue of Corollary (1), in the K-process, given the optimal prices, final decision-making regarding sectoral plans can be decentralized, while it should be centralized in the DW-process.

5. K-Process and V-Process

Unlike the K-process, the stepwise aggregation process (V-process) developed by Vakhutinsky and his group does not take full advantage of the aggregation factor. In order to clarify this statement, we consider an extreme case: (1) the initial model is a linear programming model; (2) the unknown variable of the macro-model is a scalar Z ("aggregation" of vector x into scalar Z); (3) a micro-model is set for each activity k. Then we can describe the V-process as follows.

On round $t-1$ the parameters are aggregated:

$$a_{s,t-1} = \sum_{k \in K} a_{sk} x_{k,t-1} , \tag{20}$$

$$\Pi_{t-1} = \sum_{k \in K} (\sum_{s \in S} p_{s,t-1} a_{sk} - c_k) x_{k,t-1} . \tag{21}$$

Step 1.   Solution of the macro-model:

(DC) $\max_{Z \geq 0} \{ \Pi_{t-1} Z - 2^{-1} \beta (Z-1)^2 - 2^{-1} Q_0 \sum_{s \in S} (y_s - a_{s,t-1} Z)^2 \}$,

where β is a positive parameter. The solution of this problem is denoted by Z_t.

Step 2.   Solution of the micro-model in each subsystem k:

(DL$_k$) $\max_{x_k \geq 0} \{ (\sum_{s \in S} p_{s,t-1} a_{sk} - c_k) x_k - 2^{-1} Q \sum_{s \in S} (a_{sk} x_{k,t-1} Z_t - a_{sk} x_k)^2 \}$.

Denote the solution of this problem by $\hat{x}_{kt}$.

Step 3.   The preliminary adjustment of the prices:

$$\hat{p}_{st} = p_{s,t-1} + \alpha Q (y_s - \sum_{k \in K} a_{sk} x)_k , \quad s \in S . \tag{22}$$

Step 4.   The next approximation for the variables:

$$x_{kt} = (1-\gamma) x_{k,t-1} + \gamma \hat{x}_{kt} , \quad k \in K;$$

$$p_{st} = (1-\gamma) p_{s,t-1} + \gamma \hat{p}_{st} , \quad s \in S , \tag{23}$$

where γ is a process parameter, $0 < \gamma < 1$.

It should be noted that the V-process, unlike the K-process, includes a term $-2^{-1} \beta (Z-1)^2$ in the CPB macro-model and takes a "mixed" strategy in approximating the variables.

Let us assume that $x_{k0}=\theta x_k^*$ ($\theta>0$, $\theta\neq1$; $k\in K$) and $p_{s0}=p_s^*(s\in S)$. Then Eqs. (20) and (21) can be written as

$$a_{s0}=\theta\Sigma_{k\in K}a_{sk}x_k^*\,,$$

$$\Pi_0=\theta\Sigma_{k\in K}(\Sigma_{s\in S}p_s^*a_{sk}-c_k)x_k^*\,.$$

Define the objective function of the macro-model as

$$g(z)=\Pi_0Z-2^{-1}(Z-1)^2-2^{-1}Q_0\Sigma(y_s-a_{s0}Z)^2\,,$$

and for $Z>0$

$$\partial g(Z)/\partial Z=\Pi_0-\beta(Z-1)-Q_0\Sigma_{s\in S}a_{s0}(a_{s0}-y_s)=0\,.$$

Considering $\Pi_0=0$ and $y_s=\Sigma_{k\in K}a_{sk}x_k^*$, we have

$$Z_1=\frac{Q_0R+\beta}{\theta Q_0R+\beta},\text{ where }\qquad R=\Sigma_{s\in S}y_s^2\,. \qquad (24)$$

Define the objective function of the micro-model as

$$g_k(x_k)=(\Sigma_{s\in S}p_s^*a_{sk}-c_k)x_k-2^{-1}Q\Sigma_{s\in S}(\theta a_{sk}x_k^*Z_1-a_{sk}x_k)^2\,,$$

and for $x_k>0$

$$\partial g_k(x_k)/\partial x_k=\Sigma_{s\in S}p_s^*a_{sk}-c_k-Q\Sigma_{s\in S}a_{sk}-(a_{sk}x_k-\theta a_{sk}x_k^*Z_1)=0\,.$$

Considering $\Sigma_{s\in S}p_s^*a_{sk}-c_k=0$, we have

$$\hat{x}_{k1}=\theta Z_1x_k^*\,. \qquad (25)$$

Using Eqs. (24) and (25), Eq. (28) can be re-written as

$$x_{k1}=\left\{(1-\gamma)+\gamma\cdot\frac{Q_0R+\beta}{\theta Q_0R+\beta}\right\}\theta x_k^*\,. \qquad (26)$$

It follows from $0<\gamma<1$ that

$$x_{k1}\neq x_k^*,\quad k\in\{k\,|\,x_k^*>0\}\,.$$

This implies that Proposition 2 does not hold for the V-process. Since x_{k1} is not equal to x_k^*, it follows from Eqs. (22) and (23) that p_{s1}, does not coincide with p_s^*. Namely, starting from the optimal prices, the V-process yields a set of non-optimal prices on the next round.

Assume $\beta=0$ and $\gamma=1$ in the above V-process, and we have the simplest version of K-process. Then, it follows from Eqs. (24), (25) and (26) that

$$x_{k0}=\theta x_k^* \rightarrow (Z_1=1/\theta) \rightarrow \hat{x}_{k1}=x_{k1}=x_k^*, \quad k \in K .$$

On the other hand, if β is sufficiently large in the V-process ($\beta>0$, $0< \gamma<1$), we can arrive at the stage $Z_1 \approx 1$ without the need for macrobalancing which is the main function of the macro-model.

6. Numerical Experiments

Here we offer comparative degrees of convergence speed for the K-and-V-process by simple numerical experiments, based on the framework of Section 5. The initial model is a linear programming problem:

$$\min c'x; \ Ax=y, \quad x \geq o .$$

Numerical experiments are carried out using the following data;

Example 1.

$K_1= \{1, 2\}, K_2= \{3, 4\}, K_3= \{5, 6\}; \ |J|=3, \ |K|=6, \ |S|=3,$

$$A = \begin{array}{ccc} A_1 & A_2 & A_3 \end{array}$$
$$A = \begin{bmatrix} 0.8 & 0.9 & -0.1 & -0.1 & -0.4 & -0.3 \\ -0.1 & -0.3 & 0.7 & 0.6 & -0.1 & -0.1 \\ -0.2 & -0.2 & -0.2 & -0.1 & 0.7 & 0.8 \end{bmatrix},$$

$$y = \begin{bmatrix} 3 \\ 5 \\ 3 \end{bmatrix},$$

$c' = (5.0 \quad 4.0 \ \vdots \ 4.0 \quad 4.0 \ \vdots \ 2.0 \quad 3.0),$

$Q_0=Q=10; \ \alpha=0.001$

The relative plan imbalance on round t is measured by

Table 1. Plan Imbalance Remaining After Each Round
Using Example 1

	K-process				V-process	
t	case 1	case 2	case 3	case 4	case 5	case 6
1	100.00	100.00		100.00	100.00	100.00
2	0.00	0.00	0.02	0.02	11.77	50.00
3			0.00	0.00	8.55	25.00

Table 2. Plan Imbalance Remaining After Each Round
Using Example 2

	K-process				V-process	
t	case 1	case 2	case 3	case 4	case 5	case 6
1	100.00	100.00	100.00	100.00	100.00	100.00
2	0.00	0.16	2.61	3.26	32.24	57.22

$$(\sum_k |x_{kt} - x_{k,t-1}| / \sum_k |x_{k1} - x_{k0}|) \times 100 .$$

Table 1 compares the total imbalance shift over three rounds between
the K-and-V-process in the following cases ($\theta_j > 0$; $\theta_j \neq 1, j \in J$):

Case 1 $x_{j_0} = \theta_j x_j^*$ $(j \in J)$; $p_0 = p^*$.

Case 2 $x_{j_0} = \theta_j x_j^*$ $(j \in J)$; $p_0 = p^*$.

Case 3 $x_{j_0} = \theta_j x_j^*$ $(j \in J)$; $p_0 \approx p^*$.

Case 4 $x_{j_0} \approx \theta_j x_j^*$ $(j \in J)$; $p_0 \approx p^*$.

Case 5 $x_{j_0} = \theta_j x_j^*$ $(j \in J)$; $p_0 = p^*$; $\beta = 100$; $\gamma = 1$.

Case 6 $x_{j_0} \approx \theta_j x_j^*$ $(j \in J)$; $p_0 = p^*$; $\beta = 0$; $\gamma = 0.5$.

Table 2 gives corresponding results over two rounds using numerical
data where matrix A and vector y are as follows:

Example 2.

$$
A = \begin{array}{ccccccc}
& \multicolumn{2}{c}{A_1} & \multicolumn{2}{c}{A_2} & \multicolumn{2}{c}{A_3} \\
& \left[\begin{array}{cc} 0.8 & 0.9 \end{array}\right. & \begin{array}{cc} -0.1 & -0.1 \end{array} & \begin{array}{cc} -0.4 & -0.3 \end{array}\left.\right]
\end{array}
$$

$$
A = \left[\begin{array}{cc|cc|cc}
0.8 & 0.9 & -0.1 & -0.1 & -0.4 & -0.3 \\
-0.1 & -0.3 & 0.7 & 0.6 & -0.1 & -0.1 \\
-0.2 & -0.2 & -0.2 & -0.1 & 0.7 & 0.8 \\
\hline
-0.1 & -0.1 & -0.2 & -0.2 & -0.3 & -0.3
\end{array}\right],
$$

$$
y = \left[\begin{array}{c}
3 \\
5 \\
3 \\
\hline
-5.1
\end{array}\right]
$$

For Tables 1 and 2 we can state that the K-process is speedier than the V-process, and thus provides for an effective planning process.

7. Concluding Remarks

In this chapter we have attempted to investigate a stepwise aggregation method for speeding up the optimal planning process. The planning process presented suggests a possible way for improving the mechanism of central planning along the line developed by Brus (1967), although the process presented here is inadequate in that it incorporates only aggregation of activities and does not consider the introduction of aggregation of commodities or constraint constants.

The dimensionality in a planning problem can be reduced not only by aggregation but also by omitting certain variables.[2] When we consider a stepwise aggregation process allowing for the omitting of variables and parameters, we will be able to discuss the problem of an optimal combination of planning and market in a more realistic fashion. While this is one of the most important unanswered questions for improving the mechanism of central planning and for making the planning theory much more realistic, the author feels the stepwise aggregation process presented in this chapter will constitute a step toward this goal.

In conclusion, the author would like to stress the following: The

---

[2] See Heal (1973) pp. 325–337.

stepwise aggregation method can be interpreted in two ways: (1) a simple, formal "rationalization" of hierarchical, traditional Soviet-type planning; (2) an effective method or theory for the possibility of regulating the market mechanism, based on the development of market relations and, in turn, ensuring the efficient behavior of the market mechanism. In the second case, our research on the stepwise aggregation and disaggregation process suggests that the central planning activity can be limited to instructions of a high degree of aggregates, the number of "dialogues" between the CPB and production units can be stopped on the first round and the detailed calculation of production and prices should be performed by the market mechanism itself.

Chapter 5

INPUT-OUTPUT STRUCTURES OF SOVIET

AND EAST EUROPEAN ECONOMIES:

A COMPARATIVE VIEW

1. Introduction

In this chapter and Chapter 6 we clarify the fundamental, actual input-output structures of the Soviet and East European economies, as well as the basic data structures of input-output tables of these countries. The results are shown numerically or graphically. With regard to the input-output structures of the Soviet and East European countries, even the fundamental facts have not yet been fully described. Therefore, in consideration of this situation, in this chapter and Chapter 6 we make use of only classical tools for the input-output analysis.

The East European countries considered here include Hungary, Poland, Czechoslovakia, Yugoslavia and Bulgaria. We make use of the input-output tables for each country in current prices, which cover an approximately five year span, from the period around the year 1959 to the period around the year 1975. In regard to the Bulgarian economy only the Bulgarian 1963 input-output table is used.

In these chapters we intend to perform an international and inter-temporal comparison of actual input-output structures. However, it should be noted that this chapter presents preliminary work which will require further research. Therefore, these chapters do not treat two important tasks necessary for a proper international and, or, inter-temporal comparison, namely, (1) modification of distortions of the price structures in each country in order to accurately reflect the technological structure of production, and (2) compilation of sectoral deflators of commodities.

This chapter first considers the data structures of the Soviet and East European input-output tables which are also used in the following chapter. Secondly, after briefly examining macro input-output structures, the basic computational results of standard static input-output analysis, which include intermediate input and demand ratios, and Rasmussen coefficients, using 15 to 20-sector input-output tables, are described. We further present a comparison of input-output structures of the Soviet Union and the United States, using the disaggregated 1972 commodity-by-commodity input-output tables. In Chapter 6 an input-output analysis of the foreign trade of the Soviet and East European economies is comparatively described.

2. Soviet Input-Output Tables

As is known, the prototype of the Leontief input-output table is the pioneering balance of the national economy for 1923–4 by the Soviet Statistical Administration. Professor Leontief completed the first successful description of the contemporary input-output table before the Second World War. In the Soviet Union, Stalin referred to the pioneering balance as a mere "game with figures" and the development of this statistical tool was curtailed.

The need to employ Leontief's input-output table, which was completed in the United States, was officially announced by Starovsky (1956, p. 21) three years after the death of Stalin. Let us briefly state the history of Soviet input-output tables after 1956 to the present. Three stages can be distinguished as follows:

The first stage (1956 to 1960): Soviet authorities admitted the possibility of application of input-output analysis and optimal planning theory to the centrally planned countries. The Central Economic Mathematical Institute of the U.S.S.R. Academy of Sciences compiled a preliminary version of the Soviet input-output table.

The second stage (1960 to 1970): The Central Statistical Administration compiled the first Soviet input-output table, the 1959 83-sector table, and the second Soviet input-output table, the 1966 110-sector table. The traditional MPS type of input-output table was provided with a complete mode. A large scale of commodity-establishment adjustment was carried out and the commodity-by-commodity input-output tables were compiled. Also compiled were large employment and fixed capital matrixes. These additional matrixes provide a significant improvement in the Soviet input-output tables in comparison with those of the United States. However, a strange publication method was institutionalized by the Soviet authorities, namely, only the partial first quadrant of the input-output table was made public. Due to this fact the U.S. Department of Commerce began to reconstruct and estimate the Soviet input-output table under the direction of Professor V. Treml of Duke University. It should also be noted that various types of prices were calculated in the Soviet Union by Belkin, and this work formed a basis of the revision of Soviet wholesale prices in the 1965 economic reforms.

The third stage (1970 to 1988): The Central Statistical Administration compiled the basic input-output tables for the bench mark years 1972, 1977 and 1982. Compilation of the input-output tables has since been institutionalized. Various static and dynamic input-output analysis, including computation of turnpike and optimal prices, were carried out and the national balances of accounts, based on the U.N. SNA method, were tentatively compiled. However, the actual statistical figures for these analyses and balances have not been made public. The most remarkable change of the third stage is that the Soviet authorities stopped publishing even the partial first quadrant of the input-output table starting in 1977. At the beginning of the 1980's it was said that the Soviet mathematical economists were denied the authorization to make use of input-output analysis and optimal planning theory. This reflects the Soviet attitude of secrecy in regard to statistical data. After Gorbachev assumed the position of First Secretary of the CPSU he began to reform Soviet policy regarding publication of statistical data. However, as of July of 1988, the 1977, 1982 and the latest version of the Soviet input-output tables have not yet been made public. Regardless of this fact, remarkable changes have taken place in Soviet economic attitudes. For example, proposals for the reform of the Soviet price system based on dynamic input-output analysis and optimal price theory have been put forward by scholars on the staff of the Central Economic Mathematical Institute, including Petrakov, Volkonsky and Iasin (see Chapter 8).

The basic outline of the Soviet input-output tables is shown in Table 1. It may be helpful to provide additional comments on the characteristics of the data structure of the Soviet input-output table.

As has been previously mentioned, the Soviet input-output table is compiled by use of the traditional MPS method. The activities of the "non-material" (unproductive) service sector are excluded from the value added quadrant and the intermediate transaction quadrant of the input-output table. The non-material service sectors are treated as a final demand column sector in the MPS.

In the Soviet case the activities of passenger transportation and the private use of communication facilities are excluded from the intermediate quadrant of the input-output tables. Further, all the outputs of the construction sector are placed into the final demand quadrant.

Domestically produced products are evaluated in terms of purchasers' prices, imported products are evaluated in terms of CIF prices and export products are evaluated in terms of FOB prices, excluding the turnover taxes. The supply price of each imported product is the ex-customs price, including the turnover tax.

The Soviet MPS method provides the format for the input-output table as shown in Table 3.

Each element of the first and second quadrants is specified in the total sums (T) of the domestically produced commodities use (D) and imported commodities use (I). Namely, the Soviet input-output table employs a competitive import method. The total uses and outputs are specified as the total supply (TS). However, the original Soviet input-output table sets an import row vector under the third (value added) quadrant. Therefore, we can easily convert the total supply base Soviet input-output table into the gross domestic output (GDO) base table by noting the following relation (see Table 2):

Table 1. Description of Soviet Input-Output Tables

Date	Type	No. of Industries	No. of Positions 2nd quadrant	No. of Positions 3rd quadrant	Unit of Measurement	Uses described by	Compiled by	Source
1959	MPS; Basic Com. by Com. Competitive	83 Published / 72	13 / Unpublished	10 / Unpublished	Purchasers' Prices	T; TS	TsSU	Narkhoz (1960)
1966	ibid.	110 Published / 85	13 / Unpublished	11 / Unpublished	ibid.	ibid.	ibid.	Narkhoz (1967)
1972	ibid.	112 Published / 85	13	10	ibid.	ibid.	ibid.	Narkhoz (1967)
1977	ibid.	117	n.a.	n.a.	n.a.	n.a.	ibid.	Unpublished
1982	ibid.	n.a.	n.a.	n.a.	n.a.	n.a.	ibid.	Unpublished
1959	a MPS; Estimated Com. by Com. Competitive	38	4	3	Purchasers' Prices	T; TS	Treml et al.	JEC (1966)
	b ibid.	55	3	3	ibid.	T; GDO	ibid.	JEC (1973)
1966	a ibid.	55	3	3	ibid.	ibid.	ibid.	ibid.
	b ibid.	75	5	4	ibid.	ibid.	ibid.	Treml et al. (1977)
	c ibid.	75 (Exports and imports, not specified)	3	4	Producers' Prices	T; GDO	ibid.	ibid.
1972	a ibid.	88	5	7	Purchasers' Prices	ibid.	ibid.	Gallik et al. (1983)
	b ibid.	88	5	7	Producers' Prices	ibid.	ibid.	Gallik et al. (1983) and Treml (1984)

Table 1. (continued)

Date	Type	No. of Industries	No. of Positions 2nd quadrant	No. of Positions 3rd quadrant	Unit of Measurement	Uses described by	Compiled by	Source
1977 a	ibid.	16	6	7	Purchasers' Prices	ibid.	ibid.	Gallik et al. (1984)
b	ibid.	16	3	7	Producers' Prices	ibid.	ibid.	ibid.
			(Exports and imports, not specified)					
1982	ibid.	16	1	1	Purchasers' Prices	ibid.	ibid.	Kostinsky (1985)
1959	ibid.	8	2	5	Purchasers' Prices	T; TS	Belkin	Belkin (1963)
1959	MPS; Basic Com. by Com. Competitive	7	5	2	ibid.	ibid.	TsSU	Aganbegian et al. (1968)
1959	MPS; Estimated Com. by Com. Competitive	9	13	3	ibid.	ibid.	Sverdlik	Sverdlik (1981)
1966	ibid.	ibid.	ibid.	ibid.	ibid.	ibid.	ibid.	ibid.
1972	ibid.	ibid.	ibid.	ibid.	ibid.	ibid.	ibid.	ibid.

Notes: 1. n.a.–not available; com. by com.–commodity by commodity; TS–Total supply; GDO–Gross Domestic Output; TsSU–The Soviet Central Statistical Administration; Narkhoz x–Soviet Statistical Year Book (*Narodnoe Khoziaistvo*) for the year x.

2. A "Basic" input-output table is compiled by using a full range of actual sampling data.

3. "T" implies that each element of the first and second quadrant of the input output table describes a total input or use as the sum of domestically produced ("D") and imported ("I") commodity uses or inputs.

4. "TS" ["GDO"] indicates that a grand total output, or use, vector of an input-output table is described by the total supply [gross domestic output] vector.

5. "Competitive" indicates a competitive import-type input-output table.

Table 2. Competitive Import-Type IO Table and TS [GDO] Method

Uses \ Inputs	Intermediate Demand (uses)	Gross Final Demand			TS (=TD)	Import (deduction)	Net Final Demand	GDO
		Domestic Final Demand		Export				
		Investment	Consumption					
	1	2	3	4	5 (1+2+3+4)	6	7 (2+3+4+6)	8 (5+6)
1. Intermediate Inputs	(T)	(T)	(T)	(T)	(T)	–(I)	(D)	(D)
2. Value–Added								
3. GDO (1+2)	(D)							
4. Import (≥0)	(I)							
5. TS (3+4)	(T)							

Notes: 1. TS [TD]–Total Supply [Total Demand]; GDO–Gross Domestic Output.
2. T–Total sum of domestically produced and imported uses (inputs); I–Imported use (input); D–Domestically produced use (input).

Table 3.   A Description of Soviet IO Table

	Intermediate Demand	Final Demand
Construction	0 0	
Transportation and communication		0 0
Trade, Supply and Procurement		0 0

Total supply = gross domestic output + import (non-negative).

It should be noted that in the Soviet input-output table agricultural subsidies appear as subsidies provided to the processing industries rather than to agriculture. It should also be noted that in the Soviet table the flows are assumed to be "commodity pure." The secondary products are transferred to some sector by assuming that the input coefficient showing use of commodity i to produce (characteristic)commodity j in sector j also applies to use of commodity i to produce secondary commodity j in any other sector. Namely, in the Soviet input-output table a type of "industry technology assumption" is made.

The construction and reconstruction of the Soviet input-output table have been carried out by the Treml group. The 1959, 1966 and 1972 Soviet input-output tables which are used in our computations have been so constructed. The group has also compiled the Soviet input-output tables in terms of producers' prices, and the Soviet 1977 16-sector input-output tables in terms of purchasers' and producers' prices, which are also employed in our computation, have been made available on a preliminary basis. While we cannot fully describe the reconstruction method employed by the Treml group in detail, we would like to make some remarks regarding their methodology.

In Treml's input-output table in producers' prices, the net commodity taxes and the marketing margins are excluded. The net commodity taxes of each product are placed in the lowest row of the intermediate transaction quadrant. As a result, Treml's table in producers' prices can be regarded as an input-output table in "basic values" as recommended by the U.N. rather than the usual input-output table in producers' prices.

Unlike the 1959 and 1966 table constructed by the Treml group, the most disaggregated input-output table, the 1972 88-sector input-output table developed by the group does not distinguish the metal, mining and basic metal products from the metallurgy and mining sector. This statistical defect limits the effectiveness of our analysis of the Soviet input structures and our comparative analysis to some extent.

In testing the effectiveness of Treml's construction method for the Soviet 1977 table, the original version of which has not yet been completely published, we can make use of the result of the recalculation of the input coefficient matrixes in purchasers' prices for the periods 1972 and 1977 by using the RAS method, which is described in detail in section 5.2 of this chapter. This calculation suggests that considerable estimation errors are concentrated in a residual sector, say "Industry n.e.c."

Although there are some defects in the Treml group estimation, the Soviet input-output tables developed by them provide us with the best estimation of the Soviet input-output tables available at this time.

3. East European Input-Output Tables

We can distinguish two stages in the history of East European input-output tables as follows:

The first stage (1955 to the end of the 1960's): The East European countries began to compile their input-output tables rather earlier than the Soviet Union. In the second half of the 1950's many of the East European countries completed the construction of their first input-output tables. In the mid 1960's they compiled highly reliable MPS-type input-output tables in producers' prices. Unlike the Soviet Union they have published their input-output tables with a full description. As in the Soviet Union, the East European countries, including Czechoslovakia, calculated various types of prices using input-output tables.

The second stage (1970 to the 1980's): A remarkable difference between the first and second stage is the change in methods used for compiling input-output tables. While Hungary and Poland began to compile SNA-type input-output tables, Czechoslovakia and Yugoslavia continued to compile only MPS-type input-output tables. The Polish attitude regarding the use of SNA-type tables varied. They first produced SNA-type tables, while subsequent tables were of the MPS-type. In Hungary, annual SNA-type input-output tables in basic values have been compiled in accordance with U.N. recommendations. It should be noted that we can easily derive MPS-type input-output tables from the East European SNA-type input-output tables if the latter is available. However, the converse is not true.

The standardized input-output tables of the ECE countries for the years around 1959, 1965, 1970 and 1975 have been compiled by the U.N. Statistical Commission and Economic Commission for Europe. The East European input-output tables, which are included among the ECE standardized tables and used in our computation, are shown in Table 4.

From Table 4, we can see that in most cases individual total transactions have been divided into domestically produced and imported uses. For these cases we can compile both competitive-type and perfectly noncompetitive-type input-output tables.

From Table 4 we can also see that in the Hungarian and Polish standardized input-output tables for the years around 1975 only the domestic uses are displayed as individual elements of the first and second quadrants. Namely, these tables are simple noncompetitive-types since only the import vectors are provided and the import matrixes are not supplied.

The Hungarian and Polish standardized input-output tables for the years around 1970 are missing. The Hungarian and Polish Statistical Offices have published input-output tables for the years around 1970 but the published versions limit our analysis of exports and imports presented in Chapter 6. The published Hungarian input-output tables for the 1970's are simple noncompetitive-types (B-type in Hungarian terminology). The published Polish tables for the years 1971 to 1973 are competitive-types but do not include separate export and import vectors.

The Hungarian and Polish standardized input-output tables for the years around 1975 are also simple noncompetitive-types containing import vectors but no import matrixes. Therefore, these tables limit our

Table 4.   ECE Standardized IO Tables of East European Countries

Country		Years around 1959	Years around 1965	Years around 1970	Years around 1975
Hungary	a	1959	1965	n.a.	1976
	b	MPS Competitive (T)	MPS Any Import Type (T, D, I)		Quasi-SNA Noncompetitive (D)
	c	Producers' Prices	Producers' Prices		Approximate Basic Prices
Poland	a	1962	1965	n.a.	1977
	b	MPS Any Import Type (T, D, I)	MPS Any Import Type (T, D, I)		Quasi-SNA Noncompetitive (D)
	c	Producers' Prices	Producers' Prices		Producers' Prices
Czechoslovakia	a	1962	1967	1973	1977
	b	MPS Any Import Type (T, D, I)	MPS Any Import Type (T, D, I)	MPS Any Import Type (T, D, I)	MPS Any Import Type (T, D, I)
	c	Producers' Prices	Producers' Prices	Producers' Prices	
Yugoslavia	a	1962	1966	1970	1976
	b	MPS Any Import Type (T, D, I)	MPS Competitive (T)	MPS Any Import Type (T, D, I)	MPS Any Import Type (T, D, I)
	c				

Table 4.   (continued)

Country	Years around 1959	Years around 1965	Years around 1970	Years around 1975
Bulgalia	a 1963	n.a.	n.a.	n.a.
	b MPS			
	Any Import Type			
	(T, D, I)			
	c Purchasers' Prices			

Sources: ECE (1972; 1977; 1982a; 1982b)

Notes: 1. Items a,b and c describe : a–date; b–MPS or SNA; c–unit of measurement.
2. Countries listed in Table 4 compile an industry-by-industry input-output table.
3. Imports are evaluated in CIF.
4. All the input-output tables above are simply aggregated versions of the "basic" tables. The stardardized IO tables for the years around 1959 and 1965 have been adjusted by the ECE secretariat.

analysis of exports and imports. However, they are none-the-less of interest since they are based on both SNA and MPS accounts. The framework of the Hungarian 1976 standardized table, which is similar to the official Hungarian input-output tables for the ten year period from 1970 to 1979, is shown in Table 5.

With regard to the Bulgarian case, only the standardized input-output table for the years around 1959 is available. As far as the author knows, the Bulgarian Statistical Office has not published any other input-output tables.

The sector classification codes of the published ECE standardized input-output tables are shown in Table 6. The correspondence of the code used in our computation to the ECE codes is shown in Table 7.

4. Preliminary Observation: Macro Input-Output Structures

We observe the macro input-output structures of Soviet and East European economies in order to learn the fundamental characteristics of each country's input-output tables and structures.

The macro intermediate input and demand ratios are shown in Table 8. From this Table we can find the following facts:

The macro intermediate input and demand ratios generally show an increase, but the dynamics of these ratios are stable with values of 53% or 55%. The increase of intermediate input and demand ratios is proportional to the degree of development of the social division of labor and is inversely proportional to the increase of productivity since the value added ratio is equal to the value 1 minus the intermediate input ratio.

While an increase in the intermediate input ratio, to some extent, can be regarded as a necessary condition for industrialization, it begins to be related to the inefficiency of the economy after a certain stage of development. In order to clarify this relationship we should consider the increase in the intermediate input ratio with explicit capital-and-labor related indicators. However, this task is beyond the scope of this chapter.

Secondly, the intermediate input and demand ratios for Poland, Yugoslavia, and in particular for Czechoslovakia drastically increased from the years around 1959 to 1965. This reflects some improvement in their

107

Table 5. A Description of The Hungarian Quasi–SNA Type IO Table

Uses \ Inputs	Intermediate Demand — in Material Sectors (1)	Intermediate Demand — in Service Sectors (2)	Total Inter-mediate Demand (1+2) (3)	Final Demand (4)	Import (deduction) (5)	GDO¹ (3+4+5) (6)	Commodity Tax, Net (7)	GDO² (6+7) (8)	TS (8−5) (9)
1. Intermediate inputs in Material Sectors	(D)	(D)	(D)	(D)	0	(D)	0	(D)	—
2. Intermediate inputs in Service Sectors	(D)	(D)	(D)	(D)	0	(D)	0	(D)	—
3. Commodity Tax, Net	(T)	(T)	(T)	(T)	0	0	(T)	—	—
4. Noncompetitive Imports	(I)	(I)	(I)	(I)	−(I)	0	0	0	—
5. Total Intermediate inputs (1+2+3+4)	(T)	(T)	(T)	(T)	0	0	0	0	(T)
6. Value Added	(D)	(D)	(D)						
7. GDO¹ (5+6)	(D)	(D)	(D)						
8. Total Commodity Tax, Net	—	—	(T)						
9. GDO² (7+8)	(D)	(D)	(D)						
10. Total Import	—	—	(I)						
11. TS (9+10)	—	—	(T)						

Notes: 1. Abbreviations used here are explained in Table 2.
2. GDO¹ and GDO² indicate gross domestic output in approximate basic prices and in producers' prices, respectively.

Table 6.   ECE Sectoring Code

	Code ECE	ISIC Code reference
1	Agriculture, hunting, forestry and fishing	1
2	Coal mining	21
3	Crude petroleum and natural gas	22
4	Metal ore mining	23
5	Other mining	29
6	Manufacture of food, beverages and tobacco	31
7	Textile, wearing apparel and leather industries	32
8	Manufacture of wood and wood products	33
9	Manufacture of paper and paper products, printing and publishing	34
10	Manufacture of chemicals and chemical, petroleum, coal, rubber and plastic products, except petroleum refineries	35 except 353
11	Petroleum refineries	353
12	Manufacture of non-metallic mineral products, except products of petroleum and coal	36
13	Basic metal industries	37
14	Manufacture of fabricated metal products, machinery and equipment	38
15	Other manufacturing industries	39
16	Electricity, gas and steam	41
17	Water works and supply	42
18	Construction	50
19	Distribution	61 and 62
20	Restaurants and hotels	63
21	Transport and storage	71
22	Communication	72
23	Other branches of material sphere	part of 8, and 9
24	Financing, insurance, real estate and business services	8
25	Community, social and personal services: Industries	92 to 95
26	Community, social and personal services: Government	91 to 94
27	Community, social and personal services: Other producers	92 to 95
28	Other services, non-material sphere	part of 8, and 9

Source: ECE (1982a; 1982b) Annex I.

compilation methods for the input-output tables rather than any real economic changes.

Thirdly, after the years around 1965, the Polish intermediate input and

Table 7. Correspondence between ECE Code and other Codes used

code CA	code ECE	code CB	code ECE	code CC	code ECE2	code CS	code ECE
1	1	1	1	1	1	1	1
2	2	2	2	2	2	2	2, 3, 11
3	3	3	3, 11	3	3	3	4, 5, 13
4	4	4	4, 5, 13	4	4	4	6
5	5	5	6	5	5, 6	5	7
6	6	6	7	6	7	6	8, 9
7	7	7	8, 9	7	8, 9, 10	7	10
8	8, 9	8	10	8	11	8	12
9	10	9	12	9	12	9	14
10	11	10	14, 15	10	14	10	15
11	12	11	16, 17	11	15	11	16, 17
12	13	12	18	12	16	12	18
13	14	13	19, 20	13	17	13	19, 20
14	15	14	21, 22	14	18	14	21, 22
15	16, 17	15	23, 29	15	19	15	23, 29
16	18			16	23, 24		
17	19, 20						
18	21, 22						
(a) 19	23, 29						
(b) 19	23						
20	28						
21	29, 30						
22	noncompetitive imports						

Notes: Code ECE2 is the code employed in the standardized input-output tables around the years 1959 and 1965 (ECE (1972; 1977, annex III)). Code CC is applied to the Yugoslavian input-output table around the years 1965 since the basic metal industries are included in the metal ore mining sector and petroleum refineries are included in the crude petroleum sector.

Table 8.   Macro Intermediate Input and Demand Ratios

(unit: %)

		Macro Intermediate Input Ratios				Macro Intermediate Demand Ratios			
		"1959"	"1965"	"1970"	"1975"	"1959"	"1965"	"1970"	"1975"
Soviet Union	[S]	51.95	53.43	56.39	57.13	50.41	52.19	54.20	54.36
Hungary	[H]	50.27	54.95	55.59	58.91	47.24	48.75	48.50	50.14
Poland	[P]	46.82	58.32	58.16	63.72	42.45	53.62	58.16	57.67
Czechoslovakia	[C]	38.09	55.99	56.38	58.78	34.70	50.85	50.21	51.58
Yugoslavia	[Y]	39.55	48.23	49.56	53.59	34.84	43.23	43.55	47.73
Bulgaria	[B]	44.29	n.a.	n.a.	n.a.	38.10	n.a.	n.a.	n.a.

Notes: 1. "x"—years around the year x; n.a.—not available.
2. The Soviet cases are computed by using Treml's IO tables in purchasers' prices. The Soviet macro-intermediate input ratios based on IO tables in producers' prices are lower than those in the table above: 49.78% (1966), 53.03% (1972), and 53.78% (1977).
3. Most of the East European cases are computed by using the ECE IO tables. The Hungarian and Polish cases for the years around 1970 are calculated by using the original 1972 IO Tables published by the Hungarian and Polish Statistical Office.

demand ratios were the largest and the Yugoslavian ratios the smallest. The Polish intermediate input ratios were extraordinarily large; 63.72%. This was due to the remarkable increase in the share of intermediate imported input in the gross domestic output and to the aggravation of foreign trade conditions. The share increased from 5.45% in 1965 to 11.12% in 1977.

5.   Comparative Analysis of Input-Output Structures

5.1.   Correlation Analysis of Input Structures

Let us first present the correlation coefficient of the twin-pair interme-diate input ratio compositions of the four East European countries shown in Table 9. Here the intermediate input ratio of sector j in any country k, u_j^k is defined as

$$u_j^k = \Sigma_i X_{ij}^k / X_j, \quad j = 1, 2, \cdots, n; \quad k = \text{H, P, C, Y},$$

111

Table 9. Correlation of East European Intermediate Input Ratio
Compositions

	"1965"				"1975"			
	H	P	C	Y	H	P	C	Y
H	1.000	0.783	0.841	0.727	1.000	0.313	0.767	0.924
P	0.783	1.000	0.828	0.928	0.313	1.000	0.355	0.363
C	0.841	0.823	1.000	0.733	0.767	0.355	1.000	0.830
Y	0.727	0.928	0.733	1.000	0.924	0.363	0.830	1.000

where

X_j^k: the gross domestic output of commodity j in country k.

X_{ij}^k: the intermediate input (including imports) of commodity i, used by sector j in country k.

When a simple noncompetitive-type of input-output table is employed, this ratio is defined as

$$u_j^k = (\sum_i X_{ij}^{dk} + M_j^k)/X_j^k, \quad j=1, 2, \cdots, n; \quad k=\text{H, P},$$

where

X_{ij}^{dk}: the intermediate input of commodity i domestically produced, used by sector j in country k;

M_j^k: the import of sector j in country k.

The composition of the intermediate input ratio of country k is defined as

$$\boldsymbol{u}^k = \begin{bmatrix} u_1^k \\ u_2^k \\ \cdot \\ \cdot \\ \cdot \\ u_n^k \end{bmatrix}.$$

Each element in Table 9 presents the correlation coefficient of the twin-pair vectors of $\boldsymbol{u}^H$, $\boldsymbol{u}^P$, $\boldsymbol{u}^C$ and $\boldsymbol{u}^Y$.

The results for the years around 1965 are obtained by using the 14-

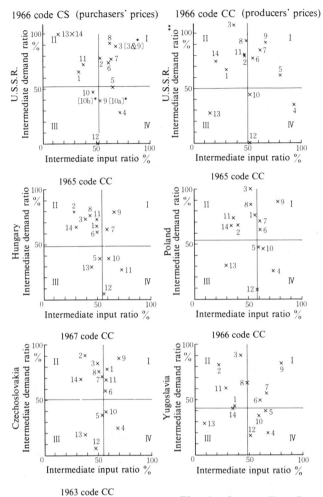

Fig. 1. Intermediate Input and Demand
Ratios Around 1965

Notes: * Sector no. 3 of code CS corresponds to
sectors no. 3 and no. 9 of code CC.
Sector no. 10 of code CC is divided
into two sectors no. 9 and no. 10 in the
case of code CS.
** This "intermediate demand ratio" is
defined as the intermediate demand divided by the gross domestic output.

113

sector input-output tables based on sectoring code C1 (the "15. Others" sector is omitted). This result shows that correlation between Poland and Yugoslavia is highest and the correlation between Hungary [Poland] and Czechoslovakia is rather high.

The computation, employing the 18-sector input-output tables for the years around 1975, based on the sectoring code CA (the "19. Other Branches of Material Production" and "20. Services" are omitted), shows that the correlation between Hungary and Yugoslavia is highest, followed by the correlation between Czechoslovakia and Yugoslavia.

From Table 9 it can also be seen that the correlations between Poland and the other three countries are particularly low. This is due to the extraordinarily high intermediate input ratios of "3. Crude Petroleum and Natural Gas" and "4. Metal Ore Mining" sectors in Poland. The ratios of each country are as follows:

		H	P	C	Y
3.	Crude Petroleum & Natural Gas	26.36	87.14	21.88	11.31
4.	Metal Ore Mining	48.99	79.15	64.48	48.52

When we omit the four sectors supplying energy and mining products, the correlation coefficients of Poland with Hungary, Czechoslovakia and Yugoslavia show a considerable increase; the values are 0.775, 0.842 and 0.810, respectively.

In order to compare the sectoral input structures of the twin-pair countries, we computed the correlation coefficient of A_i^k and $A_i^{k'}$, where A_i^k denotes the ith column of the input coefficient matrix A^k, or the input (cost) structure of industry i, in country $k[k']$. The computation results are shown in Tables 10-1, 10-2 and 10-3.

It can be seen from Table 10-1 that there is a considerable difference between the input structures of each sector supplying energy and mining products in any twin-pair country. This difference is not apparent in Table 10-2, based on the code C2 for the years around 1970, since in this table "Basic Metals" and "Other Mining" are consolidated into "Metallurgy," while "Petroleum Refineries" and "Crude Petroleum and Natural Gas" are consolidated into "Oil and Gas." The difference again appears

COMPARATIVE ANALYSIS OF INPUT-OUTPUT STRUCTURES

Table 10-1.   Correlation of East European Sectoral Input Structures in the Years around 1965

Sector Code CC		H/P	H/C	H/Y	P/C	P/Y	C/Y
1.	Agriculture	0.981	0.998	0.986	0.977	0.997	0.984
2.	Coal, Oil & Gas Fuels	0.452	0.266	0.757	0.213	0.585	0.287
3.	Other mining	0.682	0.429	0.013	0.921	0.630	0.855
4.	Food	0.982	0.990	0.993	0.997	0.981	0.986
5.	Textiles	0.997	0.987	0.991	0.990	0.989	0.963
6.	Wood & Paper	0.948	0.975	0.976	0.983	0.973	0.987
7.	Chemicals	0.887	0.974	0.911	0.961	0.975	0.975
8.	Non-metallic minerals	0.766	0.799	0.763	0.855	0.793	0.804
9.	Basic metals	0.747	0.974	0.963	0.810	0.856	0.988
10.	MBMW & industry n.e.c.	0.981	0.999	0.987	0.982	0.933	0.988
11.	Electricity	0.931	0.691	0.944	0.863	0.933	0.705
12.	Construction	0.944	0.943	0.349	0.969	0.445	0.414
13.	Distribution	0.974	0.994	0.516	0.979	0.609	0.573
14.	Transport	0.908	0.927	0.690	0.986	0.905	0.854
15.	Others	0.0	0.0	0.912	0.0	0.0	0.0

Table 10-2.   Correlation of Soviet and East European Sectoral Input Structures in the Years around 1970

Sector Code CB		C/Y	S/C	S/Y
1.	Agriculture	0.952	0.958	0.952
2.	Coal	0.963	0.891	0.878
3.	Oil & Gas	0.997	0.949	0.957
4.	Metallurgy	0.996	0.988	0.992
5.	Food	0.996	0.989	0.989
6.	Textiles	0.962	0.934	0.992
7.	Wood & Paper	0.987	0.905	0.916
8.	Chemicals	0.979	0.968	0.976
9.	Non-metallic minerals	0.744	0.727	0.831
10.	MBMW & industry n.e.c.	0.984	0.994	0.968
11.	Electricity	0.783	0.531	0.708
12.	Construction	0.354	0.842	0.332
13.	Distribution	0.511	0.306	0.018
14.	Transport	0.776	0.759	0.582
15.	Other	0.588	0.781	0.526

Table 10-3.   Correlation of East European Input Structures in the Years around 1975

Code CA		C/Y	H/P
1.	Agriculture	0.959	0.967
2.	Coal	0.417	0.758
3.	Crude Petroleum & Gas	0.486	0.040
4.	Metal ore mining	0.976	0.087
5.	Other mining	0.808	0.738
6.	Food	0.987	0.971
7.	Textiles	0.978	0.974
8.	Wood & Paper	0.992	0.908
9.	Chemicals	0.989	0.797
10.	Petroleum refineries	0.992	0.612
11.	Non-metallic minerals	0.736	0.723
12.	Basic metals	0.989	0.189
13.	MBMW	0.986	0.775
14.	Industry n.e.c.	0.753	0.729
15.	Electricity	0.940	0.625
16.	Construction	0.368	0.680
17.	Distribution	0.001	0.852
18.	Transport	0.780	0.651
19.	Other	0.872	0.127
20.	Service	—	0.940

in Table 10-3, based on the code CA, for the years around 1975.

We can further see from Table 10-1 (for the years around 1965) to 10-3 (for the years around 1975) that the Yugoslavian input structures of "Construction" and "Trade" sectors are quite different from those of the other East European countries and the Soviet Union. Comparing the Soviet sectoral input structures with the Czechoslovakian ones for the years around 1970, we find a remarkable similarity between them except for four sectors; "Non-Metallic Minerals (Construction Materials)," "Electricity," "Distribution" and "Transportation and Communication" (see Table 10-2).

Let us now compare the Hungarian sectoral (domestically produced) input structures with the Polish ones for the years around 1975 (see Table 10-3). The similarities between them are generally weak. However, we see strong similarities between the input structures of the "Service" sector of the two countries.

In order to make an inter-industry comparison of the sectoral, input structures of each country, we computed the correlation matrix of the input coefficient matrix,

$$A = (A_1 A_2 \cdots A_i \cdots A_n),$$

where A_i denotes the composition of sector i's input coefficients, or the ith column of input coefficient matrix A. However, we cannot obtain much useful information when we use aggregated 15-sector or 20-sector input-output tables. For example, when we calculate the correlation coefficient matrix (R_{ij}) between A_i and A_j for each of the Soviet and East European countries by using the 15 or 20-sector tables, we see that only the correlation coefficient between "Agriculture" and "Food" sectors is rather high (greater than 0.95). When we apply the Soviet 1972 88-sector table, we find, interestingly, that the input structure of the "Ores and Metals" sector is similar to that of "Industrial Metal Products," "Cable Products," "Bearings," "Tools and Dies," "Sanitary Engineering Products," "Other Metalwares" and "Metal Structures" sectors; the value of the correlation coefficients lies in the range from 0.938 to 0.981.

5.2. Intertemporal Analysis of Input Coefficients: An Application of the RAS Method

Let us consider the trends of changes of input coefficients only in the Soviet and Czechoslovakian cases by employing the RAS method developed by Stone (1961). The RAS method is based on the following concept (Allen (1974)): The changes in technologies and changes in relative prices which affect input coefficients of an economy are summarized by "substitution" coefficients (row modification multiplier) $r_i's$ and "fabrication" coefficients (column modification multipliers) $s_j's$.

The value of the substitution coefficient r_i greater than [smaller than] unity shows that industry i's outputs have been substituted for [replaced by] the other industries' outputs as intermediate inputs into industrial processes. On the other hand the value of the fabrication coefficient s_j

greater than [smaller than] unity shows that the outputs of industry j have come to absorb a greater [smaller] ratio of materials, fuels and other current inputs to value added in their production.

The simple RAS problem is to find:

$$A^* = RAS$$

such that $\qquad (A^*X^*)i = \tilde{x}^*i = u^*,$

and $\qquad (A^*X^*)'i = \tilde{x}^{*\prime}i = v^*,$

where

A: a base year input coefficient matrix (given);

u^*: an update year vector of total intermediate use by industry (given);

v^*: an update year vector of total intermediate input by industry (given);

R: a diagonal matrix whose ith diagonal element is the substitution coefficient r_i, namely $R = \text{diag}\{r_1, \cdots, r_n\}$;

S: a diagonal matrix whose jth diagonal element is the fabrication coefficient s_j, namely $S = \text{diag}\{s_1, \cdots, s_n\}$;

$\tilde{x}^*$: the estimated flow matrix for the update year;

X^*: a diagonal matrix of gross domestic outputs for the update year;

i: a unit aggregation column vector $(i = [11 \cdots 1])$.

The prime $(\prime)$ denotes the transpose of a vector or matrix. It should be noted that here we are interested in the value of r_i and s_j, provided that the base and update year input-output tables are given.

We first present our computation results for the Soviet case. When we recalculated the 1972 input coefficient matrix $A^*(1972)$, we used the Treml 1966 15-sector input coefficient matrix $A(1966)$ as a base year input coefficient matrix and the update year gross domestic output vector, intermediate input and demand vectors obtained from the Treml 1972 input-output table. When we calculated the 1977 input coefficient matrix $A^*(1977)$, we used the Treml 1972 15-sector input coefficient matrix $A(1972)$ as a base year input coefficient matrix and the update year gross domestic output vector, intermediate input and demand vectors obtained from the Treml 1977 input-output table.

Table 11. Changes of Soviet Input Coefficients

Sector Code CS	1966 to 1972 r_i	s_i	1972 to 1977 r_i	s_i
1. Agriculture	0.952	1.226	0.996	1.022
2. Coal, Oil & Gas [Fuels]	1.316	0.869	1.065	1.009
3. Metallurgy	1.244	0.855	1.027	0.953
4. Food	0.922	1.139	0.940	1.046
5. Textiles	0.911	1.093	0.921	1.081
6. Wood & Paper	1.002	0.965	0.953	1.058
7. Chemicals	1.118	0.931	1.104	0.913
8. Non-metallic minerals	1.131	0.955	1.052	0.985
9. MBMW	1.278	0.858	1.086	0.947
10. Industry n.e.c.	1.015	1.190	1.403	0.920
11. Electricity	1.192	0.882	0.956	0.994
12. Construction	0.0	0.858	0.0	0.928
13. Distribution	0.970	0.809	0.988	0.958
14. Transport	0.932	0.799	1.060	0.994
15. Other	0.903	1.558	1.037	0.947

The 1972 and 1977 input coefficient matrixes computed by the RAS method satisfies the following:

$$A^*(1972) = R^1 A(1966) S^1 ,$$

and

$$A^*(1977) = R^2 A(1972) S^2 .$$

R^1 and S^1 [R^2 and S^2] summarize the trend of changes of Soviet input coefficients from 1966 to 1972 [from 1972 to 1977]. Here we are interested in R and S rather than the prognosis of the 1982 input coefficients. Table 11 shows our computation results for the Soviet Union.

The substitution coefficients from 1966 to 1972 should be regarded as reflecting not only technological substitution but also the change in relative prices. With the 1967 revision of wholesale prices, the prices of energy-related sectors have been remarkably increased. The high [low] level of substitution [fabrication] coefficients of the "Fuels (coal, oil and gas)", "Metallurgy (other mining and basic metals)" and "Electricity" sectors directly reflects the price changes of the energy-related sectors. The Treml group, properly, does not use the 1966 table in estimating the 1977 table.

From Table 11 we can also see that the values of substitution and fabrication coefficients for the "Industry n.e.c." sector from 1972 to 1977 are rather strange. In terms of conventional economic thought we can assume that the industries in this sector have either enjoyed a particularly high level of economic development or have experienced a remarkable increase in the price of their products. In the opinion of the author both assumptions are suspect and this anomaly may be caused by a concentration of estimation errors in this sector.

Table 11 suggests that in the Soviet case the change of Matrix A in terms of current prices from 1972 to 1977 is very small. Namely, we can state that the so-called "oil shock" did not affect the Soviet economy, so long as we base our research on the 1977 table, estimated by using the official statistics other than the input-output tables. However, the East European countries' cases are quite different.

Table 12 presents the changes of the Czechoslovakian input coefficients in terms of R and S, computed by the RAS method, from 1973 to 1977. The input coefficient matrix at the base period is derived from the 1973 Czechoslovakian input-output table. As updated data we use the 1977 Czechoslovakian input-output table. Therefore, substitution coefficients (row multipliers) R and fabrication coefficients (column multipliers) S satisfy

$$A^*(1977) = RA(1972)S.$$

As can be seen from Table 12, the "Crude Petroleum and Natural Gas" sector displays an extraordinary value of the substitution coefficient, 3.81, due to the change of relative price and technological substitution. The substitution coefficients of "Petroleum Refineries," "Metal Ore Mining" and "Electricity" sectors are rather high; 1.66, 1.35 and 1.34, respectively. Corresponding to this, the fabrication coefficients of "Petroleum Refineries" and "Metal Ore Mining" are rather low; 0.69 and 0.52,

Table 12. Changes in Czechoslovakian Input Coefficients from 1973 to 1977

Sector Code CA	r_i	s_i
1. Agriculture	1.014	0.968
2. Coal	0.906	0.990
3. Crude Petroleum & Gas	3.811	1.302
4. Metal ore mining	1.349	0.687
5. Other mining	1.068	1.169
6. Food	1.014	1.023
7. Textiles	0.991	1.029
8. Wood & Paper	1.014	1.042
9. Chemicals	1.100	0.987
10. Petroleum refineries	1.655	0.516
11. Non-metallic minerals	0.994	1.064
12. Basic metals	0.865	1.030
13. MBMW	1.037	1.081
14. Industry n.e.c.	0.995	0.918
15. Electricity	1.343	0.930
16. Constrution	1.106	1.089
17. Distribution	1.048	0.772
18. Transport	0.835	0.993
19. Other	1.772	1.471

respectively.

5.3. Comparative Analysis of Interdependence in Production: An Application of the Chenery and Watanabe Method

We can explore the more fundamental characteristics of input-output structures of the Soviet and East European economies by employing a classical method developed by Chenery and Watanabe (1958). Their concept contains two main tools. One is the intermediate input ratio u_j which is defined as the ratio of purchased inputs to the value of total gross domestic output (see 5.1). The u_j measures the extent of indirect use of production factors. The other key concept is the intermediate demand ratio of sector i, w_i, which is defined as

$$w_i = \sum_j X_{ij}/(X_i + M_i) . \quad i = 1, 2, \cdots, n$$

121

Namely, w_i is defined as the ratio of intermediate to total demand ($=$ total supply).

Let us use an average (macro) value of w and u from each country as a basis for classifying sectors. The sectors can then be classified into four types:

Category I   −Intermediate Manufacture;
Category II   −Intermediate Primary Production;
Category III −Final Primary Production;
Category IV −Final Manufacture.

The word "final" is used for sectors with low values of w; high final demand. The word "primary" refers to sectors with low values of u; high value added (high primary input).

Figure 2 shows the distribution (u_i, w_i) for each country in the years around 1965. For reference, the Bulgarian 1963 case is also shown. From this figure we can see the common features of distribution and the characteristics of inter-dependency of production for each country. Excluding the Bulgarian case we first learn that the following sectors are placed in common in each Category with some exceptions, designated by the superscript *:

Category I   − 9.   Basic Metals
                   7.   Chemicals
                   6.   Wood and Paper*
Category II   − 3.   Other Mining
                   2.   Oil, Coal and Gas
                   8.   Non-Metallic Minerals
                14.   Transport and Communication
                   1.   Agriculture*
                11.   Electricity
Category III −13.   Trade
Category IV −10.   MBMW and Industry n.e.c.
                   4.   Food
                12.   Construction*

It is difficult to classify "5. Textiles" into any particular common category. For all countries the "Textiles" sector is part of the "final"

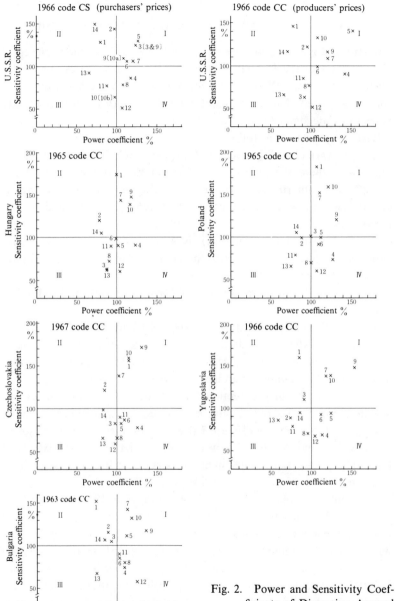

Fig. 2.   Power and Sensitivity Coefficients of Dispersion Around 1965

123

industry and is placed in Categories III or IV. This sector is placed in Category III in the Hungarian and Czechoslovakian cases, while it is placed in Category IV in the Soviet, Polish and Yugoslavian cases. It should be noted that in the capitalist countries this sector is usually placed in Category IV.

The exceptions are as follows:

1. "1. Agriculture" is placed in Category I only in the Czechoslovakian case where the intermediate demand ratio is remarkably high; 78.48%. (The intermediate demand ratio of agriculture in the Hungarian, Polish and Yugoslavian cases are 65.96%, 75.11% and 44.7% respectively).

2. "2. Fuels(Oil, Coal and Gas)" is placed in Category I in the Soviet case (in purchasers' prices) since the intermediate input ratio is higher than the average.

3. "6. Wood and Paper" is placed in Category II only in the Hungarian case.

4. "11. Electricity" is placed in Category I only in the Czechoslovakian case since the intermediate input ratio is higher than the average.

5. "12. Construction" is placed in Category III in the Czechoslovakian case and Soviet case in purchasers' prices.

The third and fourth exceptions may be due to sector consolidation and item number 5 above cannot be regarded as a special exception.

It can also be seen from Figure 2 that the intermediate input ratios of "5. Textiles" and "4. Food" sectors in the Soviet Union are extremely high. This shows that Soviet light industry, in a broad sense, can be characterized as a low value-added sector.

We would now like to comment on the Bulgarian 1963 case shown in Figure 2. The machine building and metalworking sector with low intermediate input ratio is placed in Category IV. The chemical industry with rather low intermediate input ratio is placed on the borderline between Categories I and II. This reflects the lower level of Bulgarian industrialization in comparison with the other countries. Figure 2 also graphically shows that the intermediate demand of the construction sector in Bulgaria is set at zero as in the Soviet Union. In other words, only the Soviet and Bulgarian statistical offices assume that the construction sector does not supply any intermediate goods. A similar pattern of inter-dependency in production can be seen for the years around 1959, 1970 and 1975. A notable exception is the movement in the position of the crude petroleum and natural gas sector in Poland from Category II to I, which can be seen from the Polish 1977 input-output table.

5.4. Power and Sensitivity Coefficients of Dispersion: the Rasmussen Coefficients

Rasmussen (1956) developed two concepts in order to clarify, with relation to the average dispersion of an economy, the role that each industry plays in the reproduction process of the economy. One is the power coefficient of dispersion and the other is the sensitivity coefficient of dispersion. Together they are called the Rasmussen coefficients.

The total amount of outputs directly and indirectly induced by one unit of final demand for sector j is given by $\sum_i b_{ij}$ $(j=1, 2, \cdots, n)$, where b_{ij} is the i-jth element of the Leontief inverse matrix $B=(I-A)^{-1}$. Their average can be defined as

$$\bar{b}=\sum_i \sum_j b_{ij}/n .$$

Sector j's power coefficient of dispersion is defined as

$$U_j=\sum_i b_{ij}/\bar{b}, j=1, 2, \cdots, n .$$

The value of U_j reflects a relative degree of economy-wide output inducement by one unit of final demand for sector j, namely a relative degree of sector j's power of dispersion for the whole economy. When U_j is greater [smaller] than unity, sector j is assumed to have a stronger [weaker] power of dispersion than the average; sector j draws heavily [slightly] (i.e. compared to the sectors in general) on the system of sectors.)

Sector i's sensitivity coefficient of dispersion is defined as

$$U^i=\sum_j b_{ij}/\bar{b}, i=1, 2, \cdots, n .$$

U^i shows sector i's output directly and indirectly induced by one unit of

125

final demand for each industry. The value of U^i measures a relative degree of sector i's sensitivity of dispersion to an economy-wide level of final demand. When U^i is greater [smaller] than unity, sector i is assumed to be more [less] sensitive to other industries' production ; the system of sectors draws on sector i to a relatively large [small] extent.

Using U_j and U^i, the sectors can be classified into four types:

Category I $[U_i > 1$ and $U^i > 1]$

Category II $[U_i < 1$ and $U^i > 1]$

Category III $[U_i < 1$ and $U^i < 1]$

Category IV $[U_i > 1$ and $U^i < 1]$

Before describing our computation results we should refer to the content of the Leontief inverse matrix.

As is known, there are several types of Leontief inverse matrixes. For competitive import-type input-output tables, the following two types of inverse matrix are typical:

$$B^1 = (I - A)^{-1},$$

$$B^2 = [I - (I - \hat{M})A]^{-1},$$

where A is an n by n matrix of input (domestically produced and imported) coefficient, and $\hat{M} = \mathrm{diag}\{m_i\}$ is an n by n diagonal matrix whose diagonal element m_i denotes the ratio of commodity i's import to sector i's domestic demand (intermediate input plus domestic final demand, domestically produced and imported).

We computed both B^1 and B^2 for competitive-type input-output tables. However, we are mainly concerned with the Rasmussen coefficients in the case of B^1-type inverse matrixes.

Figure 3 presents the distribution (U_i, U^j) for each country in the years around 1965. The Bulgarian case is also presented for reference. We are able to see the common features of distribution from this figure. We first see that the following sectors are placed in common in each Category:

Category I   −10.   MBMW and Industry n.e.c.

               9.   Basic Metals

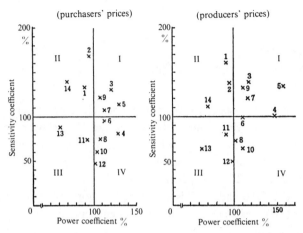

Fig. 3. Power and Sensitivity Coefficients of Dispersion: U.S.S.R. (1977); code CS

	7.	Chemicals
Category II	−14.	Transportation and Communication*
	2.	Fuels(Oil, Coal and Gas)*
Category III	−13.	Distribution
	11.	Electricity
	3.	Other Mining*
Category IV	− 4.	Food
	5.	Textiles*
	6.	Wood and Paper
	12.	Construction

In the above, the superscripted asterisk "*" following the sector indicates the existence of exceptions.

It is difficult to classify "1. Agriculture" into any particular common category. The "Agriculture" sector has a rather high value of sensitivity coefficient of dispersion for all countries (unit:%):

Soviet union	146 (using IO table in producers' prices)
	128 (using IO table in purchasers' prices)

Hungary	174
Poland	182
Czechoslovakia	155
Yugoslavia	160
Bulgaria	152

However, with respect to the power coefficient of dispersion of the agriculture sector, the value in the Soviet and Yugoslavian case is low and the values in the Polish and Czechoslovakian cases are relatively high. The Hungarian and Bulgarian power coefficients of the agriculture sector are neutral. The exceptions are as follows:

1. "2. Oil, Coal and Gas" is placed in Category III in the Yugoslavian and Polish cases since the sensitivity coefficient, as well as the power coefficient, is low.

2. "3. Other Mining" is placed in Category II in the Yugoslavian case with the low power coefficient (as in the Bulgarian case).

3. "5. Textiles" is placed in Category I in the Soviet case (in both producers' and purchasers' prices) since the sensitivity coefficient, as well as the power coefficient, is remarkably high (as in the Bulgarian case).

4. "6. Wood and Paper" is placed in Category IV in the Hungarian case.

5. "14. Transport and Communication" is placed in Category II in the Czechoslovakian and Yugoslavian cases.

A pattern similar to the distribution of (U_i, U^i) in Figure 3 can be seen from the period around 1959 to the period around 1975.

Figure 4 describes the distribution of (U_i, U^i) for the Soviet cases in 1977. The distribution pattern is the same as in 1966 with three exceptions: "4. Food" (a shift from IV to I), "6. Wood and Paper" (a shift from Category I to IV) and "10. Other industries" (a shift from Category III to IV).

Of course, there are changes of values of U_i and U^j from 1966 to 1977. For example, the "2. Coal, Oil and Gas" sector's sensitivity coefficient increased from 143% to 169% and the "5. Textiles" sector's sensitivity coefficient decreased from 130.35% to 115.42%.

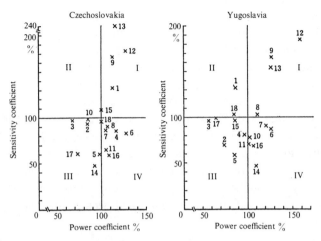

Fig. 4. Power and Sensitivity Coefficients of Dispersion: Czechoslovakia (1977) and Yugoslavia (1976); code CA

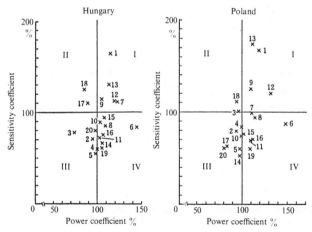

Fig. 5. Power and Sensitivity Coefficients of Dispersion: Hungary (1976) and Poland (1977); code CA

Regarding the changes of distribution of the Rasmussen coefficients through conversion of purchasers' prices into producers' prices, both in the Soviet 1966 and 1977 cases, we can see that the power and sensitivity coefficients of light industry increase, the sensitivity coefficient of agriculture increases and that of the energy industry decreases.

Figure 5 shows the distribution of the Rasmussen coefficients in the Czechoslovakian and Yugoslavian cases for the years around 1975. Although there are slight differences between the sectoring codes for the years around 1965 and 1975 (the Rasmussen coefficients are not independent of the aggregation method), we can see a common pattern between the distributions for the sectors around 1965 and 1975. It can also be seen that additional disaggregated sectors are placed in the following categories.

		Czechoslovakia	Yugoslavia
2.	Coal	III	III
3.	Crude Petroleum and Natural Gas	III	III
4.	Metalworking	IV	III
5.	Other Mining	III	III
10.	Petroleum Refineries	III	IV

Comparing the two countries, we can state from Figure 5 that the Czechoslovakian sensitivity coefficient of "13. MBMW" is relatively high and the Yugoslavian power coefficient of "12. Basic Metals" is relatively high.

It should be noted that in the Czechoslovakian case in 1965 the sensitivity coefficient of the basic metal industry is greater than that of the machine building and metalworking industry, but in 1975 the latter is much greater than the former as in the 1973 case.

A simple non-competitive type input-output table assumes the following type of Leontief inverse matrix.

Let us define the non-competitive type input coefficient matrix as

$$\tilde{A}^d = \left(\begin{array}{c|c} A^d & 0 \\ \hline m & 0 \end{array}\right),$$

where $\tilde{A}^d$ and m denote the input (only domestically produced) co-efficient matrix and the import coefficient row vector, respectively.

Then, the Leontief inverse matrix can be defined as

$$B^3 = (\tilde{I} - \tilde{A}^d)^{-1},$$

where $\tilde{I}$ is a unit matrix of rank $(n + 1)$. Simple calculation results in

$$(\tilde{I} - \tilde{A}^d)^{-1} = \left(\begin{array}{c|c} I - A^d & 0 \\ \hline -m & 1 \end{array}\right)^{-1} = \left(\begin{array}{c|c} (I - A^d)^{-1} & 0 \\ \hline m(I - A^d)^{-1} & 1 \end{array}\right).$$

Applying the B^3-type inverse matrix to the Hungarian and Polish economies for the years around 1975, we obtain Figure 6. From this figure we can first see that the distribution patterns of the Rasmussen coefficients in both countries are similar except for "3. Petroleum and Natural Gas," "7. Textiles," "10. Petroleum Refineries," "14. Other Industries," and "17. Distribution." Secondly, the power and sensitivity of dispersion for "7. Textiles" are remarkably high in the Hungarian case and the power of dispersion for "13. MBMW" is considerably high in the Polish case.

With regard to the "20. Non-Material Services" sector, the power of dispersion for this sector in the Hungarian case is higher than in the Polish case, while the Rasmussen coefficients in both countries are placed in Category III.

We have briefly observed the input-output structures from the view point of output inducement effect.

In conclusion, we would like to state that one of the main characteristics of the Soviet and East European input-output structures is that the two fundamental sectors for the national economy, namely the machine building and metalworking sectors, show high values for the sensitivity of dispersion. This feature is independent of the type of Leontief inverse matrix selected; B^1, B^2 and B^3. When we select B^2 and compute the Rasmussen coefficients in the years around 1975, we have the following

coefficients of sensitivity of dispersion for the agriculture and MBMW
sectors (unit:%):

		Agriculture	MBMW
Soviet Union	(1977; code CS)	133	118
Czechoslovakia	(1977; code CA)	149	197
Yugoslavia	(1976; code CA)	144	128
Hungary	(1965; code CC)	178	121
Poland	(1965; code CC)	181	141

Normally, an industry with high power and sensitivity of dispersion is
considered to be a sector which supplies basic materials such as the basic
metals sector. On the other hand, the MBMW products appear as goods
which satisfy final demand. In fact, the MBMW sectors in the United
States and Japan are placed in Category IV. Judging from these considerations, the placement of the Soviet and East European MBMW sectors
in Category I strikes the author as strange, but may be caused in part by
the poor quality of the data compilation methods employed. With regard
to this point, further research is required regarding the basic metals and
the metalworking industry including very disaggregated sectors, consolidated into the basic metals industry and metalworking industry. In
terms of this point, further investigation is also required regarding the
Soviet and East European method of consolidating very disaggregated
sectors into the basic metals and metalworking industry sectors since
these sectors are not clearly distinct at the present time.

6. Comparison of the Soviet Union and the United States: A Dis-aggregated Case

When making an input-output analysis, the greater the degree of
disaggregation, the better able we are to make concrete analysis of the
input-output structure of an economy.

The most detailed input-output table for the Soviet Union is the 88-
order version compiled by Treml, Kostinsky and Gallik (1983). We
employ this version in producers' prices to compare the Soviet input-
output structure with that of the United States.

In the case of the United States we employ the 85-order commodity-by-commodity table compiled by merging the make and use tables of the BEA(see Kuboniwa et al.(1986) and the Appendix of the book). For both countries, very few studies have been conducted in terms of direct comparisons to date. Therefore, we employ the original codes presently used in both countries.

6.1. *Power and Sensitivity of Dispersion*

Table 13. Power of Dispersion: The Ten Highest Sectors

1972 U.S.S.R. (Producers' Prices) (unit: %)

Rank		Sector Treml's 88-Order Code	
1.	65	Wool materials	183.43
2.	66	Flax materials	181.32
3.	70	Other light industry products	150.98
4.	67	Hosiery & knitwear	148.66
5.	72	Meat products	147.43
6.	78	Vegetable oils	136.43
7.	68	Other textile products	134.62
8.	69	Sewn goods	131.66
9.	46	Paints & lacquers	131.55
10.	77	Confections	128.51

1972 U.S. (Producers' Prices) (unit: %)

Rank		Sector BEA's 85-Order Code	
1.	33	Leather tanning and finishing	135.39
2.	1	Livestock and livestock products	134.68
3.	14	Food and kindred products	130.69
4.	17	Miscellaneous textile goods and floor coverings	128.67
5.	38	Primary nonferrous metals manufacturing	125.96
6.	18	Apparel	125.39
7.	19	Miscellaneous fabricated textile products	125.24
8.	16	Broad and narrow fabrics, yarn and thread mills	123.82
9.	39	Metal containers	119.04
10.	59	Motor vehicles and equipment	118.90

Table 14.   Power of Dispersion: The Ten Lowest Sectors

1972 U.S.S.R. (Producers' Prices)   (unit: %)

Rank		Sector Treml's 88-Order Code	
1.	6	Oil extraction	52.33
2.	87	Trade & distribution	57.67
3.	8	Gas	57.68
4.	85	Forestry	59.49
5.	86	Transportation & communications	62.16
6.	83	Animal husbandry	65.99
7.	88	Other branches of material production	68.06
8.	49	Logging	69.94
9.	60	Construction ceramics	73.25
10.	10	Oil shales	73.82

1972 U.S. (Producers' Prices)   (unit: %)

Rank		Sector BEA's 85-Order Code	
1.	66	Communications except radio and TV	63.08
2.	71	Real estate and rental	64.49
3.	69	Wholesale and retail trade	68.39
4.	67	Radio and TV broadcasting	71.29
5.	78	Federal Government enterprises	72.38
6.	8	Crude petroleum and natural gas	75.84
7.	77	Health educ., & social serv. and nonprofit org.	77.05
8.	73	Business services	79.21
9.	65	Transportations and warehousing	83.69
10.	70	Finance and insurance	85.18

We first compare the Soviet and U.S. input-output structures by employing the Rasmussen Coefficients, based on the B^1-type Leontief inverse matrix. Tables 13 and 14 present the ten highest and lowest sectors of power of dispersion in the Soviet Union and the United States. Tables 15 and 16 show the ten highest sectors of sensitivity of dispersion in these two countries. From these tables we can state that there are similarities between the Soviet and U.S. technology structures, even

Table 15.   Sensitivity of Dispersion: The Ten Highest Sectors

1972 U.S.S.R. (Producers' Prices)   (unit: %)

Rank		Sector Treml's 88-Order Code	
1.	1	Ores & metals	643.12
2.	83	Crops	438.27
3.	86	Transportation & communications	367.46
4.	5	Coal	260.13
5.	11	Electric & thermal power	255.38
6.	84	Animal husbandry	244.24
7.	65	Wool materials	227.61
8.	63	Cotton materials	226.27
9.	33	Electronics	214.03
10.	66	Flax materials	181.82

1972 U.S. (Producers' Prices)   (unit: %)

Rank		Sector BEA's 85-Order Code	
1.	37	Primary iron and steel manufacturing	322.05
2.	73	Business services	296.40
3.	69	Wholesale and retail trade	282.06
4.	65	Transportation and warehousing	265.78
5.	71	Real estate and rental	249.24
6.	38	Primary nonferrous metals manufacturing	246.98
7.	27	Chemicals and selected chemical products	234.37
8.	68	Electric, gas, water, sanitary services	213.46
9.	20	Lumber and wood products, except containers	165.97
10.	14	Food and kindred products	165.89

though there are many differences in the methods used for compiling the databases.

In both countries the power coefficients of dispersion for the sectors supplying textiles and meat are very high. In other words these sectors draw heavily on the system of industries in both countries. On the other hand, the sensitivity coefficients of dispersion for the producing of basic metals, food, electricity and transport services are also very high. These

135

Table 16. Sensitivity of Dispersion: The Ten Lowest Sectors

1972 U.S.S.R. (Producers' Prices) (unit: %)

Rank		Sector Treml's 88-Order Code	
1.	82	Construction	45.10
2.	76	Bread & bakery products	45.66
3.	25	Printing M & E	45.73
4.	58	Asbestos-cement & slate	45.95
5.	17	Casting M & E	46.02
6.	59	Roofing materials	46.06
7.	60	Construction ceramics	46.64
8.	16	Forging-pressing M & E	46.89
9.	36	Metal structures	47.05
10.	24	Food industry M & E	47.07

1972 U.S. (Producers' Prices) (unit: %)

Rank		Sector BEA's 85-Order Code	
1.	11	New construction	49.20
2.	67	Radio and TV broadcasting	49.21
3.	23	Other furniture and fixtures	50.79
4.	13	Ordnance and accessories	51.36
5.	22	Household furniture	51.42
6.	34	Footwear and other leather products	51.62
7.	79	State and local government enterprises	52.27
8.	21	Wood containers	52.32
9.	54	Household appliances	52.56
10.	44	Farm and garden machinery	54.32

sectors only seem to influence the system of industries to a relatively small extent. It should also be noted that unlike the U.S. input-output table, the Soviet input-output table does not make distinction between ferrous and non-ferrous metals.

It can also be seen that in both countries the power coefficients of dispersion for the sectors supplying petroleum, natural gas and distribution services are remarkably low. It appears that the system of industry as a whole draws heavily on these sectors.

Conversely, the sensitivity coefficient of dispersion for the construction sector is the lowest in each country. This sector is therefore only slightly affected by a general increase in final demand.

In regard to the distribution of the Rasmussen coefficient we can see the following similarity between the Soviet Union and the United States: industries producing basic metals, meat, textiles and plastics are placed in Category I (high power and sensitivity of dispersion).

A well known exception is shown in Table 15; "33. Electronics" for the Soviet Union shows a very high coefficient of sensitivity of dispersion. From the computation we can also learn that " 13. Electrotechnical M & E (machine and equipment)" shows a rather high coefficient of sensitivity of dispersion, while "Electronics" and "Electrotechnical M & E" sectors for the Soviet Union show rather low coefficients of power of dispersion.

Thus these sectors are placed in Category I. We can assume, therefore, that the "Electronics" and " Electrotechnical M & E" sectors are heavily drawn upon by the Soviet system of industries as a whole and at the same time the "Electronics" and "Electrotechnical M & E" sectors draw heavily on the Soviet system of industries as a whole. In the U.S. case all industries belonging to the MBMW sector are placed in either Category III or IV. Namely, the U.S. MBMW industries show rather low coefficients of sensitivity of dispersion and thus are only slightly affected by a general increase in final demand.

With regard to the distribution of the Rasmussen coefficients of the MBMW industries, excluding "Electronics" and "Electro-technical M & E," we can see similarities between the Soviet Union and the United States. In both countries the industries which supply farm machinery, construction and mining machinery and transportation equipment are placed in Category IV, while the precision instrument and general industrial M & E industries are placed in Category III.

From the above observation we are now in a position to answer the question posed in Section 5.4 of this chapter: Why, with regard to the coefficients of sensitivity, does the MBMW sector show a relatively high value in the Soviet and East European economies? In the Soviet case the answer to this question is that the "Electronics" and "Electrotechnical M & E" industries, particularly "Electronics," show very high coefficients of sensitivity of dispersion.

Chapter 6

INPUT-OUTPUT ANALYSIS OF THE
STRUCTURE OF SOVIET FOREIGN
TRADE: A COMPARATIVE VIEW

1. Introduction

This chapter presents a "skyline" chart analysis of the Soviet and East European economies in order to investigate the patterns and changes of the foreign trade of these countries from a comparative view.

As is well known, the "skyline" concept in input-output analysis was conceptualized by Leontief (1963) as a tool to study the structure of the economic development and foreign trade patterns of developing countries. We apply this concept to clarify foreign trade characteristics of the Soviet and East European economies.

A primary reason for employing the "skyline" concept is that one of the most useful ways to see how these countries stand today is to construct a model of the economy as it would appear if it enjoyed self-sufficiency; namely, to determine the structure of production these economies would have to attain in order to maintain their present actual consumption and investment without access to foreign trade. The "skyline" chart graphically depicts these features, and also shows the degree of import and export activity of each economy.

2. Basic Description of the Composition of a "Skyline" Chart

In the "skyline" chart, the vertical axis of the chart represents the self-sufficiency rate. The self-sufficiency rate is defined as the actual gross domestic output (GDO) divided by the hypothetical GDO, which is induced by domestic final demand. The hypothetical GDO is the GDO directly and indirectly required to produce domestic final demand, which consists of consumption plus investment, including imported consumption and investment goods. The hypothetical GDO is based on the assumption that all outputs required to meet domestic final demand are produced domestically, with no imports.

The horizontal axis represents the hypothetical GDO of each sector. In the "skyline" chart all hypothetical GDO's are assumed to be 100% (100% self-sufficiency rate). Atop each GDO block is added a direct and indirect "export" block.

Direct and indirect "imports" are subtracted from the direct and indirect "export" block, and the remainder is added to the GDO to derive the final configuration of the sector block. This procedure is performed for each industrial sector. The actual industrial structure is therefore described by the solid line which has the appearance of a city skyline.

Let us explain the mathematical background for "skyline" chart analysis.

Define

$X=(X_i)$: a gross domestic output (GDO) vector;
$Y=(Y_i)$: a domestic final demand vector;
$E=(E_i)$: an export vector;
$M=(M_i)$: an import vector.

Using an input coefficient matrix A, a standard competitive-type input-output model can be written as

$$X=AX+Y+E-M.\qquad(1)$$

Hence we have

$$X=(I-A)^{-1}(Y+E-M).\qquad(2)$$

Let

$$X_Y=BY;\quad X_E=BE;\quad X_M=BM,\qquad(3)$$

where $B=(I-A)^{-1}$.

X_Y, X_E and X_M are a hypothetical GDO vector, and direct and indirect "export" and "import" vectors, respectively.

Eq. (2) can be written as

$$X_i = X_{Yi} + X_{Ei} - X_{Mi} . \tag{4}$$

Define

$$s_i = X_i / X_{Yi};$$

$$e_i = X_{Ei} / X_{Yi};$$

$$m_i = X_{Mi} / X_{Yi} .$$

It follows from these definitions and Eq. (4) that

$$s_i = 1 + e_i - m_i . \tag{5}$$

The s_i is the sector i's self-sufficiency rate. The e_i and m_i are respectively direct and indirect "export", and "import", ratios of the sector i.

We have from Eq. (5)

$$s_i X_{Yi} = 1 \times X_{Yi} + e_i X_{Yi} - m_i X_{Yi} .$$

The left-hand side of this equation shows "the final configuration of the sector block." The first, second and third term of the right-hand side show the hypothetical GDO, "export" block and "import" block, respectively.

3. A Description of the Data

We here also use the data employed in Chapter 5. In the case of the Soviet Union we use Soviet 1959, 1966, 1972, 1977 Input-Output Tables constructed or reconstructed by Professor Treml and his associates.

In the reconstructed tables in producers' prices, export and import vectors are not separated, with the exception of the 1972 input-output table, which is the most disaggregated version of the tables provided by the Treml group. Therefore, in the aggregated 15-sector input-output analysis we must use the input-output data in purchasers' prices furnished by Professor Treml and his associates.

In estimating separate export and import vectors many problems present themselves. Primarily, we must adjust the official trade data in order to make it consistent with national accounts and input-output accounts. The problem, therefore, is to devise a method for determining the conversion rates of the official foreign trade prices to the domestic prices. Treml and his associates have made great efforts to determine these conversion rates. These rates are the only reliable tools we have at this time to make any type of accurate assessment of the Soviet economy. However, the conversion rates published in several monographs are not always consistent. This has limited the accuracy of the Soviet data, but given the scarcity of accurate data, we must use whatever is available.

In the input-output analysis of East European economies we mainly use input-output tables provided by the ECE. The ECE has published standardized input-output tables for the years around 1959, 1965, 1970 and 1975. In the ECE tables we can find Hungarian, Polish, Czechoslovakian, Yugoslavian and Bulgarian input-output tables. Only the 1963 Bulgarian table is available. The Hungarian and Polish input-output tables for the years around 1970 are missing. The Hungarian and Polish statistical offices have published the original input-output tables, but they are not available for analysis. The original Hungarian input-output tables for the 1970's are non-competitive types (B-type in Hungarian terminology). The original Polish tables for the years 1971 to 1973 are competitive types, but they do not include separate export and import vectors. Further, the Hungarian and Polish ECE tables for the years around 1975 are not available. Most of ECE tables employed in this chapter are in producers' prices or basic prices. It should be noted that most of the Soviet input-output tables are compiled on the basis of purchasers' prices. Therefore, when the Soviet economy is compared with other economies, inconsistencies may occur.

In the case of the United States we use the commodity-by-commodity input-output tables compiled by merging the U.S. 1972 and 1977 make and use tables. In the case of Japan, original tables published by the Japanese Government are used. In the case of West Germany, the 1975 ECE standardized input-output table compiled by the Federal Statistical

Office is used.

As has been stated, most of the available Soviet input-output tables with separate export and import vectors are compiled in purchasers' prices, as is the case with France. Most other countries, including the CMEA countries, compile their tables in producers' prices. More importantly, when compiling input-output data, the CMEA countries usually evaluate imports in CIF prices, but employ data which does not realistically reflect world prices. This fact is especially true in the case of the Soviet Union.

4. "Skylines" of Soviet and East European Economies

"Skyline" chart analysis was first developed to study changes of input-output structure of an economy with its economic development from the viewpoint of the degrees of domestic production and import substitution by sector, and assuming that final demand by sector is given. In this section we apply this method in order to investigate macro and multi-sectoral analysis of foreign trade of the centrally planned economies.

Table 1 presents macro foreign trade structures and Leontief self-sufficiency rates of the six centrally planned economies. From this table the following three facts can easily be seen.

First, the self-sufficiency rate of each country shows a uniformly declining trend, with some fluctuations. This self-sufficiency rate around 1975 is about 95%. A decrease in the self-sufficiency rate from 1970 to 1975 seems to be caused by the deterioration of trade conditions due to the first "oil shock" in 1973. We can also see the degree of decline in the self-sufficiency rate of Hungary, which accounted for the highest decline, and of Czechoslovakia, which was the most stable.

Secondly, both export and import ratios of Hungary and Czechoslovakia were very high in each bench-mark year, and the growth rates of these ratios were also high over this period of time.

Thirdly, the export and import ratios of the Soviet Union are remarkably lower than the other five planned economies in each bench-mark year over this period. The import ratios of the Soviet Union, while low in

Table 1. Macro-Structure of Foreign Trade: Selected MPS Countries

(unit: %)

	around 1959			around 1965			around 1970			around 1975		
	e	m	s	e	m	s	e	m	s	e	m	s
S	3.60	6.22	97.38	3.16	5.02	98.14	5.08	8.94	96.14	6.30	11.36	95.44
H	27.11	14.54	112.57	31.69	28.97	102.72	34.54	33.31	101.23	36.71	40.79	95.92
P	18.07	19.18	98.90	19.18	20.98	98.20				23.48	27.69	95.79
C	17.12	15.96	101.15	27.24	23.92	103.32	31.09	28.81	102.29	33.03	33.78	99.25
Y	20.83	22.10	98.73	19.40	21.80	97.60	18.97	25.54	93.43	18.06	24.71	93.35

Notes: S = Soviet Union
H = Hungary
P = Poland
C = Czechoslovakia
Y = Yugoslavia
e = direct and indirect "export" ratio
m = direct and indirect "import" ratio
s = self-sufficiency rate $(1 + e - m)$

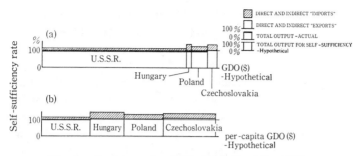

Fig. 1. An International "Skyline" Chart for 1975

comparison with the other five, show a marked increase.

In terms of this third fact, it appears that the Soviet Union is a self-sufficing economy without access to foreign trade. However, we must keep in mind that economic data for Soviet exports and imports is statistically suspect and biased toward the low side.

Figure 1 shows an "international skyline chart" of four countries, in and around 1975. In this chart each country is regarded as an industrial sector for input-output analysis. From this figure we can see that the line showing the self-sufficiency rate for each country is rather flat. The shaded area of the "silhouette" for imports and the import expansion of the three countries, with the exception of the Soviet Union, is remarkably large. Also shown is the much greater gross domestic output of the Soviet Union, in comparison with the other three. Further, when we depict gross domestic output-per-capita horizontally, each country's share of gross domestic output-per-capita tends to be equalized.

We will now turn to our main subject, an input-output "skyline" chart analysis.

Unlike the macro analysis, it should be noted that the input-output "skyline" chart analysis assumes the existence of competitive import-type input-output tables on the GDO base, and the analysis requires use of the $(I-A)^{-1}$-type Leontief inverse, and not the $(I-(I-\hat{M})A)^{-1}$ or $(I-A^d)^{-1}$-type inverse. Therefore, we do not describe the Hungarian "skyline" chart for the 1970's, and the Polish "skyline" chart for 1976, because the published input-output tables for these countries for the 1970's are non-competitive import-types. (The Polish input-output tables for 1971–3 do not have separate import and export columns, although they are competitive import-type tables).

Figure 2 shows a "skyline" chart of the Soviet and East European economies using 14 to 19-sector input-output tables. Sector classification codes for East European countries are not identical, except for the years in and around 1959 and 1965. However, the sector classification codes are the same vertically but not horizontally. The "skyline" charts of the Soviet Union in Figure 2 are based on input-output data in purchasers' prices. In Figure 3 is shown the 1972 Soviet "skyline" chart based on producers' prices.

For convenience, the horizontal dimensions of each country's "skyline" chart are the same, so that the share of each industry's GDO can be seen.

From Figure 2, it can be seen that the "skyline" of the Soviet Union is rather flat over time, while the "skylines" of the East European economies, particularly that of Yugoslavia, show remarkable jumps and drops. For each country we can show the following characteristics:

U.S.S.R.

The self-sufficiency rates of the energy, mining and basic metals industries are rather high, while the rates for light industry, particularly the textile, apparel and leather industry are low. This is a basic, constant feature of the Soviet "skyline" over time. The self-sufficiency rate of agriculture shows a decline in the 1970's. Both the exports and imports of the machinery industry increase over time. It should be noted, however, that the changes in the shapes of the Soviet "skylines" are rather static in nature.

Czechoslovakia

The self-sufficiency rate of the machinery industry decreases over time, and the rate around 1975 drops below 100%. The rates of agriculture and the food industries are consistently low, and the rate of the energy sector is remarkably low. The rates of the textile, apparel and leather industry and the non-metallic mineral products industries are rather

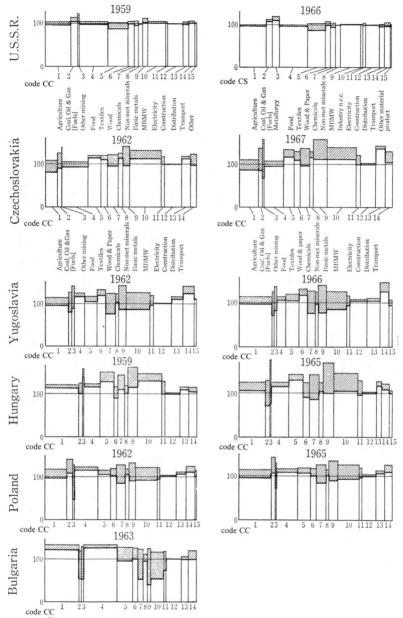

Fig. 2. Sky-line Charts of Soviet & East European Economies

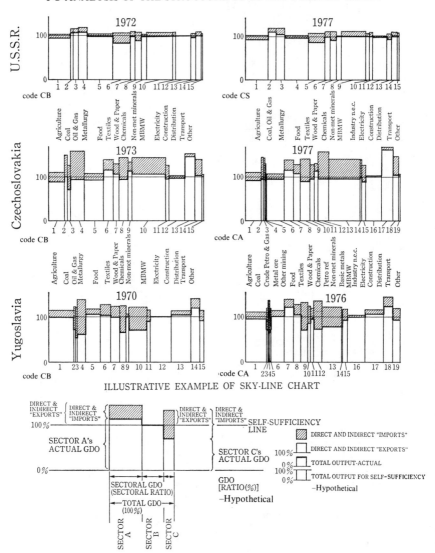

Fig. 2. Sky-line Charts of Soviet & East European Economies (continued)

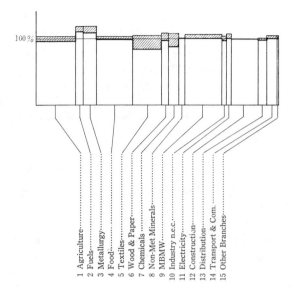

Fig. 3.   Sky-line Chart: 1972 U.S.S.R. (Producers' Prices)

high, over 100%. The fact that the output share and export and import ratios of the metal block, namely basic metals and machinery, are remarkably high compared with other East European countries shows the high level of Czechoslovakian economic development. The horizontal shape of the "skyline" tends to be rather flat, except for the distribution sector.

Yugoslavia

The low level self-sufficiency rate of the metal block and the large shaded area for metal block imports suggest that Yugoslavia remains a typically developing country. The rate of light industry, particularly the textile, apparel and leather industry, is over 100%. The rate of agriculture is below the 100% line, except for around 1970. The rate of the energy sector is remarkably low. The shape of the "skyline" is remarkably jagged over time.

Hungary

Although the self-sufficiency rates of the agriculture, mining and manufacturing industries, especially the metal block and energy industries, remarkably decrease from around 1959 to 1965, the rates of the agriculture and machinery industries remained over 100%. The rate of the textile, apparel and leather industry increased, while the export and import ratios of the industry declined. The complexity of the shape of the Hungarian "skylines" tends to decrease over time, although the "skylines" show the greatest degree of change in comparison with the other East European economies.

Poland

The self-sufficiency rate of the energy sector around 1959 and 1965 is rather high, but the rates of agriculture and the food industry decreased.

Bulgaria

The shape of the Bulgarian "skylines" is jagged, and the shape of the "skyline" is quite particular compared with other East European countries. This is due to the fact that the output shares of agriculture and the food industry are both large, the export ratios of these sectors are high and the import ratios are low. Only Bulgaria shows a remarkable contrast between the self-sufficiency rate of agriculture and the food industry and that of the metal block sector.

In addition to the above facts, the self-sufficiency rates of the energy and natural resources sectors of East European countries are generally low, although there are some exceptions; for example, the self-sufficiency rate of Poland around 1959 and 1965, and of Hungary around 1959.

Let us turn to a "skyline" chart of the major Western economies.

Figures 4, 5 and 6 show a "skyline" chart of the U.S., Japanese and FRG economies based on 15-sector input-output tables. The sector classification corresponds to a standard industry classification employed in the CMEA countries. However, it should be noted that the "other branches" sector is mainly occupied by a service sector in the case of the Western SNA countries.

From Figure 4, it can be seen that the 1972 "skyline" of the United States features the characteristic shape of a highly developed country; a fact first pointed out by Leontief (1963). The "skyline" is mostly flat in shape and graphically reflects the large output share accounted by the

Sky-Line Chart: 1972 U.S.

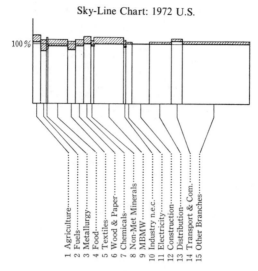

Sky-Line Chart: 1977 U.S.

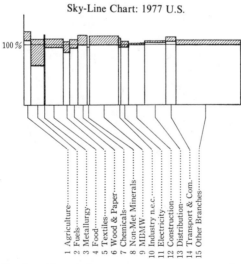

Fig. 4.   Sky-line Charts of the United States (15-Sector Versions)

151

Sky-Line Chart: 1970 JAPAN

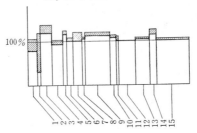

Sky-Line Chart: 1975 JAPAN

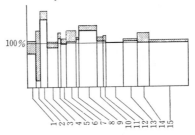

Sky-Line Chart: 1980 JAPAN

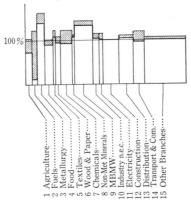

Fig. 5.   Sky-line Charts of Japan

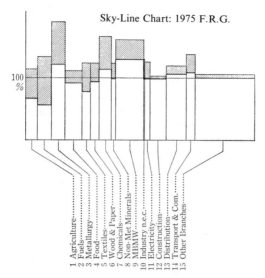

Fig. 6.   Sky-line Chart of the F.R.G.

service sector. The U.S. 1977 "skyline" shows a remarkable change in shape because the self-sufficiency rates of the fuels (energy) and metallurgy sectors have shown a much greater decrease. The other sectors have shown positive growth of both "export" and "import" ratios while the textiles and electricity sectors show a greater increase in the "import" ratio. It should be noted that a rather higher level of the self-sufficiency rate of the agriculture sector is one of the constant features of the U.S. economy over time.

From Figures 5 and 6 we can see that the "skylines" of the Japanese and FRG economies displays some rather remarkable jumps and drops while that of Japan, with exception of the fuels sector, is flatter in shape. The most conspicuous difference between the "skylines" of the two countries is in that the "import" ratios (shaded areas), "import" ratios, of the machine building and metalworking (MBMW) and metallurgy sectors of the FRG are much greater than those of Japan, while the self-sufficiency rates of these sectors in the two countries show a remark-

Table 2. Changes in Soviet Foreign Trade: Difference between
Two Periods   (unit: %)

Sector	Output Ratios-Actual	"Export" Ratios	"Import" Ratios	Self-Sufficiency Rates
1972—1966				
1 Agriculture	−2.51	1.32	4.46	−3.14
2 Fuels	1.10	2.88	3.84	−.96
3 Metallurgy	1.02	−.60	2.14	−2.73
4 Food	−2.35	1.42	2.88	−1.46
5 Textiles	−.53	1.18	6.64	−5.46
6 Wood & Paper	.01	.27	5.72	−5.45
7 Chemicals	.54	2.05	9.06	−7.01
8 Non-Met Minerals	.17	.66	2.15	−1.48
9 MBMW	1.38	3.21	3.26	−.04
10 Industry n.e.c.	.27	1.35	2.69	−1.34
11 Electricity	.25	2.27	3.54	−1.27
12 Construction	.99	.00	.00	.00
13 Distribution	.00	1.39	4.34	−2.95
14 Transport & Com.	−.15	1.49	3.92	−2.41
15 Other Branches	−.19	2.41	5.24	−2.83
1977—1972				
1 Agriculture	−.29	.13	2.70	−2.58
2 Fuels	.19	3.68	1.56	2.12
3 Metallurgy	−.22	.52	5.18	−4.67
4 Food	−.93	−.20	3.42	−3.63
5 Textiles	−.36	2.03	.14	1.90
6 Wood & Paper	−.23	1.90	1.62	.28
7 Chemicals	.46	2.84	2.33	.51
8 Non-Met Minerals	−.13	.45	.46	−.01
9 MBMW	1.08	4.65	5.03	−.39
10 Industry n.e.c.	.77	1.32	.64	.68
11 Electricity	−.02	2.39	1.91	.47
12 Construction	−.58	.00	.00	.00
13 Distribution	−.02	.98	2.69	−1.70
14 Transport & Com.	.20	2.16	2.43	−.29
15 Other Branches	.08	1.02	−.04	1.06

ably high level. This difference has became more striking since the self-sufficiency rate of the Japanese MBMW sector has shown a much greater increase. As for Japan. it should also be noted that the output share of the service sector has shown much greater growth from 1970 to 1980.

Let us now move from a general description of the "skyline" chart to a more detailed description.

First we analyze the changing trade pattern of the Soviet Union over a period of time. Table 2 shows the differences in rates of output, "export," and "import" ratios, and the self-sufficiency rates between 1966 and 1972, and also between 1972 and 1977. It should be noted that these tables are based on data in current purchasers' prices. With regard to the difference in "export" and "import" ratios between 1972 and 1966, we can see that all sectors, with the exception of metallurgy, have shown positive growth of "export" and "import" ratios.

In all sectors the growth of "import" ratios is greater than the growth of "export" ratios. Therefore, the self-sufficiency ratios of all sectors decrease. The chemical industry shows the greatest decrease, followed by light industry, wood and chapter, and agriculture. The machine building and metalworking (MBMW) sector shows the lowest decline. It should be noted, that while the construction sector shows a zero rate of decrease, this sector is treated as a non-export and non-import sector. With regard to the difference in "export" and "import" ratios between 1977 and 1972, we can see that all sectors, with the exception of the food industry and other material branches, have shown positive growth of "export" and "import" ratios. Unlike the dynamic decreasing trend from 1966 to 1972, during the period 1972 to 1977, some sectors, including energy and light industry, show a slight increase in self-sufficiency rates. The metallurgy sector shows the greatest decline in self-sufficiency rates, followed by food industry and agriculture. The MBMW sector shows a slightly greater decrease compared to the period 1966 to 1972, but the growth rates of "export" and "import" ratios of this sector are the highest.

Let us now compare the foreign trade patterns of the Soviet Union

Table 3. A Comparison of Soviet and East European Foreign Trade
(unit: %)

	Sector	Output Ratios-Actual	"Export" Ratios	"Import" Ratios	Self-Sufficiency Rates
		1977 Czechoslovakia—1977 U.S.S.R.			
1	Agriculture	−4.52	8.02	7.83	.20
2	Fuels	−1.03	15.72	63.26	−47.54
3	Metallurgy	2.48	33.53	53.83	−20.30
4	Food	−3.66	5.33	4.79	.55
5	Textiles	−4.72	35.04	3.11	31.91
6	Wood & Paper	1.12	18.53	10.09	8.45
7	Chemicals	2.28	31.53	30.64	.89
8	Non-Met Minerals	−.68	30.84	16.85	13.99
9	MBMW	4.40	31.60	32.33	−.73
10	Industry n.e.c.	−1.76	35.89	11.02	24.87
11	Electricity	1.07	18.22	28.06	−9.83
12	Construction	.75	2.45	4.35	−1.90
13	Distribution	4.45	63.32	−4.97	68.28
14	Transport & Com.	−.15	38.12	32.43	5.70
15	Other Branches	−0.03	1.21	2.40	−1.19
		1976 Yugoslavia—1977 U.S.S.R.			
1	Agriculture	−1.19	6.80	3.78	3.03
2	Fuels	−2.60	2.66	56.53	−53.87
3	Metallurgy	1.20	14.04	47.38	−33.33
4	Food	−6.59	10.43	4.23	6.21
5	Textiles	−4.76	33.36	−2.69	36.04
6	Wood & Paper	1.59	16.42	11.54	4.88
7	Chemicals	.55	20.40	40.28	−19.87
8	Non-Met Minerals	−1.23	15.64	22.26	−6.61
9	MBMW	−3.20	11.30	32.96	−21.65
10	Industry n.e.c.	−2.33	7.57	26.14	−18.57
11	Electricity	1.19	6.89	16.61	−9.71
12	Construction	2.16	2.20	1.62	.58
13	Distribution	9.08	7.93	−2.75	10.67
14	Transport & Com.	2.23	31.88	11.48	20.41
15	Other Branches	3.91	10.00	19.86	−9.86

Table 4.   A comparison in the Foreign Trade Patterns of the U.S.S.R., the U.S.A and the F.R.G.   (unit: %)

Sector	"Export" Ratios	"Import" Ratios	Self-Sufficiency Rates
	1977 U.S.A.—1977 U.S.S.R.		
1 Agriculture	21.03	2.58	18.46
2 Fuels	−9.50	30.94	−40.44
3 Metallurgy	−1.35	15.64	−16.98
4 Food	9.22	5.18	4.05
5 Textiles	.78	−4.01	4.78
6 Wood & Paper	−.71	.47	−1.18
7 Chemicals	7.05	−4.35	11.40
8 Non-Met Minerals	7.77	8.84	−1.07
9 MBMW	5.31	1.68	3.63
10 Industry n.e.c.	6.48	8.50	−2.02
11 Electricity	−3.74	−.93	−2.80
12 Construction	2.01	2.39	−.38
13 Distribution	1.31	−10.04	11.34
14 Transport & Com.	1.88	−4.86	6.75
	1975 F.R.G.—1977 U.S.S.R.		
1 Agriculture	10.87	34.99	−24.10
2 Fuels	14.01	66.12	−52.11
3 Metallurgy	70.01	51.56	18.46
4 Food	8.97	10.85	−1.88
5 Textiles	17.66	24.09	−6.44
6 Wood & Paper	12.44	15.87	−3.43
7 Chemicals	55.13	29.76	25.37
8 Non-Met Minerals	21.32	20.86	.46
9 MBMW	49.88	17.76	32.12
10 Industry n.e.c.	24.15	49.86	−25.70
11 Electricity	16.36	16.94	−.57
12 Construction	3.53	4.23	−.70
13 Distribution	14.24	1.07	13.16
14 Transport & Com.	26.87	16.41	10.47

with the East European countries. Table 3 shows the difference in "export," and "import" ratios, and self-sufficiency rates between the 1977 Czechoslovakian economy and the 1977 Soviet economy.

As can be seen in Table 3, all sectors of the Czechoslovakian economy, with the exception of the distribution sector, show much greater "export" and "import" growth rates. Compared with the Soviet Union, the self-sufficiency rate of the Czechoslovakian distribution sector shows a remarkable increase, followed by the light industry and non-metallic mineral products sectors. In contrast, the energy sector shows the greatest decrease, followed by the metallurgy sector. As for the relative deviation of "export" ratios between Czechoslovakia and the Soviet Union, the non-metallic mineral product sector shows the greatest value; 1733%. Also, for the relative deviation of "import" ratios, this sector shows the second greatest value; 503%. The MBMW "export" and "import" ratios show a much greater increase, but the self-sufficiency rate shows a slight decrease.

Let us next compare the foreign trade patterns of the Soviet Union with the Western economies.

Table 4 shows the difference in "export" and "import" ratios and self-sufficiency rates between the 1977 U.S. economy and the 1977 Soviet economy. Table 4 also shows the difference in "export" and "import ratios and self-sufficiency rates between the 1975 FRG economy and the 1977 Soviet economy.

From Table 4 we can see that the U.S. agriculture sector shows a much greater "export" ratio, followed by food, non-metallic mineral products and chemicals. The U.S. fuels sector shows a much greater "import" ratio, followed by the metallurgy and non-metallic mineral products sectors. Consequently, the U.S. self-sufficiency rates of the fuels and metallurgy sectors have shown a much greater decrease, while the U.S. self-sufficiency rates for the agriculture sector has shown a greater increase.

From Table 4 we can also see that the FRG metallurgy sector shows a much greater "export" ratio, 70%, followed by the wood, chapter and non-metallic minerals sectors. Unlike the comparison of the U.S. and Soviet foreign trade pattern, all sectors of the FRG economy show much greater "export" and "import" ratio increases. The FRG fuels sector shows a much greater "import" ratio, 66%, followed by the metallurgy and agriculture sectors. Consequently, the self-sufficiency rates of the FRG fuels and agriculture sectors show a much greater decrease, while

Table 5. Self-Sufficiency Rates: The Ten Highest Sectors

1972 U.S.S.R. (Producers' Prices)

(unit: %)

Rank	Sector Treml's 88-Order Code	Output Ratios-Actual (-hypothetical)	"Export" Ratios	"Import" Ratios	Self-Sufficiency Rates
1	6 Oil extraction	0.62 (0.47)	37.32	10.10	127.22
2	39 Mineral chemistry products	0.09 (0.07)	40.10	21.43	118.68
3	71 Fish products	0.96 (0.83)	12.74	1.62	111.12
4	2 Coke products	0.37 (0.32)	23.50	13.91	109.60
5	20 Mining & metallurgical M & E	0.33 (0.29)	20.20	11.16	109.04
6	12 Energy & power M & E	0.21 (0.19)	19.15	10.40	108.75
7	1 Ores & metals	4.93 (4.36)	19.78	11.20	108.57
8	5 Coal	1.43 (1.28)	17.90	10.79	107.11
9	7 Oil refining	1.12 (1.01)	13.30	6.49	106.80
10	34 Sanitary engineering products	0.19 (0.17)	6.99	1.04	105.96

Table 5. (continued)

1972 U.S.A. (Producers' Prices)

(unit: %)

Rank	Sector BEA's 85-Order Code	Output Ratios-Actual (-hypothetical)	"Export" Ratios	"Import" Ratios	Self-Sufficiency Rates
1	45 Construction & mining machinery	0.39 (0.29)	37.72	5.65	132.07
2	60 Aircraft & parts	0.84 (0.68)	27.70	5.44	122.26
3	51 Office, computing & accounting machines	0.41 (0.35)	28.21	12.80	115.41
4	2 Other agricultural products	1.74 (1.53)	19.82	6.93	112.88
5	15 Tobacco manufactures	0.47 (0.42)	13.16	1.23	111.93
6	43 Engines & turbines	0.29 (0.26)	20.59	11.12	109.47
7	7 Coal mining	0.28 (0.26)	17.15	8.58	108.57
8	52 Service industry machines	0.41 (0.39)	8.97	3.43	105.53
9	65 Transportation & warehousing	3.90 (3.69)	11.80	6.58	105.22
10	57 Electronic components & accessories	0.44 (0.42)	23.53	18.49	105.04

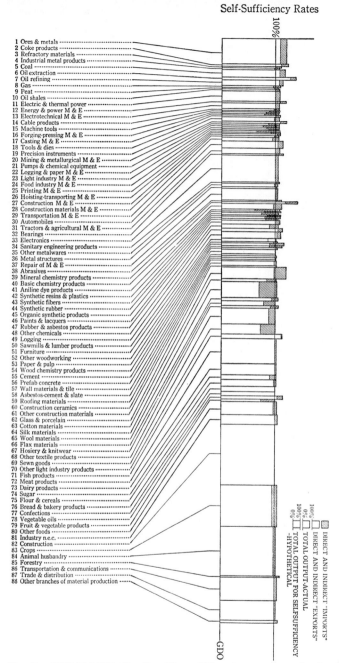

Self-Sufficiency Rates

1 Ores & metals
2 Coke products
3 Refractory materials
4 Industrial metal products
5 Coal
6 Oil extraction
7 Oil refining
8 Gas
9 Peat
10 Oil shales
11 Electric & thermal power
12 Energy & power M & E
13 Electrotechnical M & E
14 Cable products
15 Machine tools
16 Forging-pressing M & E
17 Casting M & E
18 Tools & dies
19 Precision instruments
20 Mining & metallurgical M & E
21 Pumps & chemical equipment
22 Logging & paper M & E
23 Light industry M & E
24 Food industry M & E
25 Printing M & E
26 Hoisting-transporting M & E
27 Construction M & E
28 Construction materials M & E
29 Transportation M & E
30 Automobiles
31 Tractors & agricultural M & E
32 Bearings
33 Electronics
34 Sanitary engineering products
35 Other metalwares
36 Metal structures
37 Repair of M & E
38 Abrasives
39 Mineral chemistry products
40 Basic chemistry products
41 Aniline dye products
42 Synthetic resins & plastics
43 Synthetic fibers
44 Synthetic rubber
45 Organic synthetic products
46 Paints & lacquers
47 Rubber & asbestos products
48 Other chemicals
49 Logging
50 Sawmills & lumber products
51 Furniture
52 Other woodworking
53 Paper & pulp
54 Wood chemistry products
55 Cement
56 Prefab concrete
57 Wall materials & tile
58 Asbestos-cement & slate
59 Roofing materials
60 Construction ceramics
61 Other construction materials
62 Glass & porcelain
63 Cotton materials
64 Silk materials
65 Wool materials
66 Flax materials
67 Hosiery & knitwear
68 Other textile products
69 Sewn goods
70 Other light industry products
71 Fish products
72 Meat products
73 Dairy products
74 Sugar
75 Flour & cereals
76 Bread & bakery products
77 Confections
78 Vegetable oils
79 Fruit & vegetable products
80 Other foods
81 Industry n.e.c.
82 Construction
83 Crops
84 Animal husbandry
85 Forestry
86 Transportation & communications
87 Trade & distribution
88 Other branches of material production

GDO

DIRECT AND INDIRECT "IMPORTS"
DIRECT AND INDIRECT "EXPORTS"
TOTAL OUTPUT-ACTUAL
TOTAL OUTPUT FOR SELFSUFFICIENCY -HYPOTHETICAL

Fig. 7. 1972 U.S.S.R. Sky-line Chart (88-sector: producers' prices)

161

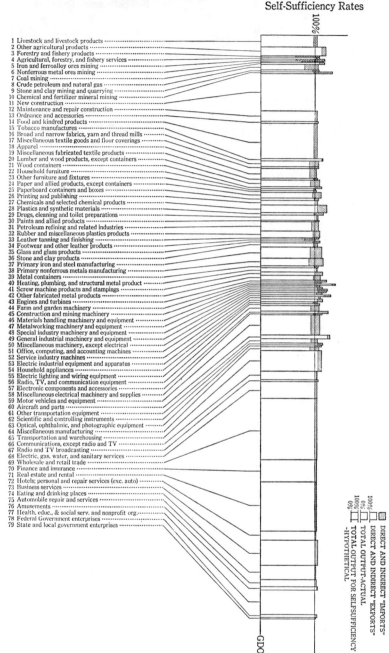

Self-Sufficiency Rates

1 Livestock and livestock products
2 Other agricultural products
3 Forestry and fishery products
4 Agricultural, forestry, and fishery services
5 Iron and ferroalloy ores mining
6 Nonferrous metal ores mining
7 Coal mining
8 Crude petroleum and natural gas
9 Stone and clay mining and quarrying
10 Chemical and fertilizer mineral mining
11 New construction
12 Maintenance and repair construction
13 Ordnance and accessories
14 Food and kindred products
15 Tobacco manufactures
16 Broad and narrow fabrics, yarn and thread mills
17 Miscellaneous textile goods and floor coverings
18 Apparel
19 Miscellaneous fabricated textile products
20 Lumber and wood products, except containers
21 Wood containers
22 Household furniture
23 Other furniture and fixtures
24 Paper and allied products, except containers
25 Paperboard containers and boxes
26 Printing and publishing
27 Chemicals and selected chemical products
28 Plastics and synthetic materials
29 Drugs, cleaning and toilet preparations
30 Paints and allied products
31 Petroleum refining and related industries
32 Rubber and miscellaneous plastics products
33 Leather tanning and finishing
34 Footwear and other leather products
35 Glass and glass products
36 Stone and clay products
37 Primary iron and steel manufacturing
38 Primary nonferrous metals manufacturing
39 Metal containers
40 Heating, plumbing, and structural metal product
41 Screw machine products and stampings
42 Other fabricated metal products
43 Engines and turbines
44 Farm and garden machinery
45 Construction and mining machinery
46 Materials handling machinery and equipment
47 Metalworking machinery and equipment
48 Special industry machinery and equipment
49 General industrial machinery and equipment
50 Miscellaneous machinery, except electrical
51 Office, computing, and accounting machines
52 Service industry machines
53 Electric industrial equipment and apparatus
54 Household appliances
55 Electric lighting and wiring equipment
56 Radio, TV, and communication equipment
57 Electronic components and accessories
58 Miscellaneous electrical machinery and supplies
59 Motor vehicles and equipment
60 Aircraft and parts
61 Other transportation equipment
62 Scientific and controlling instruments
63 Optical, ophthalmic, and photographic equipment
64 Miscellaneous manufacturing
65 Transportation and warehousing
66 Communications, except radio and TV
67 Radio and TV broadcasting
68 Electric, gas, water, and sanitary services
69 Wholesale and retail trade
70 Finance and insurance
71 Real estate and rental
72 Hotels; personal and repair services (exc. auto)
73 Business services
74 Eating and drinking places
75 Automobile repair and services
76 Amusements
77 Health, educ., & social serv. and nonprofit org.
78 Federal Government enterprises
79 State and local government enterprises

100%
100% 0%
100% 0%

DIRECT AND INDIRECT "IMPORTS"
DIRECT AND INDIRECT "EXPORTS"
TOTAL OUTPUT–ACTUAL
TOTAL OUTPUT FOR SELFSUFFICIENCY
–HYPOTHETICAL

GDO

Fig. 8.   1972 U.S. Sky-line Chart (79-Sector; producers' prices)

162

Table 6. Self-Sufficiency Rates: The ten Lowest Sectors

1972 U.S.S.R. (Producers' Prices)

(unit:%)

Rank	Sector Treml's 88-Order Code	Output Ratios -Actual (-hypothetical)	"Export" Ratios	"Import" Ratios	Self-Sufficiency Rates
1	41 Aniline dye products	0.05 (0.08)	7.90	46.15	61.75
2	25 Printing M & E	0.01 (0.01)	7.59	42.20	65.39
3	65 Wool materials	1.97 (2.70)	2.35	32.29	70.05
4	70 Other light industry products	1.25 (1.65)	1.16	28.55	72.60
5	79 Fruit & vegetable products	0.32 (0.42)	1.14	28.10	73.04
6	43 Synthetic fibers	0.27 (0.35)	4.87	30.65	74.21
7	22 Logging & paper M & E	0.04 (0.05)	6.91	30.07	76.84
8	65 Hosiery & Knitwear	0.68 (0.83)	0.58	22.32	78.26
9	42 Synthtic resins & plastics	0.25 (0.30)	9.32	30.25	79.07
10	17 Casting M & E	0.01 (0.01)	4.76	25.26	79.50

Table 6. (continued)

1972 U.S.A (Producers' Prices)

(unit: %)

Rank	Sector BEA's 85-Order Code	Output Ratios- Actual (-hypothetical)	"Export" Ratios	"Import" Ratios	Self- Sufficiency Rates
1	3 Forestry & fishery products	0.11 (0.17)	8.33	44.01	64.32
2	5 Iron & ferroalloy ores mining	0.07 (0.11)	17.19	52.53	64.66
3	6 Nonferrous metal ores mining	0.11 (0.14)	13.96	38.37	75.59
4	33 Leather tanning & finishing	0.05 (0.06)	6.86	29.56	77.01
5	8 Crude petroleum & natural gas	0.85 (1.04)	5.91	24.92	80.99
6	34 Footwear & other leather products	0.23 (0.28)	0.90	19.77	81.12
7	38 Primary nonferrous metals manufacturing	1.19 (1.34)	13.86	25.64	88.22
8	16 Broad & narrow fabrics yarn & thread mills	0.88 (0.98)	5.90	16.79	89.11
9	17 Miscellaneous textile goods & floor coverings	0.31 (0.34)	5.57	15.64	89.93
10	64 Miscellaneous manufacturing	0.58 (0.64)	6.71	16.48	90.24

the self-sufficiency rates of the FRG MBMW, chemical and metallurgy sectors show a much greater increase.

5. A Comparison of the Soviet Union and the United States: A Disaggregated Case

When making an input-output analysis, the greater the degree of disaggregation, the better able we are to make concrete analysis of the input-output structure of an economy.

The most detailed input-output table for the Soviet Union is the 88-order version compiled by Treml, Kostinsky and Gallik (1983). We employ this version, incorporating the 88-order export and import vectors, in producers' prices to compare the Soviet foreign trade pattern with that of the United States.

In the case of the United States we employ the 85-order commodity-by-commodity table compiled by merging the make and use tables of the BEA. For both countries, very few studies have been conducted in terms of direct comparisons to date. Therefore, we employ the original codes presently used in both countries.

Figure 7 and Figure 8 show the "skyline" charts of the Soviet Union and the United States, respectively. In the 1972 aggregated 15-sector versions both "skyline" charts are very flat. However, in the disaggregated version the charts of both countries are complex in shape. Table 5 shows the ten highest sectors of the self-sufficiency rates for the Soviet Union and the United States. From this table we can see that the Soviet Union uses the terms "Energy and Power Machinery and Equipment," and "Mining and Metallurgical Machine and Equipment", while the United States uses the terms "Energy and Turbines" and "Construction and Mining Machinery" for the same respective categories. These two sectors and the coal sector show the relatively high self-sufficiency rates in both countries.

Secondly, Table 5 shows that the Soviet Union has a high self-sufficiency rate in such basic resources-related sectors as "Oil Extraction" and "Metallurgy and Ore. " For the United States, the "Aircraft" and "Office, Computing and Accounting Machines" sectors show a high degree of self-sufficiency in these high-technology related areas.

Thirdly, with regard to sectors related to agriculture and fisheries, it can be seen that in the case of the Soviet Union, the self-sufficiency rate for "Fish Products" is very high. In the United States the "Other Agricultural Products" sector, which covers fruits and vegetables, and "Tobacco Manufactures" show a high self-sufficiency rate.

Sectors which reflect a high rate of self-sufficiency usually account for high direct and indirect "exports;" namely, the ten highest sectors shown in the Table 6 are also high export sectors.

The Soviet sector with the highest self-sufficiency rate, "Oil Extraction," reflects the second highest "export" ratio. This sector's "import ," actual, and hypothetical output ratios are respectively 10.10, 0.62 and 0.47%.

The second highest self-sufficiency sector in the Soviet economy, "Mineral Chemistry Products," reflects the highest "export" ratio, 40.10%. This sector' s "import," actual, and hypothetical output ratios are respectively 21.43, 0.09, and 0.07%. The output share of this sector is rather low, and hence, this sector does not effectively impact on the economy as a whole.

The third highest self-sufficiency sector, "Fish Products," does not reflect the relatively high "export" ratio, but rather, reflects the low "import" ratio. This sector's "export," "import," actual and hypothetical output ratios are respectively 12.74, 1.62, 0.96, and 0.83%.

The highest self-sufficiency sector for the United States,"Construction and Mining Machinery," reflects the highest "export" ratio, a remarkable 37.72%. This sector's "import," actual and hypothetical output ratios are respectively 5.65, 0.39, and 0.29%.

The second highest self-sufficiency sector. "Aircraft and Parts," reflects the fourth highest" export" ratio, 27.70%. This sector's "import," actual and hypothetical output ratios are respectively 5.44, 0.84, and 0.68%. The sector, "Oil Shales," shows the second highest "export" ratio, 33.55%. Therefore, the self-sufficiency rate of this sector is below 100%.

The third highest self-sufficiency sector, "Office, Computing and Accounting Machines , " reflects the third highest "export" ratio, 28.21%.

This sector's "import," actual and hypothetical "output" ratios are respectively 12.80, 0.41, and 0.35%.

The fourth highest self-sufficiency sector, "Other Agricultural Products," reflects the eighth highest "export" ratio, 19.82%. This sector's actual and hypothetical "output" ratios are rather high; 1.74 and 1.53% respectively.

Let us now turn to the ten sectors with the lowest self-sufficiency rates. From Table 6 and the "skyline" chart it can be seen that for both the United States and the Soviet Union "Leather Tanning and Finishing" and "Other Light Industry Products" (U.S.S.R.) have the fourth lowest self-sufficiency rates. The U.S. sector "Footwear and Other Leather Products," which is included in the Soviet sector "Other Light Industry Products," has the sixth lowest self-sufficiency rate. Secondly, with regard to the agriculture and fisheries- related sectors the "Fruit and Vegetable Products" sector (U.S.S.R.) is the fifth lowest sector of the Soviet economy. This is in great contrast to the American case. In the case of the United States "Forestry and Fishery Products" is the lowest self-sufficiency sector.

Thirdly, in contrast with the Soviet Union, the U.S. sectors related to basic resources are among the four lowest sectors. Among these sectors are included "Iron and Ferroalloy Ores Mining," "Nonferrous Metal Ores Mining," "Crude Petroleum" and "Natural Gas," and "Primary Nonferrous Metals Manufacturing." The "export" ratios of these sectors, with the exclusion of "Crude Petroleum" and "Natural Gas," are not particularly low, but the "import" ratios are very high. The "Iron and Ferroalloy Ores Mining" and "Nonferrous Metal Ores Mining" sectors have the highest and third highest "import" ratios; 52.53 and 38.37% respectively.

Unlike the United States, there is no sector among the ten lowest sectors in the Soviet Union with an "export" ratio higher than 10%. The highest "export" ratio of the ten lowest self-sufficiency sectors in the Soviet Union is recorded by the "Synthetic Resins and Plastics" sector: 9.32%.

Finally, the Soviet sectors, "Aniline Dye Products" and "Synthetic

Resins and Plastics" constitute the lowest and ninth lowest self-sufficiency sectors; 61. 75 and 79.07%. The former sector's "import" ratio is the highest; 46.15%. The latter sector's "import" ratio is the second highest; 42.20%.

Chapter 7

APPLYING TURNPIKE MODELS

TO THE SOVIET ECONOMY

1. Introduction

This chapter attempts an application of two proto-types of a dynamic input-output model for optimal planning and presents turnpike and optimal paths for the Soviet economy.

A proper application of a dynamic input-output model requires a set of data, namely a matrix of current input coefficients, a matrix of depreciation coefficients, a matrix of capital coefficients, a matrix of inventory coefficients, and so on. Using Soviet and American contributions to the Soviet input-output database, we will compile a set of 1966 year data for use with the dynamic Leontief model.

It is said that many Soviet economists have attempted to determine a balanced growth path or optimal growth path by solving an eigenvalue problem or a linear programming problem, although the results of these computations have not been published except in a few cases. Efimov and Movshovich (1971, 1973) and Kantorovich and Makarov (1976) performed and published a computation of the Neumann path (turnpike) of the Soviet economy by using unpublished 1965 input-output data compiled by the Institute of Economics of Gosplan (NIEI *pri Gosplane*). However, they did not consider and examine the so-called *turnpike property*, namely the catenary movement of the optimal paths toward the turnpike. Cheremnykh (1982) also published the results of an examination of turnpike properties using a dynamic Leontief model for optimal accumulation and 1966 input-output data. It should be noted that his description is based on an unpublished doctoral dissertation written by an Egyptian scholar, Al'-Ashkar (1974).[1]

In this chapter we explicitly describe the input-output database, and further, present simulation results of a consumption turnpike model as well as a dynamic Leontief model for optimal accumulation. Our research represents the first comprehensive attempt to clarify the Soviet turnpike properties. Our computation also provides the reader with a method for judging the results of the Soviet studies mentioned above.

Compiling the input-output data using the Soviet statistical method, a matrix of capital coefficients B, which is defined as the sum of a fixed capital coefficient matrix and an inventory coefficient matrix, does not satisfy the nonsingularity condition, namely det $B=0$. Usually, empirical analysis of turnpike properties assumes the nonsingularity of the matrix B.[2] For example, Tsukui and Murakami (1979, p. 9) wrote that the nonsingularity of B "is rather a controversial assumption. However, if we consider the fact that our capital coefficient must be the sum of both coefficients of fixed capital and of inventory, this nonsingularity assumption seems to be satisfied by actual data." In this chapter we attempt to perform an empirical analysis of the Soviet economy and a computerized simulation analysis of the turnpike properties without assuming the nonsingularity of the matrix B.

2. Models and Programs

The models employed in this chapter belong to the prototype models

---

[1] This chapter is based on my paper, "Turnpike and Optimal Path in the Soviet Economy," *The Economic Review* (*Keizai Kenkyu*), July 1983 (in Japanese).

At the time this paper was written the author did not know of the existence of an unpublished doctoral dissertation by an Egyptian scholar by the name of Al'-Ashkar. During discussions with Professor Cheremnykh of the Moscow State University in 1987 it was learned that Cheremnykh's computations were based on the work of one of his former students, Al'-Ashkar. Having read Al'-Ashkar's dissertation at the Lenin Library in Moscow the author learned that he had developed his own database for a computerized simulation of the final state turnpike model, using the works of Treml, Belkin and Tsukui, as is the case with the material in this chapter.

[2] Singular dynamic Leontief systems have been studied by Luenberger and Arbel (1977) and Meyer (1982).

developed by Kantorovich (1959), DOSSO (1958), Brody (1970) and, among others, Tsukui and Murakami (1979). For the purpose of clarifying the results of our computations, we provide the reader with a brief description of the models. All the programs for our computerized simulation are provided in Kuboniwa et al. (1987). While they are simplified versions of the programs employed for the calculation of this chapter, they are adequate enough to obtain computation results and can be compiled with either mainframe or personal computers.

2.1. Final State Turnpike Model

The final state turnpike model is a linear programming version of the closed dynamic input-output system without alternative techniques, where the planning target is the maximization of the value of capital stocks in the final (terminal) planning period evaluated by given prices. The final state turnpike model is a model for optimal accumulation.

The final state turnpike model can be written as the following large scale linear programming problem:[3]

(TK) max $\bar{p}Bx(T)$

$$x(t) \geq \tilde{A}x(t) + B(x(t+1) - x(t)) \quad (t=0, 1, \ldots, T),$$

$$x(t) \geq o \quad (t=0, 1, \ldots, T),$$

where

$x(t)$: an n-dimensional column vector of output levels in period t $(t=0, 1, \ldots, T)$;

$\tilde{A}$: an n by n matrix of augmented input coefficients;

B: an n by n matrix of capital coefficients;

$\bar{p}$: an n-dimensional row vector of prices given such that $\bar{p}B \geq o$.

The matrixes A and B are defined as

$$\tilde{A} = A + cw,$$

$$A = A^{(1)} + A^{(2)},$$

---

[3] The FORTRAN program for solving the final state turnpike model is described in Kuboniwa et al. (1987)(PROGRAM T).

and

$$B = B^{(1)} + B^{(2)},$$

where

    A: an n by n matrix of input coefficients;

    $A^{(1)}$: an n by n matrix of current input coefficients;

    $A^{(2)}$: an n by n matrix of depreciation or amortization coefficients;

    c: an n-dimensional column vector of consumption coefficients;

    w: an n-dimensional row vector of wage coefficients;

    $B^{(1)}$: an n by n matrix of fixed capital coefficients;

    $B^{(2)}$: an n by n matrix of inventory coefficients.

All the vectors and matrixes introduced above are assumed to be semi-positive. The wage coefficient vector w is assumed to be strictly positive. Further, $x(0)$ is assumed to be given by the initial condition such that $(I - \tilde{A} + B)x(0) > o$, where I is a unit matrix of rank n.

The turnpike (Neumann) output vector x^*, which constitutes a possible solution of the problem (TK), is determined by the equation[4]

$$x = (\tilde{A} + gB)x; \quad ex = 1, \tag{1}$$

where g is the positive balanced (Neumann) growth rate and e is an aggregation vector $(e = (11...1))$. The second equation of Eq. (1) is the normalization condition for outputs. Eq. (1) can be written as

$$g^{-1}x = (I - \tilde{A})^{-1}Bx.$$

We make the assumption:

(A1) $(I - \tilde{A})^{-1} > O$ and each column of B has at least one positive element.

Since $(I - \tilde{A})^{-1}B > O$ by this assumption, we can state, by virtue of the Perron-Frobenius theorem of the positive matrix, that the matrix $(I - \tilde{A})^{-1}B$ yields the unique positive eigenvalue λ^* with the largest absolute value and the unique positive right-hand eigenvector x^* associated with

---

[4] The FORTRAN program for solving this equation is given in Kuboniwa et al. (1987) (PROGRAM N1).

λ^*. Therefore, the economically significant turnpike (Neumann growth path) is defined by the half line $\{\alpha x^* | \alpha \geqq 0\}$ in the n-dimensional output space, which is referred to as the Neumann ray, or the accumulation turnpike. The turnpike growth rate g^* on this path is given by $1/\lambda^*$.

We further make the assumptions

(A2)   det $B \neq 0$

and

(A3)   det $(I + (I - \tilde{A})B^{-1}) \neq 0$. Eigenvalues, $\rho_1, \rho_2, \ldots, \rho_n$, of $(I + (I - \tilde{A})B^{-1})$ are simple and $\rho_1 = 1 + \lambda^{*-1} \neq \rho_i$: $(i = 2, \ldots, n)$.[5]

For sufficiently large time-horizon T and any $x(0)$ and $\bar{p}$, we then obtain the following weak and/or strong turnpike theorem which characterizes the relationship between the (accumulation) turnpike (the balanced growth path, or the Neumann growth path) and the optimal path as the solution of the linear problem (TK):

Weak Turnpike Theorem: *any optimal path stays outside of a well-selected neighborhood of the turnpike no longer than a certain number T_o of periods determined independently of T.*

Strong Turnpike Theorem: *any optimal path stays consecutively in the neighborhood of the turnpike except for certain periods at the beginning and at the end of the planning horizon.*

The dual equation of Eq. (1) yields the turnpike (Neumann) price (index) system[6]:

$$p = p(\tilde{A} + rB); \quad pe' = p(0)e [= n] , \tag{2}$$

where

p: an n-dimensional row vector of price indexes;

---

[5]   This is Tsukui's condition to avoid any possibility of non-dampened oscillation in the non-negative space of the output path. This condition can be substituted for by using Morishima's 'primitive' condition (Morishima (1961)).

[6]   Kuboniwa et al. (1987)(PROGRAM N2).

$p(0)$:   an n-dimensional row vector of the initial price indexes at the base period $(p(0)=(11...1))$;

e':   the transpose of the vector e.

If we make the assumption (A1), we can state that the equilibrium profit rate r^* is given by the reciprocal of the unique positive eigenvalue λ^*, with the largest absolute value, of the matrix $(I-\tilde{A})^{-1}B$. Further, the unique positive left-hand eigenvector associated with λ^* yields the turnpike price index system p^*.

Using Eq. (1) and Eq. (2), we easily obtain

$$g^*=r^*=p^*(I-\tilde{A})x^*/p^*Bx^*. \tag{3}$$

Therefore, when we denote the perturbations of $\tilde{A}$ and B as $d\tilde{A}$ and dB, respectively, we have the following relation (Brody (1970), pp. 127–128)):

$$dg^*=-p^*(d\tilde{A}+g^*dB)x^*/p^*Bx^*. \tag{4}$$

It follows from this equation that an increase [decrease] of $\tilde{A}$ or B causes a decrease [increase] of the turnpike growth rate. This implies that an increase [decrease] of consumption coefficient vector c results in a decrease [increase] of the turnpike growth rate, namely the level of the turnpike growth rate depends on the extent to which c is augmented into $\tilde{A}$.

Eq. (4) also states that the computed value of the turnpike growth rate is not particularly sensitive to measurement errors of input coefficients in comparison with those of capital coefficients. Normally, since it is very difficult to obtain accurate capital coefficients data, the above sensitivity relation is desirable for empirical analysis. However, it should be noted that in the Soviet case a much more difficult task is the obtaining of reliable data on input coefficients because a full description of the first quadrant of the Soviet input-output table has not yet been published. Therefore, a sensitivity relationship is not particularly desirable for empirical analysis of the Soviet economy.

2.2. Consumption Turnpike Model

From a practical view of management of socialist economies, the final-state turnpike model is not useful since it limits factors of growth constraints only to capital accumulation and its sole objective is the maximization of the final accumulation of capital. The main objective of socialist economies should be to increase consumption in the course of economic growth. Further, the Soviet and East European countries have faced a serious shortage of labor since the end of the 1960's.

The consumption turnpike model is one of the models which attempt to maximize consumption in the course of growth, subject to labor supply constraint, which is the basic limiting factor for economic growth.

For the convenience of statistical measurement and preservation of the economic significance of the price system, we employ wage coefficients in place of labor input coefficients. Corresponding to this treatment, we substitute labor supply constraint for wage fund constraint.

Let $W(t)$ ($W(0)$ given) and g be the total amount of wage funds in the period t and its growth rate given exogenously, respectively. Then we have $W(t) = (1+g)^t W(0)$.

g is determined by the growth rate of the labor population, g_1, and the growth rate of average wage level, g_2 ($g = g_1 + g_2 + g_1 g_2$). When we assume that the growth rate of the average wage level results from an increase in labor productivity, namely the Harrod-neutral technological progress, our treatment of the labor constraint can be regarded as plausible for empirical analysis.

Let us employ a dynamic version of Kantorovich's objective function (Kantorovich (1959)) where the consumption composition is constant over the planning periods and the present value of the total sum of levels of such consumption is maximized.

The consumption turnpike model can also be written as the following large scale linear programming problem[7]:

(TC) $\qquad\qquad \max \sum_{t=0}^{T} (1+\delta)^{-t} \theta(t)$

[7]   PROGRAM CTURN in Kuboniwa et al. (1987).

$$x(t) \geqq Ax(t) + B(x(t+1) - x(t)) + \theta(t)q ,$$

$$wx(t) \geqq (1+g)^t W(0) ,$$

$$x(t) \geqq o, \quad \theta(t) \geqq 0 \ (t=0, 1, \ldots, T) ,$$

where

    q: an n-dimensional column vector of consumption composition ($eq=1$);

    $\theta(t)$:   the level of consumption in the period t;

    δ: discount rate.

$x(0)$ and $x(T+1)$ are given such that $(I-A+B)x(0) > O$ and $x(T+1) \geqq o$.

We make the assumption:

    (A1-C) $(I-A)^{-1} > O$ and $(I-A-gB)^{-1} > O$.

When we further make the assumption (A2) and some additional assumptions, as in the case of the final state turnpike, we can *expect* to obtain the weak and/or strong turnpike theorem which characterizes the relationship between the (consumption) turnpike and the optimal path as the solution of the linear program (TC). If the objective function is strictly concave and $g=\delta$, we can prove the turnpike theorem. However, it should be noted that in the case of $g \neq \delta$ or the linear objective function, any general and strict proof for the turnpike theorem has not been given. Theoretically, in the case of the linear objective function, the turnpike property may be weakened since the 'value loss' decreases. (For a further description of the above statement, see Tsukui and Murakami (1979, Chs. 2 and 7).)

The consumption turnpike is given by

$$x^*(t) = (1+g)^t x^*; \quad \theta^*(t) = (1+g)^t \theta^* . \tag{5}$$

(x^*, θ^*) is the unique positive solution of the turnpike equation[8]:

---

[8]   PROGRAM CN1 in Kuboniwa et al. (1987).

$$x = Ax + gBx + \theta q; \quad wx = W(0) . \tag{6}$$

In this chapter, the output vector $x(T+1)$ is set as follows:

$$x(T+1) = x^*(T+1) = (1+g)^{T+1}x^*. \tag{7}$$

This setting implies that our computerized simulation for the consumption turnpike property is focused only on the initial output-consumption adjustment.

The turnpike price system, which is the dual equation[9] associated with Eq. (6), can be written as

$$p = pA + w + rpB; \quad r = g . \tag{8}$$

3. Data

We compiled the Soviet 1966 7-sector database for the dynamic input-output model. The sectors consist of

1. heavy industry
2. light industry
3. food industry
4. construction
5. agriculture
6. transport and communication (T & C)
7. trade and others.

The term 2. 'light industry', as used in this chapter, refers to light industry in a narrow sense, and is composed of the textile and apparel industries and others, except for the food industry. 7. 'trade and others' includes the forestry industries.

The transaction matrix of intermediate goods, in terms of purchasers' prices, is an aggregated version of Sverdlik's Soviet input-output table (see Sverdlik (1981) pp. 81–85). The transaction matrix of intermediate goods, in terms of producers' prices, is an aggregated version of Treml's Soviet input-output table (see Treml et al. (1973, 1977)).

---

[9] PROGRAM CN2 in Kuboniwa et al. (1987).

The amortization matrix is our estimation using the fixed capital matrix, which is described later in this section. We first calculate the amortization rates of the fixed capital supplied by the heavy industry and construction industry by making a weighted average of the fixed capital by categories, published in *Narkhoz* (1967, p. 220). The weights of these are the total amounts of the fixed capital by categories given by the published fixed capital stock balance (*Narkhoz* (1968)). Therefore, we set the amortization rates of the fixed capital by the heavy industry and the construction industry as 10.7% and 4.2% respectively. We set the amortization rate of the fixed capital supplied by the agriculture sector as 7.1%, which is the published sectoral amortization rate.

We next multiply these amortization rates by the respective rows of the fixed capital matrix. As a result, we obtain an amortization matrix. When we compare the sum of each column of the amortization matrix with the amortization row given by Sverdlik's input-output table, we find that only in the construction sector is the value of the former much greater than the value of the latter. Therefore, we reduce the column of the amortization matrix for the construction sector by multiplying the column by a unique rate so as to equalize the value of the former to the value of the latter.

In regard to the fixed capital matrix, we compile it using an aggregated version of Belkin's fixed capital matrix (Belkin (1972, pp. 104–105)) with one modification. The basic material for compiling the fixed capital matrix is obtained through the transpose of the published fixed capital stock balance (84 industries by 27 categories of capital stock). However, the published fixed capital stock balance suffers from two insufficiencies. First, it does not make a distinction between 'structures' and 'transmission devices'. As is known, structures are supplied by the construction sector while transmission devices are supplied by heavy industry. Secondly, the published fixed capital stock balance is compiled in terms of 1955 constant prices, not in terms of current prices. To avoid these insufficiencies, Belkin compiled his fixed capital matrix. However, it should be noted that the value of the element (4.4) for agriculture in Belkin's matrix, 11.166 billion rubles, is quite different from the value obtained by

DATA

Table 1. Soviet 1966 Dynamic Input-Output Data

(unit: billion rubles)

Intermediate Transaction Matrix (at purchasers' prices)

	Industry	1	2	3	4	5	6	7	Total
1.	Heavy industry	72.4	2.2	2.4	21.3	5.7	3.9	1.8	109.7
2.	Light industry	1.9	27.0	0.5	0.6	0.3	0.2	0.3	30.8
3.	Food industry	0.9	0.7	22.1	0.1	0.9	0.0	0.3	25.0
4.	Construction	0.0	0.0	0.0	0.0	0.0	0.0	0.0	0.0
5.	Agriculture	0.7	5.4	31.2	0.0	17.6	0.0	0.1	55.0
6.	T & C	15.9	0.4	1.5	0.1	0.9	0.0	0.2	19.0
7.	Trade and others	4.6	1.7	7.0	0.5	2.9	0.0	0.4	17.1
	Total	96.4	37.4	64.7	22.6	28.3	4.1	3.1	256.6

Amortization Matrix

	Industry	1	2	3	4	5	6	7	Total
1.	Heavy industry	6.8	0.4	0.7	1.6	2.2	1.7	0.6	14.0
2.	Light industry	0.0	0.0	0.0	0.0	0.0	0.0	0.0	0.0
3.	Food industry	0.0	0.0	0.0	0.0	0.0	0.0	0.0	0.0
4.	Construction	3.2	0.1	0.3	0.2	1.3	1.1	0.6	6.8
5.	Agriculture	0.0	0.0	0.0	0.0	1.2	0.0	0.0	1.2
6.	T & C	0.0	0.0	0.0	0.0	0.0	0.0	0.0	0.0
7.	Trade and others	0.0	0.0	0.0	0.0	0.0	0.0	0.0	0.0
	Total	10.0	0.5	1.0	1.8	4.7	2.8	1.2	22.0

Fixed Capital Matrix

	Industry	1	2	3	4	5	6	7	Total
1.	Heavy industry	64.0	3.5	6.5	8.6	20.5	16.1	5.8	125.0
2.	Light industry	0.0	0.0	0.0	0.0	0.0	0.0	0.0	0.0
3.	Food industry	0.0	0.0	0.0	0.0	0.0	0.0	0.0	0.0
4.	Construction	75.0	3.1	6.5	3.2	30.5	25.2	13.9	157.4
5.	Agriculture	0.6	0.2	0.5	0.2	16.2	0.9	0.2	18.8
6.	T & C	0.0	0.0	0.0	0.0	0.0	0.0	0.0	0.0
7.	Trade and others	0.0	0.0	0.0	0.0	0.0	0.0	0.0	0.0
	Total	139.6	6.8	13.5	12.0	67.2	42.2	19.9	301.2

Table 1.   (continued)

Inventory Matrix

Industry	1	2	3	4	5	6	7	Total
1. Heavy industry	37.7	6.1	4.3	4.9	4.6	1.2	14.0	72.8
2. Light industry	0.0	1.6	0.0	0.0	0.0	0.0	17.7	19.3
3. Food industry	0.0	0.0	3.4	0.0	0.0	0.0	18.2	21.6
4. Construction	0.0	0.0	0.0	0.8	0.0	0.0	0.0	0.8
5. Agriculture	0.1	0.0	0.1	0.0	21.8	0.0	9.2	31.2
6. T & C	0.0	0.0	0.0	0.0	0.0	0.0	0.0	0.0
7. Trade and others	0.0	0.0	0.0	0.0	0.0	0.0	0.0	0.0
Total	37.8	7.7	7.8	5.7	26.4	1.2	59.1	145.7
Wages	30.4	4.5	3.5	15.9	38.0	6.5	9.9	108.7
Gross Output	166.9	57.0	90.6	43.5	83.0	19.0	19.7	479.7

Sources: The intermediate matrix and the wage and output vectors are based on Sverdlik (1981, pp. 82–83). The amortization matrix is based on the author's estimation. The fixed capital and inventory matrixes are from Belkin (1972, pp. 108–109).

Notes: The above matrixes and vectors are explained in the text.

the published balance, 16.166...billion rubles. Therefore, we adopt the value of the published balance as the value of the element for agriculture.

The inventory matrix is an aggregated version of Belkin's inventory matrix (Belkin (1972) pp. 108–109).

The wage row and gross output row, in terms of purchasers' prices, are compiled by using Sverdlik's input-output table. The wage row and gross output row, in terms of producers' prices are compiled by employing Treml's input-output table.

Table 1 displays the basic matrixes in terms of purchasers' prices. From these matrixes we can easily calculate the current input coefficient matrix, amortization coefficient matrix, fixed capital coefficient matrix, inventory coefficient matrix and wage coefficient vector. From these coefficient matrixes we can also obtain input coefficient matrix A, wage coefficient vector w and capital coefficient matrix B, which are exhibited in Table 3. These matrixes in terms of producers' prices are shown in Table 6.

Table 2. Input Coefficient Matrix $A = A^{(1)} + A^{(2)}$ and Wage Coefficient Vector w Using Data in Terms of Purchasers' Prices

A	1	2	3	4	5	6	7
1. Heavy industry	0.47454	0.04561	0.03422	0.52644	0.09518	0.29474	0.12183
2. Light industry	0.01138	0.47368	0.00552	0.01379	0.00361	0.01053	0.01523
3. Food industry	0.00539	0.01228	0.24393	0.00230	0.01084	0.0	0.01523
4. Construction	0.01917	0.00175	0.00331	0.00460	0.01566	0.05789	0.03046
5. Agriculture	0.00419	0.09474	0.34437	0.0	0.22651	0.0	0.00508
6. T & C	0.09527	0.00702	0.01656	0.00230	0.01084	0.0	0.01015
7. Trade and others	0.02756	0.02982	0.07726	0.01149	0.03494	0.0	0.02030
w	0.18214	0.07895	0.03863	0.36552	0.45783	0.34211	0.50254

Table 3. Capital Coefficient Matrix $B = B^{(1)} + B^{(2)}$ Using Data in Terms of Purchasers' Prices

B	1	2	3	4	5	6	7
1. Heavy industry	0.60935	0.16842	0.11921	0.31034	0.30241	0.91053	1.00508
2. Light industry	0.0	0.02807	0.0	0.0	0.0	0.0	0.89848
3. Food industry	0.0	0.0	0.03753	0.0	0.0	0.0	0.92386
4. Construction	0.44937	0.05439	0.07174	0.09195	0.36747	1.32632	0.70558
5. Agriculture	0.00419	0.00351	0.00662	0.00460	0.45783	0.04737	0.47716
6. T & C	0.0	0.0	0.0	0.0	0.0	0.0	0.0
7. Trade and others	0.0	0.0	0.0	0.0	0.0	0.0	0.0

In order to apply the turnpike models to the Soviet economy we further need the data for consumption coefficient vector c and consumption composition vector q. These vectors are compiled by using the final demand quadrant of Sverdlik's input-output table (Table 4). The results are shown in Table 5. The results in producers' prices are shown in Table 7. The difference between case 1 and case 2 in Table 5 results from the treatment of the 'other expenditures' category of the final demand table. In case 1 the consumption column excludes 'other expenditures'. In case 2 it includes 'other expenditures.'

Table 4.   Final Demand Table in Current Purchasers' Prices

(unit: billion rubles)

Industry	8	9	10	11	12	13	14	15	16	Total
1. Heavy industry	14.7	7.9	17.7	2.4	3.4	0.4	9.2	7.3	−5.8	57.2
2. Light industry	27.5	1.3	0.0	0.0	0.2	0.0	1.4	0.9	−5.1	26.2
3. Food industry	62.0	2.3	0.0	0.0	1.7	0.0	1.0	1.0	−2.4	65.6
4. Construction	0.0	0.0	24.0	19.5	0.0	0.0	0.0	0.0	0.0	43.5
5. Agriculture	21.1	0.7	0.8	0.0	6.2	0.0	0.8	0.4	−2.0	28.0
6. T & C	—	0.0	0.0	0.0	0.0	0.0	0.0	0.0	0.0	0.0
7. Trade and others	2.4	0.2	0.0	0.0	0.0	0.0	0.0	0.0	0.0	2.6
Total	127.7	12.4	42.5	21.9	11.5	0.4	12.4	9.6	−15.3	223.1

Notes: 1.   This table has been constructed by the author, using the data in Sverdrik (1981, pp. 82–85).

2.   Each column of this table shows:

   8: Private Consumption
   9: Social Consumption
   10: Productive Fixed Capital Formation
   11: Unproductive Fixed Capital Formation
   12: Productive Inventory Formation
   13: Unproductive Inventory Formation
   14: Other Expenditures
   15: Exports
   16: Imports

4.   Computation of the Turnpike and the Optimal Path: the Final State Turnpike Model

4.1.   The Accumulation Turnpike

We first state the computational results when we use the final state turnpike model and the data in terms of purchasers' prices (see Table 8-1).

The turnpike balanced growth rate g^* is 10% in case 1 of the consumption coefficients of Table 5. The rate g^* is 7.5% in case 2. The latter growth rate is closer to the actual Soviet macro growth rate than the former. The actual annual average Soviet growth rate of gross social product(GSP) was 7.4% from 1966 to 1970.

As can be seen, the balanced growth rate is dependent on the extent to which the final demand is augmented into the matrix A. In other words,

Table 5. Consumption (C), Consumption Coefficients (c) and Consumption Composition (q) Using Data in Terms of Purchasers' Prices

		case 1			case 2		
		C billion rubles	c	q	C	c	q
1.	Heavy industry	26.9	0.247	0.172	36.1	0.332	0.213
2.	Light industry	24.6	0.226	0.157	26.0	0.239	0.154
3.	Food industry	62.9	0.579	0.401	63.9	0.588	0.378
4.	Construction	19.5	0.179	0.124	19.5	0.180	0.115
5.	Agriculture	20.2	0.186	0.129	21.0	0.193	0.124
6.	T & C	0.0	0.0	0.0	0.0	0.0	0.0
7.	Trade and others	2.6	0.024	0.017	2.6	0.024	0.015
		156.7	1.441	1.000	169.1	1.556	1.000

Notes: This table is derived from Table 4.
Case 1: Column 17 − (column 10 + column 12 + column 14) = comsumption column.
Case 2: Column 17 − (column 10 + column 12) = consumption column.
Each column number of the left-hand side shown here is the same as the column number of Table 4.

the computation of the turnpike growth rate has an arbitrary quality. When we change the system from a completely closed system to a quasi-closed system by adding the fixed consumption part to the closed system, the balanced growth rate does not change so long as matrixes A and B do not change. Therefore, to avoid the arbitrary nature of the computation, g^* should be computed through the augmentation of all the final demand factors except for productive accumulation into matrix A. At any rate, we can judge the computations provided by Soviet scholars by using our results. The balanced growth rate calculated by Efimov and Movshovich ($g^*=8\%$) is very close to our computation in case 2 when we take into consideration the difference in each base period 1965 and 1966. The Cheremnykh balanced growth rate ($g^*=10.1\%$) corresponds to our case 1, while the Kantorovich and Makarov balanced growth rate ($g^*=9.3\%$) takes an intermediate method between our case 1 and 2.

The turnpike output ratio is closer to the actual output ratio in the base period in case 1, but the difference between the two ratios is very small in both case 1 and 2. From Table 8-1 actual outputs of heavy and light

Table 6.   Input Coefficient Matrix A, Wage Coefficient Vector w and Capital Coefficient Matrix B Using Data in Terms of Producers' prices

A	1	2	3	4	5	6	7
1. Heavy industry	0.48665	0.05334	0.04558	0.42379	0.08751	0.22148	0.11715
2. Light industry	0.01722	0.51091	0.00859	0.01315	0.00364	0.00791	0.01415
3. Food industry	0.00874	0.01558	0.28806	0.00326	0.01080	0.00069	0.01639
4. Construction	0.02285	0.00263	0.00444	0.00540	0.01671	0.05670	0.02970
5. Agriculture	0.00475	0.11785	0.49184	0.00071	0.22357	0.00062	0.00484
6. T & C	0.05174	0.00995	0.01587	0.08851	0.01108	0.02258	0.01644
7. Trade and others	0.01495	0.00620	0.01985	0.01827	0.01119	0.00571	0.00941
w	0.21131	0.08761	0.05077	0.36479	0.48522	0.31649	0.41566

B	1	2	3	4	5	6	7
1. Heavy industry	0.72302	0.21764	0.17769	0.31144	0.31476	0.91000	0.36912
2. Light industry	0.0	0.03675	0.0	0.0	0.0	0.0	0.09039
3. Food industry	0.0	0.0	0.05506	0.0	0.0	0.0	0.09278
4. Construction	0.53301	0.07088	0.10737	0.09221	0.38294	1.32058	0.70604
5. Agriculture	0.00444	0.00039	0.00151	0.00037	0.47642	0.00455	0.48117
6. T & C	0.0	0.0	0.0	0.0	0.0	0.0	0.0
7. Trade and others	0.0	0.0	0.0	0.0	0.0	0.0	0.0

industries are less than the corresponding theoretical turnpike production and the actual outputs of food, construction and agriculture are greater than the corresponding turnpike production. However, it should be noted that these facts result from the compilation of input-output data by the direct use of base period data and from setting the consumption coefficient of heavy industry at a rather high level, second only to the consumption coefficient of the food industry.

In comparison with output ratios the turnpike price system p^* is far from the actual 1966 price indexes.[10] The computation implies that the

[10]   The Neumann price system corresponds to the "production price" system. The first comprehensive computation of this price system using the Soviet 1966 data was carried out by Belkin (1972, pp. 83–161). The computation performed by Seton (1981) in the case of the Soviet 1966 economy does not provide us with reasonable results. In the paper in Japanese the author has commented that necessary data is missing in Seton's calculation. Later it was learned that his computer program contained some serious errors.

Table 7. Consumption Coefficients (c), Consumption Composition (q) and Initial Output ($x(0)$) Using Data in Terms of Producers' prices

		case 1		case 2		$x(0)$
		c	q	c	q	billion rubles
1.	Heavy industry	0.144	0.115	0.144	0.134	140.7
2.	Light industry	0.164	0.131	0.164	0.136	44.1
3.	Food industry	0.381	0.304	0.381	0.357	61.0
4.	Construction	0.185	0.148	0.0	0.0	43.3
5.	Agriculture	0.198	0.158	0.198	0.186	79.6
6.	T & C	0.047	0.037	0.047	0.044	19.1
7.	Trade and others	0.134	0.106	0.134	0.125	19.6
Total		1.253	1.000	1.068	1.000	407.5

Notes: This table is obtained by using the Aggregated 7-sector version of Treml's 75-sector input-output tables (Treml et. al. (1977, pp. 31–44)).

Case 2 is derived when the consumption column vector here is set as the sum of the 'private consumption' column and the 'public consumption' column in the Treml table.

Case 1 is followed when the construction element of the consumption vector in case 1 is increased by 19.5 billion rubles, which is the unproductive investment by the construction sector, shown in Table 5. Each consumption coefficient vector is calculated by dividing the respective consumption vector by the total wage fund, $w(0) = 105.34$ billion rubles.

prices of light, and food industries should be decreased and the prices of agriculture and trade should be increased.

Next, we state the computational result using the data in terms of producers' prices (see Table 8-2).

The balanced growth rate, g^*, is 9.6% in case 1 and 13.9% in case 2. Case 2 is an example in which consumption demand for the construction sector is set to 0. The computation result in case 2, namely, a very high rate of balanced growth, suggests that case 2 is not a realistic assumption. In case 2, where the turnpike output ratio is closer to the actual output ratio in the base period, the actual outputs of heavy industry and construction are greater than the corresponding turnpike outputs, and the actual outputs of the light and food industries and agriculture are less than the corresponding turnpike outputs. This confirms that the actual Soviet growth policy is biased toward heavy industry.

Table 8-1. Accumulation Turnpike Using Data in Terms of Purchasers' Prices

	$x(0)$ billion rubles (%)	case 1 $g^*=10.0\%$		case 2 $g^*=7.5\%$		case 1 $r^*=10.0\%$ p^*	case 2 $r^*=7.5\%$ p^*
		$x^*(\%)$	$x_i^*/x_i(0)$	$x^*(\%)$	$x_i^*/x_i(0)$		
1. Heavy industry	166.9 (34.8)	171.9 (35.8)	1.030	175.3 (36.5)	1.050	0.989	0.974
2. Light industry	57.0 (11.9)	57.3 (12.0)	1.005	58.5 (12.2)	1.027	0.647	0.655
3. Food industry	90.6 (18.9)	89.2 (18.6)	0.985	89.1 (18.6)	0.983	0.833	0.840
4. Construction	43.5 (9.1)	42.2 (8.8)	0.971	38.2 (8.0)	0.877	1.074	1.099
5. Agriculture	83.0 (17.3)	80.0 (16.7)	0.964	79.3 (16.5)	0.955	1.165	1.194
6. T & C	19.0 (4.0)	19.4 (4.0)	1.022	19.7 (4.1)	1.039	1.048	1.027
7. Trade and others	19.7 (4.1)	19.6 (4.1)	0.995	19.6 (4.1)	0.996	1.244	1.212
Total	479.7 (100)	479.7 (100)	[0.143]	479.7 (100)	[0.304]	7.0	7.0

Notes: 1. x^* in terms of rubles is calculated by using the normalization condition $ex^*=ex(0)$.

2. $[\,\cdot\,]=\sum_1^7|x_i^*/x_i(0)-1|$

Table 8-2. Accumulation Turnpike Using Data in Terms of Producers' Prices

	$x(0)$ billion rubles (%)	case 1 $g^*=9.6\%$		case 2 $g^*=13.9\%$		case 1 $r^*=9.6\%$ p^*	case 2 $r^*=13.9\%$ p^*
		$x^*(\%)$	$x_i^*/x_i(0)$	$x^*(\%)$	$x_i^*/x_i(0)$		
1. Heavy industry	140.7 (34.5)	136.3 (33.5)	0.968	143.8 (35.3)	1.022	0.988	1.016
2. Light industry	44.1 (10.8)	47.4 (11.6)	1.076	48.6 (11.9)	1.103	0.743	0.725
3. Food industry	61.0 (15.0)	63.5 (15.6)	1.041	64.2 (15.8)	1.052	1.049	1.020
4. Construction	43.3 (10.6)	41.0 (10.1)	0.947	29.1 (7.1)	0.671	1.045	1.005
5. Agriculture	79.6 (19.6)	81.1 (19.9)	1.019	84.5 (20.7)	1.061	1.131	1.072
6. T & C	19.1 (4.8)	18.7 (4.6)	0.979	18.0 (4.4)	0.943	0.934	0.971
7. Trade and others	19.6 (4.8)	19.5 (4.8)	0.993	19.3 (4.7)	0.982	1.110	1.191
Total	407.5 (100)	407.5 (100)	[0.248]	407.5 (100)	[0.642]	7.0	7.0

Notes: See the notes for Table 8-1.

Concerning the turnpike price system, the computation suggests that only the price of light industry should be drastically changed. Namely, even after subtracting the turnover tax from the price of each industry, the actual producers' price of light industry does not reflect the real situation.

4.2. The Turnpike Property

Using the data in terms of purchasers' prices from Tables 9 and 10, in cases 1 and 2, the optimal path quickly converges to the turnpike in the first or second planning period, remains on the turnpike for several intermediate periods and then enters into the terminal adjustment from the seventh planning period. Therefore, this calculation reflects the strong turnpike property. Although in actuality the terminal adjustment is unrealistic, the milder initial adjustment in case 1 should be noted. In case 2 the initial adjustments of the construction and the transport and communication sectors are very pronounced. In both cases, due to the difference between the turnpike and the initial actual output ratios, at the beginning of the time horizon the heavy industry sector displays slightly more rapid growth. It is also noted that in case 2, due to the violent initial adjustment of the construction sector, the macro growth rate is remarkably low from the initial period to the first period.

Employing the data in terms of producers' prices from Table 11, we can also confirm the strong turnpike property. Concerning the initial adjustment, it should be noted that the light and food industries display more rapid growth from the initial period to the first period, but in the next period, on the contrary, the heavy industry and the construction sectors grow more rapidly. In both cases 1 and 2 the violent initial adjustments of the construction and transport and communication sectors should be especially noted.

5. The Computation of the Turnpike and the Optimal Path: The Consumption Turnpike Model

Employing the consumption turnpike model, unlike the case in which the final state turnpike model is used, the balanced growth rate, g, can be

Table 9. Optimal Output Ratios and Optimal Growth Rates: Case 1 ($g^* = 10\%$)

	Heavy industry 1	Light industry 2	Food industry 3	Construction 4	Agriculture 5	T & C 6	Trade & others 7	[.]
0	34.793	11.882	18.887	9.068	17.302	3.961	4.107	[1.204]
1	35.809	11.949	18.604	8.794	16.710	4.046	4.087	[0.048]
2	35.771	11.954	18.612	8.786	16.746	4.043	4.088	[0.157]
3	35.688	11.966	18.629	8.767	16.824	4.036	4.090	[0.206]
4	35.506	11.991	18.666	8.725	16.995	4.022	4.095	[0.444]
5	35.105	12.052	18.751	8.632	17.365	3.989	4.106	[0.971]
6	34.214	12.231	18.960	8.392	18.156	3.917	4.131	[2.174]
7	32.037	12.910	19.559	7.840	19.722	3.741	4.191	[5.079]
8	26.920	16.578	21.996	4.572	22.207	3.341	4.386	[13.864]
9	9.239	32.745	31.550	0.0	19.694	1.895	4.877	[37.563]
10	0.0	0.0	0.0	0.0	0.0	10.407	89.593	[91.867]

	1	2	3	4	5	6	7	Macro Growth Rates
0– 1	10.359	7.829	5.621	3.989	3.552	9.537	6.698	7.225
1– 2	9.916	10.079	10.078	9.924	10.269	9.949	10.060	10.032
2– 3	9.779	10.138	10.135	9.798	10.549	9.851	10.095	10.035
3– 4	9.479	10.273	10.262	9.514	11.157	9.639	10.173	10.040
4– 5	8.814	10.620	10.560	8.892	12.455	9.169	10.353	10.059
5– 6	7.336	11.762	11.352	7.057	15.145	8.146	10.805	10.130
6– 7	3.651	16.844	14.194	3.417	20.248	5.710	12.307	10.695
7– 8	−4.886	45.358	27.301	−33.987	27.456	1.091	18.447	13.194
8– 9	−51.941	176.588	100.858	−100.000	24.183	−20.557	55.729	40.034
9–10	−100.000	−100.000	−100.000	0.0	−100.000	23.504	313.220	−77.506

Note: $[\,.\,] = \sum \left| \dfrac{x^*}{ex^*} - \dfrac{x_i(0)}{ex(0)} \right|$. This value measures the distance between the turnpike and the optimal path.

Table 10. Optimal Output Ratios and Optimal Growth Rates: Case 2 ($g^* = 7.5\%$)

	Heavy industry 1	Light industry 2	Food industry 3	Construction 4	Agriculture 5	T & C 6	Trade & others 7	
0	34.793	11.882	18.887	9.068	17.302	3.961	4.107	[2.244]
1	36.233	12.258	18.616	7.404	16.591	4.816	4.083	[0.873]
2	36.490	12.211	18.577	7.944	16.578	4.109	4.092	[0.083]
3	36.421	12.221	18.591	7.927	16.644	4.103	4.094	[0.166]
4	36.266	12.243	18.623	7.891	16.790	4.091	4.098	[0.369]
5	35.915	12.297	18.697	7.808	17.114	4.063	4.108	[0.831]
6	35.118	12.458	18.884	7.588	17.824	3.998	4.130	[1.913]
7	33.116	13.081	19.434	7.079	19.270	3.836	4.186	[4.586]
8	28.290	16.518	21.728	3.987	21.649	3.459	4.369	[12.881]
9	10.712	32.077	30.987	0.0	19.362	2.018	4.844	[35.887]
10	0.0	0.0	0.0	0.0	0.0	13.972	86.028	[91.813]

	1	2	3	4	5	6	7	Macro Growth Rates
0– 1	5.495	4.505	-0.154	-17.293	-2.867	23.164	0.723	1.301
1– 2	8.832	7.649	7.840	15.947	7.986	-7.790	8.291	8.066
2– 3	7.303	7.591	7.589	7.288	7.931	7.361	7.557	7.507
3– 4	7.052	7.703	7.695	7.012	8.453	7.181	7.621	7.510
4– 5	6.483	7.999	7.952	6.391	9.599	6.777	7.775	7.523
5– 6	5.190	8.988	8.650	4.544	12.042	5.875	8.169	7.576
6– 7	1.905	13.470	11.213	0.823	16.831	3.682	9.515	8.067
7– 8	-5.777	39.276	23.319	-37.885	23.917	-0.546	15.141	10.296
8– 9	-48.583	163.704	93.656	-100.000	21.444	-20.789	50.529	35.791
9–10	-100.000	-100.000	-100.000	0.0	-100.000	56.343	300.998	-77.423

Notes: See the note for Table 9.

Table 11. Optimal Growth Rates Using Data in Terms of Producers' Prices

case 1 ($g^*=9.6\%$)

	Heavy industry 1	Light industry 2	Food industry 3	Construction 4	Agriculture 5	T & C 6	Trade & others 7	Macro Growth Rates
0– 1	–7.454	10.698	6.250	–35.295	4.632	87.156	–1.156	0.701
1– 2	17.874	9.838	10.739	64.918	10.450	–40.956	13.525	12.167
2– 3	9.225	9.661	9.680	9.333	10.095	9.445	9.610	9.560
3– 4	8.864	9.783	9.822	9.091	10.692	9.328	9.676	9.571
4– 5	8.095	10.040	10.122	8.579	11.928	9.081	9.814	9.593
5– 6	6.446	10.593	10.752	7.469	14.450	8.554	10.102	9.641
6– 7	2.817	12.102	12.214	4.789	19.421	7.386	10.691	9.777
7– 8	–4.365	39.538	27.235	–34.068	28.856	–0.413	9.930	12.008
8– 9	–71.774	243.289	145.573	–100.000	34.479	–8.991	20.472	49.791
9–10	–100.000	–100.000	–100.000	0.0	–100.000	53.119	414.533	–76.605

case 2 ($g^*=13.9\%$)

	1	2	3	4	5	6	7	
0– 1	–4.472	16.744	9.942	–85.576	11.855	153.495	–1.836	2.081
1– 2	28.937	14.359	15.854	460.814	15.243	–55.060	20.954	18.432
2– 3	13.598	14.056	14.078	13.556	14.521	13.810	14.002	13.946
3– 4	13.253	14.181	14.225	13.167	15.116	13.684	14.071	13.959
4– 5	12.549	14.433	14.522	12.372	16.300	13.428	14.212	13.985
5– 6	11.100	14.960	15.124	10.699	18.622	12.903	14.493	14.040
6– 7	8.050	16.458	16.528	6.633	23.038	11.762	15.039	14.194
7– 8	2.455	44.998	32.185	–53.204	31.204	3.640	14.039	16.643
8– 9	–59.026	234.207	144.166	–100.000	33.882	1.956	26.912	54.324
9–10	–100.000	–100.000	–100.000	0.0	–100.000	205.433	392.582	–73.374

Table 12-1.   Consumption Turnpike Using Data in Purchasers' Prices

	x(0) billion rubles (%)	case 1		case 2			
		g = 10% x*(%)	g = 7% x*(%)	g = 7.5% x*(%)	r = 10% p*	r = 7% p*	r = 7.5% p*
1. Heavy industry	166.9 (34.8)	173.2 (35.8)	164.4 (33.8)	178.3 (36.5)	0.989	0.971	0.974
2. Light industry	57.0 (11.9)	57.8 (12.0)	61.1 (12.6)	59.6 (12.2)	0.647	0.656	0.655
3. Food industry	90.6 (18.9)	90.0 (18.6)	97.3 (20.0)	90.6 (18.6)	0.833	0.841	0.840
4. Construction	43.5 (9.1)	42.5 (8.8)	39.3 (8.1)	38.8 (8.0)	1.074	1.104	1.099
5. Agriculture	83.0 (17.3)	80.7 (16.7)	85.2 (17.5)	30.7 (16.5)	1.165	1.199	1.194
6. T & C	19.0 (4.0)	19.6 (4.0)	18.9 (3.9)	20.1 (4.1)	1.048	1.023	1.027
7. Trade and others	19.7 (4.1)	19.8 (4.1)	20.6 (4.2)	20.0 (4.1)	1.244	1.205	1.212
Total	479.7 (100)	483.5 (100)	486.8 (100)	488.0 (100)	7.0	7.0	7.0
Optimal consumption level	{156.7 (case 1), 169.1 (case 2)	156.9	172.0	169.1			
Total optimal consumption when $\delta = 10\%$	—	1693.8	1639.4	1602.9			

Table 12-2. Consumption Turnpike Using Data in Producers' Prices

| | x(0) billion rubles (%) | case 1 | | case 2 | | | |
		g = 8% x*(%)	g = 5% x*(%)	g = 8% x*(%)	g = 5% x*(%)	r = 8% p*	r = 5% p*
1. Heavy industry	140.7 (34.5)	132.3 (32.2)	122.7 (29.9)	125.5 (30.3)	115.6 (27.8)	1.001	0.975
2. Light industry	44.1 (10.8)	49.0 (11.9)	51.2 (12.5)	51.1 (12.3)	53.5 (12.9)	0.767	0.774
3. Food industry	61.0 (15.0)	66.5 (16.2)	71.4 (17.4)	78.8 (19.0)	84.9 (20.4)	1.083	1.095
4. Construction	43.3 (10.6)	39.7 (9.7)	36.8 (9.0)	19.5 (4.7)	14.6 (3.5)	1.085	1.105
5. Agriculture	79.6 (19.6)	84.1 (20.5)	88.4 (21.5)	98.6 (23.8)	104.1 (25.0)	1.183	1.211
6. T & C	19.1 (4.7)	18.8 (4.6)	18.7 (4.6)	18.1 (4.4)	18.0 (4.3)	0.945	0.910
7. Trade and others	19.6 (4.8)	20.4 (5.0)	21.8 (5.3)	23.3 (5.6)	25.0 (6.0)	0.935	0.931
Total	407.5 (100)	410.8 (100)	411.0 (100)	414.8 (100)	415.7 (100)	7.0	7.0
Optimal consumption level	—	138.9	152.2	141.7	155.8		
Total optimal consumption when $\delta = 10\%$	—	1375.7	1304.9	1085.1	1270.7		

Table 13. Optimal Growth Rates of Outputs And Consumption Using The Data in Terms of Purchasers' Prices

case 1 ($g = 8.0\%$; $\delta = 10\%$)

	1	2	3	4	5	6	7	Macro Growth Rates	Consumption Growth Rates
0– 1	14.288	0.800	−7.221	10.883	−1.780	11.356	−2.618	4.724	−12.0
1– 2	9.870	21.703	29.547	6.674	19.768	11.916	25.101	16.483	37.6
2– 3	10.000	9.999	10.001	10.000	10.000	10.000	10.004	10.000	10.0
3– 4	10.000	10.001	9.999	10.043	10.007	10.000	9.598	9.989	10.0
4– 5	10.052	10.000	10.000	10.010	10.011	10.000	10.000	10.021	10.0
5– 6	10.003	10.000	10.000	10.010	10.028	10.054	10.000	10.009	10.0
6– 7	9.993	10.000	10.000	10.011	10.061	9.996	10.000	10.009	10.0
7– 8	9.953	10.000	10.000	9.979	10.159	9.983	10.000	10.007	10.0
8– 9	10.000	10.000	10.000	9.948	9.655	9.968	10.000	9.936	10.0
9–10	10.000	10.000	10.000	10.000	9.897	10.000	10.000	9.983	10.0
10–11	10.000	10.000	10.000	10.000	10.183	10.000	10.000	10.030	10.0

case 2 ($g=8.0\%$; $\delta=5\%$)

	1	2	3	4	5	6	7		
0– 1	3.077	17.112	17.614	−15.266	11.108	37.310	9.760	8.847	22.4
1– 1	9.431	5.090	4.724	22.160	5.820	−16.922	9.207	6.850	4.4
2– 3	7.011	6.693	6.734	7.056	6.869	6.980	6.895	6.888	6.8
3– 4	6.976	7.236	7.168	6.939	7.101	7.000	7.190	7.076	7.1
4– 5	6.954	6.936	6.955	6.975	6.969	6.999	6.654	6.953	7.0
5– 6	6.988	7.014	7.169	6.858	6.999	6.973	7.098	7.012	7.3
6– 7	6.965	6.764	6.641	7.053	6.776	6.974	6.758	6.848	6.5
7– 8	7.120	6.977	7.068	7.010	6.962	6.982	7.057	6.995	7.2
8– 9	6.515	6.844	6.629	7.016	6.748	7.029	7.133	6.911	6.4
9–10	7.471	7.276	7.032	6.523	7.193	7.105	6.953	6.874	7.5
10–11		7.033	7.433	7.564	7.276	6.919	6.984	7.340	

case 2 ($g=7.5\%$; $\delta=10\%$)

	1	2	3	4	5	6	7		
0– 1	13.636	−8.739	−22.364	5.450	−11.575	8.802	−14.242	−2.263	−31.6
1– 1	8.687	32.799	49.194	−2.202	27.196	12.262	36.494	20.431	69.0
2– 3	7.474	7.077	7.287	7.499	7.334	7.456	8.096	7.394	7.5
3– 4	7.501	7.531	7.481	7.512	7.496	7.500	6.752	7.470	7.4
4– 5	7.500	7.500	7.500	7.500	7.500	7.500	7.699	7.508	7.5
5– 6	7.500	7.500	7.500	7.500	7.500	7.500	7.500	7.500	7.5
6– 7	7.500	7.500	7.500	7.500	7.500	7.522	7.500	7.501	7.5
7– 8	7.500	7.500	7.500	7.500	7.500	7.478	7.500	7.499	7.5
8– 9	7.500	7.500	7.500	7.500	7.500	7.500	7.500	7.500	7.5
9–10	7.500	7.500	7.500	7.500	7.500	7.500	7.500	7.500	7.5
10–11	7.500	7.500	7.500	7.500	7.500	7.500	7.500	7.500	7.5

arbitrarily given so long as it satisfies the assumption (A1-C). We set several values (5%, 7%, 7.5%, 8% and 10%) for the growth rate of wage fund, g. The values 7.5% and 10% were selected in order to compare the computation using the final state turnpike model with the computation using the consumption turnpike model. The values 7% and 8% were selected because they reflect the actual annual growth rate of the wage fund of the Soviet national economy. Although we set many values (-30%, -15%, -10%, 0%, 10%, 15% and 30%) for the discount rate w, here we can only show a part of our computational results due to space limitations.

5.1. The Consumption Turnpike

Using the data in terms of purchasers' prices, it can be seen from Table 12-1 that actual outputs of the heavy industry and the construction sector are greater than the corresponding turnpike outputs, and the actual output of the light and food industries and agriculture are less than the corresponding turnpike outputs when we set $g=7\%$ as a plausible growth rate for wage funds. Further, it can be seen that when making full use of wage funds, the total amounts of turnpike outputs and turnpike consumption, where $g=7\%$, are greater than those where $g=10\%$.

Regarding the turnpike system p^*, the computation result is similar to the case of accumulation turnpike in Table 8-1. Namely, the prices of light and food industries should be decreased and the prices of agriculture should be increased.

Employing the data in terms of producers' prices, it can be seen from Table 12-2 that actual outputs of the heavy industry and the construction sector are greater than the corresponding turnpike outputs when we set $g=8\%$ or $g=5\%$. These values for g for the balanced growth rate are less than the balanced growth rate using the final state turnpike model.

The computation of the turnpike price system implies that the price of light industry should be remarkably decreased and the price of agriculture should be increased by approximately 20%.

5.2. The Turnpike Property

Using the data in terms of purchasers' prices, from Table 13, in case 1

Table 14. Optimal Growth Rates of Outputs And Consumption Using The Data
in Terms of Producers' Prices

case 1 ($g=10\%$; $\delta=10\%$)

	1	2	3	4	5	6	7	Macro Growth Rates	Consumption Growth Rates
0–1	−0.432	36.606	16.883	−7.505	13.699	46.158	−3.399	10.216	−7.7
1–2	6.221	−15.448	7.193	3.020	6.816	0.180	56.382	5.048	44.8
2–3	11.900	21.143	9.724	21.261	9.581	−15.344	−13.344	9.686	−0.8
3–4	7.990	8.297	8.020	8.035	8.026	7.910	7.650	8.023	7.7
4–5	7.873	7.709	8.145	7.858	8.007	8.134	8.507	7.967	8.7
5–6	8.042	8.045	7.698	8.073	7.839	7.832	7.450	7.909	7.3
6–7	7.990	7.888	8.075	7.871	8.021	8.077	8.237	8.003	8.3
7–8	7.928	7.998	7.865	8.014	7.942	7.882	7.892	7.933	7.7
8–9	7.917	8.073	8.082	7.941	8.087	7.966	7.946	8.003	8.1
9–10	7.892	8.061	8.076	8.124	8.042	8.040	8.078	8.011	8.1
10–11	8.396	8.007	8.025	8.135	8.014	8.140	8.050	8.157	

case 2 ($g=8.0\%$; $\delta=15\%$)

	1	2	3	4	5	6	7	Macro Growth Rates	Consumption Growth Rates
0–1	−3.724	−2.861	−0.758	−23.290	12.727	139.310	0.123	4.839	−10.1
1–2	−8.194	76.864	55.085	−100.000	33.405	24.962	11.310	15.340	23.3
2–3	22.365	−33.985	19.781	0.0	8.789	−55.932	84.432	4.988	114.3
3–4	16.005	68.863	−16.676	550.015	−1.763	−12.008	−49.566	10.145	−61.8
4–5	0.842	−28.842	38.343	−77.421	18.250	31.209	124.683	5.993	195.0
5–6	15.082	60.978	−14.396	394.171	−0.739	−10.147	−45.095	9.912	−56.8
6–7	1.447	−25.695	34.786	−72.374	17.282	28.526	106.946	6.166	161.5
7–8	13.918	56.608	−11.563	299.997	0.529	−8.728	−40.946	9.978	−52.3
8–9	0.315	−19.199	35.022	−68.209	16.080	26.909	95.286	6.952	140.6
9–10	17.018	18.637	−17.002	213.013	−4.163	−5.578	−31.447	4.188	−39.6
10–11	5.274	10.582	23.907	−16.868	16.642	14.877	31.994	12.003	

Table 15.   Dampened Ocillation of Optimal
Growth Path

Year	Macro Growth Rates	Consumption Growth Rates
0– 1	4.884	− 10.0
1– 1	15.218	24.5
2– 3	5.082	110.7
3– 4	10.139	− 60.9
4– 5	6.024	187.3
5– 6	9.853	− 55.7
6– 7	6.253	155.3
7– 8	9.682	− 51.0
8– 9	6.432	131.3
9–10	9.520	− 46.6
0–11	6.590	112.5
10– 1	9.355	− 42.3
11– 1	6.727	97.4
12– 3	9.217	− 38.3
13– 4	6.855	84.8
14– 5	9.083	− 34.5
15– 6	6.959	74.4
16– 7	9.074	− 31.0
17– 8	7.441	67.0
18– 9	5.866	− 22.4
19–20	10.205	
20–21		

($g=7\%$ or 10%) and case 2 ($g=7.5\%$) the optimal paths quickly converge to the turnpike in the second planning period, and then remain on the turnpike. Focussing on the initial adjustment, in case 1 ($g=10\%$) and case 2 ($g=7.5\%$), where the actual output of heavy industry is less than the turnpike output and the actual outputs of the light and food industries are greater than the turnpike outputs, heavy industry displays a more rapid rate of growth from the initial period to the first period. In contrast, the light and food industries display more rapid rates of growth from the first period to the second period.

In case 1 ($g=7\%$), where the actual output of heavy industry is greater than the corresponding turnpike output and the actual outputs of the light and food industries are less than the corresponding outputs, the light and food industries display more rapid growth from the initial period to the first period. In contrast, heavy industry displays more rapid growth from the first period to the second period.

Concerning the optimal growth rates of consumption, in case 1 ($g = 10\%$) and case 2 ($g = 7.5\%$), the rate considerably decreases from the initial period to the first period and drastically increases from the first period to the second period. In case 1 ($g = 7\%$), the rate considerably increases from the initial period to the first period and drastically decreases from the first period to the second period.

Taking into consideration the movement of the macro optimal growth rate and consumption growth rate, case 1 ($g = 7\%$) is more desirable for use as an optimal development policy measure. However, it should be noted that in any case, the initial adjustment oscillation is pronounced.

Employing the data in terms of producers' prices, our computation shows that in cases where $g = 5\%$, 8% or 9%; $g = 10\%$, the optimal path converges to the turnpike in the second period. Further, the output of light industry displays more rapid growth from the initial period to the first period, drastically decreases from the first period to the second period, and then again considerably increases from the second period to the third period. It is also seen that the optimal growth rate for consumption decreases from the initial period to the first period, considerably increases from the first period to the second period, and then slightly decreases from the second period to the third period. Table 14 illustrates these facts in the case where $g = 8\%$.

Case 2 provides an interesting experimental result with regard to the turnpike property. When we set $g = 8\%$ and $\delta = 0\%$ or 10%, the optimal path converges to the turnpike from the third period. However, when we set $g = 8\%$ and $\delta = 15\%$ or 30%, it can be seen from Table 14 that the computation displays an oscillation phenomenon. In order to investigate this oscillation phenomenon in detail, we enlarge the time horizon and set $T = 20$. It can be seen from Table 15 that while the optimal path does not converge to the turnpike within the twenty periods, the oscillation is dampened and the optimal path gradually approaches the turnpike.

When we set $\delta = -10\%$, -15%, or -30%, only the construction sector displays a drastic form of oscillation. As previously stated, we can ignore case 2. Therefore, the cycle phenomena with dampened oscillation of the optimal path, dependent on the value of the discount rate, should be evaluated from the view point of pure numerical experiments for the turnpike property.[11]

6. Concluding Remarks

Up to now we have investigated the Soviet turnpike property using the Soviet 1966 dynamic input-output database. We have confirmed the strong turnpike property in all cases, with a few exceptions. It should be noted, however, that this strong turnpike property can be obtained through a violent adjustment of the output. On the contrary, the introduction of some additional conditions in order to reduce the need for a dramatic output adjustment, for example, $x(t) \geqq x(t-1)$, may weaken the turnpike property and result, in some cases, in a situation where there is no feasible solution.

One of the most important tasks for management in a socialist economy is ensuring that the actual economy conforms to the turnpike.

The realization of turnpike growth should be considered as one of the requirements for the introduction of marketization, as well as for the rationalization of planning. It should be noted that computation of turnpike growth ensures equilibrium growth in a weak sense, since the technological coefficients employed for the computation are not optimal, namely, they reflect the actual economy in the base period. This chapter provides a preliminary consideration for carrying out this main task.

---

[11] We computed the optimal path using the final state turnpike model and the Hungarian 5-sector data developed by Brody (1970). This optimal path does not converge to the turnpike but diverges from the turnpike. This may be caused by the problem of relative instability inherent in the dynamic Leontief system.

Chapter 8

PROSPECTS FOR RESTRUCTURING

THE SOVIET PRICE AND

FINANCE SYSTEM

1. Introduction

The radical economic *Perestroika* (restructuring) plan was presented to the Central Committee Plenum in June of 1987 (*"Osnovnye..."*, 1987). One of the crucial tasks to ensure full implementation of the plan is the fundamental changing of Soviet price and finance structures. Soviet authorities have therefore stated their intention to carry out a comprehensive reform of the price and finance systems. Price reform will include higher industrial wholesale prices for fuels, the incorporation of rents for natural resources into the price system, a reduction in agricultural subsidies and some decentralization of pricing[1]. This chapter describes the price reform proposals put forward by Soviet mathematical economists who have provided the theoretical foundation for the new policy.

---

[1] The Soviet authorities decided on July 17, 1987 to undertake an extensive revision of industrial wholesale prices and to introduce rents, or payments, for natural resources (*O korennoi perestroike...*, 1987). The new price lists will become effective on January 1, 1990. In the past 20 years Soviet authorities have carried out such a comprehensive revision of industrial wholesale prices only two times; in 1967 and 1982 (the last agricultural price revision became effective in 1983). The 1967 price revision was associated with a significant change in the fundamental scheme for price formation, including the introduction of payment for capital stock, while the 1982 price revision modifies the price structure to a slight extent. For the 1967 price reform and the 1982 price revision, see Schroeder (1969) and Bornstein (1987).

2. Price Reform Proposal of the Central Economic Mathematical Institute (TsEMI)

One of the fundamental characteristics of the Soviet-type centralized management system is that state enterprises enjoy viability and growth, regardless of their degree of profitability (Kornai (1981)). Price levels in some sectors fail to reflect the cost of extended reproduction, and in some cases even the cost of simple reproduction. These sectors, however, remain viable. This can be possible only when the pricing policy is completely subordinate to national fiscal policy. Soviet authorities have managed the economy by means of the so-called "dual-price system;" namely the industry wholesale price and the enterprise wholesale price, the difference of which constitutes the turnover tax. On the one hand, they collect the turnover tax from numerous sources, including the power generation and consumption goods sectors. On the other hand, the Soviet Union executes a redistribution of considerable sums through the state budget[2]. As a result, serious price distortions, as well as chronic shortages of goods occur, which in turn hinder the directing of the economy to a more intensive growth path.

A feature of the Soviet price system is the artificially low price levels of primary raw materials in comparison with the price of manufactured products.[3] The input-output of all products in an economy are interrelated. Therefore, price distortions of primary intermediate goods lead to an over-all distortion of the price structure through the interindustrial input-output inducement effect. As a result, price distortions appear,

[2]   Recently, Khovalova (1988) posed a completely retrogressive, conservative opinion that the pure type of "dual-price" system established in the Stalin era should be re-established in the Soviet Union. As is stated in Belkin (1988), she seems to have missed the point that under the "dual-price" system the price is deprived of its fundamental function of comparative calculation of costs and results (benefits).

[3]   The 1982 price revision raised the level of prices for the extractive industries. However, the coal industry still operates at a "planned loss." Some high-cost enterprises in the extractive industries also operate at a planned loss in selling their products at prices based on planned sector average cost (see Bornstein, ibid.).

[4]   The new chairman of the Soviet State Prices Commission, Pavlov, properly posed this relation in an article. See Pavlov (1987).

which cause price levels of the machine building industry to be considerably high as compared with the products of the extraction industry. In turn, this distortion causes: (1) wasteful use of raw materials and slow implementation of resource-saving technology (2) stagnation in the rate of modernization of the machine building industry (3) centralized administrative intervention in the profit formation and investment activities in each industry through large-scale redistribution of the state budget.

The TsEMI proposal for reform of the system is as follows:[5]

Soviet mathematical economists seek to apply the optimal price (marginal cost) formation principle throughout the Soviet economy. However, recognizing the enormity of this task, they have suggested that the optimal price formation principle be applied initially only to the extraction (primary raw materials) industries, including coal mining, metal ore mining, crude petroleum extraction and the natural gas industries.

The price levels of these raw materials should be raised considerably by switching the price formation principle for the extractive industries from one based on average costs to one based on marginal costs. By adopting this procedure Soviet planners hope to increase the role of profits as an efficiency indicator for all industries, to increase the incentives for general energy savings and to provide the means for the introduction of energy-saving technologies. They also seek to raise Soviet domestic energy prices to more closely reflect world energy market price levels (as is the case in the developed capitalist countries, Soviet prices of manufactured products can be expected to be low in relation to the Soviet prices of raw materials). They further seek to lay the groundwork for a redirecting of the Soviet export structure from one based on energy exports to one based on machinery exports, as is the case in advanced capitalist countries, including Japan and the United States.

In order to develop the price formation for extractive industries, based on marginal costs, it is necessary to precisely establish the rates for rents

---

[5] The following discussions are based on Petrakov (1987a;1987b), Petrakov et al. (1987), Vavilov (1986), Vavilov et al. (1986), Volkonsky and Vavilov (1987), and Volkonsky et al. (1987).

on natural resources ("natural production conditions") and incorporate these rents into the raw material prices of the extraction industries. The rents are then paid to the State, the sole owner of all natural resources. It is also necessary to abolish or decrease subsidies for the extractive industries, and to abolish or decrease the turnover tax and tax for profits which are used to finance subsidies for these industries and which are paid for by other industries. Namely, the marginal pricing of raw materials caused by incorporating the rents on natural resources into the prices of raw materials results in a change in the state budget revenue structure from one dependent on the turnover tax and profit deduction to one dependent on rents. It also requires a decrease in the share of subsidies and state-centralized investment in budget expenditures.

3. Theory of Rents and Marginal-Cost-Prices in an Input-Output System

Let us assume that a product of the extraction or agriculture industry can be produced in $i = 1, 2, \cdots, N$ sites (plots or deposits). It is assumed that each site i can increase output within a certain limit by switching to more intensive methods, and the costs of an additional unit of output increases as the amount of output increases. We define an average cost (AC) for site i, including capital charges, per single unit of the product as $\bar{P}(x_i)$, where x_i denotes the output in site i. Then, the marginal cost (MC); the cost of production of an additional unit in site i, is derived from $d\bar{P}(x_i)/dx_i (= MC_i(x_i))$. Let us assume that the optimal plan is given by the solution of the following cost minimization problem:

$$\min \sum_{i=1}^{N} \int_0^{x_i} MC_i(q)dq \tag{1}$$

$$\sum_{i=1}^{N} x_i \leq X, \tag{2}$$

$$0 \leq x_i \leq \bar{x}_i, \quad (i = 1, 2, \cdots, N), \tag{3}$$

where

[6] Vavilov (1986, Ch. 2) and Vavilov et al. (1986, pp. 784–785) considered this problem.

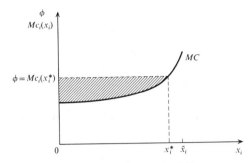

Fig. 1.   Marginal Costs and Rents

$\bar{x}_i$:   the maximum output capacity in site i;

X: the planned demand for the product.

We assume that the MC curve is depicted as shown in Figure 1. This assumption corresponds to the actual state of the Soviet extraction and agriculture sectors.

The Lagrangean corresponding to the above problem can be written as

$$L = -\sum_{i=1}^{N}\int_{0}^{x_i}MC_i(q)dq + \phi(X - \sum_{i=1}^{N}x_i)$$
$$+ \sum_{i=1}^{N}\lambda_i(\bar{x}_i - x_i); \phi \geq 0, \lambda_1, \lambda_2, \cdots, \lambda_N \geq 0,$$

where

ϕ: the shadow price associated with Eq. (2) (the price of the product);

λ_i: the shadow price associated with Eq. (3) (in Marxian terminology, differential rent I).

For simplicity, we assume that $x_i^* < \bar{x}_i$ for all i. By virtue of complementary slackness, we have $\lambda_i^* = 0$ for all i. Then the marginal costs are equal for all sites:

$$\phi = MC_i(x_i^*) \quad i = 1, 2, \cdots, N. \tag{4}$$

Namely, we have the marginal cost price (MC price) ϕ of the product at the moment of extraction. It should be noted that average costs $\bar{P}_i$ are usually different even under the optimal regime since each site differs in terms of quality. The difference between the MC price and the individual average costs defines the rents (in Marxian terminology, differential rent II). The shaded area in Figure 1 shows the sums of the rents for site i.

We denote by $S_i = \phi_i / \bar{P}_i(x_i)$ the "static" rent coefficient of site i. A greater [smaller] value of S_i shows that site i is a better [worse] one in terms of quality.

In the Soviet intra-sectoral practice[7] the static, or direct, marginal cost of a product is calculated by

$$\phi = C_o + EK , \qquad (5)$$

where

C_o: the marginal current cost (including amortization);
K: the marginal capital intensity;
E: the time discount rate.

On the other hand, the average cost of a product in a site is computed by

$$\bar{P} = \bar{C}_o + E\bar{F} , \qquad (6)$$

where

$\bar{C}_o$: the average current cost (including amortization);
$\bar{F}$: the average capital intensity.

At the present time, Soviet mathematical economists focus on the fact that for the last 10 to 15 years both average and marginal costs in the extraction industries, particularly in the petroleum extraction industry, have increased as the amount of more easily recoverable deposits have decreased and as new deposits are discovered which are further from industrial centers. In this case the (dynamic) marginal cost of extracting an exhaustible resource, $P(t)$ at the moment t includes not only the direct (static) marginal cost $\phi(t)$ but also the present-value total of additional costs in the future, $\Delta(t)$, associated with the need to increase the rate of extraction and to extract resources from less productive deposits. The present-value total of these additional costs in the future is also a type of

---

[7] A detailed description is given by Vavilov (1986, Ch. 2).

differential rent which must be applied to "cheaper" deposits. Some noted Soviet economists have labeled this rent "dynamic rent (*dinamicheskaia renta*)."[8] It should be noted that in agriculture there is no such impact on future costs.

We now describe mathematical formulas for the dynamic marginal cost and the dynamic rent. The increment of static marginal cost of an extraction output for the period $[\tau, \tau+d\tau]$ $(\tau>t)$, which is caused by extracting an additional unit of the exhaustible resource, can be denoted by $d\phi(\tau)$ $(=\phi'(\tau)d\tau)$.

Let E denote the discount rate. Then, the present-value total of incremental marginal costs for the time horizon $[t, \infty]$ is expressed as follows:

$$\Delta(t)=\int_t^\infty \phi'(\tau)\exp\{-E(\tau-t)\}d\tau.$$

Therefore, the marginal cost concept for an extraction output is redefined as a "dynamic" concept:[9]

$$P(t)=\phi(t)+\Delta(t)=E\int_t^\infty \phi(\tau)\exp\{-E(\tau-t)\}d\tau. \tag{7}$$

With regard to the (static) marginal cost path, two cases are considered:
Case 1: Assume that the (static) marginal cost increases over periods with a constant growth rate ρ, i.e., $\phi(t)=(0)\exp(\rho t)$.[10] Then by Eq. (7) we have

---

[8] Vavilov et al. (1986, p. 785). The author also uses the terminology "dynamic" and "static" marginal costs for convenience of description.

[9] Vavilov (1986, p. 52) and Vavilov et al. (1986, p. 785).

[10] As is mentioned by Vavilov (1986) and Vavilov et al. (1986), Shchevelev (1984, p. 1110) first posed the dynamic rent concept. He presented the following formula for the dynamic marginal cost.

$$p=\phi+\frac{1}{E}\dot{p}.$$

Assuming $\dot{p}=\rho p$, we can easily obtain Eq. (8) in the text.

$$P(t) = \frac{E}{E-\rho} \phi(t) \ . \tag{8}$$

Case 2: Assume that the (static) marginal cost increases, up to period T, with a constant rate ρ_1 and after that with a different rate ρ_2, i.e.,

$$\phi(t) = \begin{cases} \phi(0) \exp(\rho_1 t) & (t \leq T) \\ \phi(T) \exp\{\rho_2(t-T)\} & (t > T) \ . \end{cases}$$

In this case Eq. (7) can be written as

$$P(t) = \frac{E}{E-\rho_1} \phi(t)$$

$$- \exp\{-E(T-t)\} \left(\frac{E}{E-\rho_1} - \frac{E}{E-\rho_2} \right) \phi(T) \ . \tag{9}$$

Let the dynamic rent coefficient be denoted by $D(t)$:

$$D(t) = P(t)/\phi(t) \ .$$

Then the hybrid rent coefficient $Z(t)$, the ratio of the (dynamic) marginal cost to average cost, is defined by

$$Z(t) = P(t)/\bar{P}(t) \ ,$$

or

$$Z(t) = D(t)S(t) \ ,$$

where $S(t) = \phi(t)/\bar{P}(t)$ (static rent coefficient).

Table 1 shows the Soviet estimation of the dynamic rent coefficients D (1982) for petroleum and gas extraction, based on Eq. (8) or Eq. (9), for $E = 0.1$ and $E = 0.08$. From this table we can first see that the dynamic rent coefficient, hence the value of dynamic rent, is affected to a large extent by the selected discount rate E, particularly in case 1 for petroleum, and the dynamic rent coefficient for petroleum extraction is estimated to be much higher than for coal extraction. Selected values on the growth rates ρ of (static) marginal costs are based on Soviet energy production forecasts (Melent'ev and Makarov (1983)).

Table 1.   Dynamic Rent Coefficients (D) for Petroleum and Gas
Extraction, 1982

Discount rate (E)	Gas	Crude petroleum	
	$\rho=0.019$	case 1 $\rho_1=0.068$ $\rho_2=0.047$	case 2 $\rho_1=0.068$ $\rho_2=0.025$
$E=0.08$	1.31	2.79	1.90
$E=0.1$	1.23	2.15	1.71

Sources: Vavilov (1986, p. 55) and Vavilov et al. (1986, p. 786)
Notes: In the author's calculation the dynamic rent coefficients are slightly higher than those shown
above by approximately 0.02.

For crude petroleum Eq. (9) is applied ($t=1982$ and $T=1990$). Cases 1 and 2 in Table 1 both assume that high growth rates of average costs and incremental capital-intensities in petroleum extraction, which have prevailed for the last 15 years, will be maintained until 1990. The changes in extraction costs in subsequent periods are estimated differently: (case 1 assumes that the high growth rates observed today will be maintained even after 1990; case 2 assumes that the growth rates will decrease after 1990 as other forms of energy, such as coal, are used as substitutes for petroleum. Economists of TsEMI support the case 2 theory. However, if the proposed price revisions are not maintained, the growth rate of marginal and average costs for petroleum extraction would remain rather high. Conversely, the overall annual growth rate of static marginal cost for extraction and transportation is assumed unchanged over time and set equal to 1.9%.

Table 2 shows the values of the marginal costs and rent coefficients for fuels, calculated by Gosplan, based on sectoral optimization models. In regard to coal and gas extraction, two regions are identified; the European and Asian regions of the Soviet Union. Table 2 provides us with important data for the Soviet economy which has not previously been available to scholars in the West (however, the sectoral models used and the database have not yet been published by the Soviet authorities as far as the author knows). Table 2 also constitutes part of the initial data for

Table 2. Prices, Costs and Rent Coefficients for Fuels, 1982: Sectoral Analysis

(unit: rubles/s.f. 1 ton)

	Actual prices (P^0)	Average costs ($\bar{P}$)	Static MC (ϕ)	Static rent coefficients (S)	Growth rates of static MC ($\rho \cdot 100$)	Dynamic rent coefficients (D)	Rent coefficients (Z)	MC prices
Coal (European region)	25.0	29.4 [28.7]	40.9 [36.7]	1.39 [1.28]	0	1	1.39 [1.28]	40.9 [36.7]
Coal (Asian region)	12.72	14.9 [14.6]	20.0 [18.1]	1.34 [1.24]	0	1	1.34 [1.24]	20.0 [18.1]
Gas (European region)	23.75	26.9 [24.7]	31.5 [28.7]	1.17 [1.16]	1.9	1.23 [1.31]	1.44 [1.52]	38.8 [37.6]
Gas (Asian region)	13.82	15.7 [14.4]	18.4 [16.7]	1.17 [1.16]	1.9	1.23 [1.31]	1.44 [1.52]	22.6 [21.9]
Crude Petroleum	21.77	20.15 [19.4]	25.7 [24.0]	1.28 [1.25]	6.8–4.7	2.15 [2.79]	2.74 [3.43]	55.3 [67.0]
Heavy fuel oil	26.4	n.a.	n.a.	n.a.	n.a.	n.a.	n.a.	44.6 [56.0]

Sources: Vavilov (1986, p. 61)
Notes: 1. s.f.-the standard fuel unit used in the Soviet Union; n.a.-not available.
2. [ ] shows the values for $E=0.08$.

TsEMI's calculation. As can be seen in Table 2, the sectoral calculation shows the need to increase the current purchasers' prices of fuels to a considerable extent (approximately 200%).

From the sectoral estimates of marginal and average costs, Soviet mathematical economists derive a hypothesis in which gas is considered as the marginal fuel for the European region of the Soviet Union, while coal is the marginal fuel for the Asian region. It should be noted that with regard to replacing oil with energy substitutes, they are of the opinion that only coal and gas should be considered, and further, that gas will replace oil only when their proposals for price revision are implemented.

Making use of the results of sectoral analysis (ignoring interindustry relations), Soviet mathematical economists further proceed to an input-output analysis of the price system. For the empirical analysis of sector average prices, they employ one of the following "two-channel" price systems, both of which satisfy the requirements for measurement of the price inducement effects and for the "self-financing" principle at the sector level:

"Production prices": $\qquad \bar{p} = \bar{p}\bar{A} + \bar{w} + \mu\bar{p}\bar{F}$, $\qquad\qquad$ (10)

or

"Self-financing prices": $\qquad \bar{p} = \bar{p}\bar{A} + \bar{w} + \nu\bar{p}\bar{K}$, $\qquad\qquad$ (11)

where

$\bar{p} = (\bar{p}_j)$: an n-dimensional row vector of sector price indexes in relation to actual prices $(\bar{p}_j = \bar{P}_j/P_j^o)$;

$\bar{w} = (\bar{w}_j)$: an n-dimensional row vector of wage coefficients, including social security funds (in the following calculations $\bar{w}$ is set as $1.14 \times$ actual wage coefficient vector without social security funds);

$\bar{A} = (\bar{a}_{ij})$: an n by n matrix of average input coefficients, including amortization;

$\bar{F} = (\bar{f}_{ij})$: an n by n matrix of average capital coefficients;

$\bar{K} = (\bar{k}_{ij})$: an n by n matrix of average net-investment coefficients;

211

μ: a nation-wide average profit rate (given by the data in the Soviet Statistical Yearbook (*Narkhoz*));

ν: a proportional factor showing the ratio of total net-investment to total profit, not less than unity (given by the data in *Narkhoz*).

"Production prices" are well known. Belkin (1963; 1972) made use of Eq. (10) in calculating the 1959 and 1966 Soviet sector price indexes. "Self-financing prices" were first presented by Petrakov (1983). In "self-financing prices", the following identical equation is satisfied in each sector:

$$\text{amortization} + \text{profits} = \text{investment} + \text{other expenditures.}$$

Namely, the "self-financing" principle is ensured directly at the sector level when "self-financing" sector average prices prevail. Also under this price system growth-priority sectors which receive greater amounts of investment funding can earn higher profits. These profits may not accrue as the result of efficient production and management, but may simply be due to the higher level of investment funding. When $\nu > 1$, Eq. (11) shows that "other expenditures" in a sector are formed in proportion to net investment. When $\nu = 1$, sector profit is identically equal to net investment.

In the author's opinion, the case where $\nu = 1$ is more reasonable from a purely theoretical point of view because we can also introduce this type of proportional factor into "production prices," Eq. (10) to show the formation of "other expenditures." For example, we can redefine Eq. (10) as

$$\bar{p} = \bar{p}\bar{A} + \bar{w} + \nu(\mu\bar{p}\bar{F}) \ .$$

The author feels that a superficial consideration of Eqs. (10) and (11) will lead to an understanding of the similarity of the two types of prices, since both include a uniform proportional factor. However, further consideration will show the fundamental difference between "production prices" and "self-financing prices." In the former the proportional factor μ directly reflects profitability as one of the main indicators of economic efficiency, and each sector obtains profits in a manner uniquely proportional to its capital stock. On the other hand, in the case of "self-financing prices" the proportional factor does not reflect the profitability or investment efficiency of the economy as a whole. Under this price system the profit rate of each sector usually differs. Namely, we can re-write Eq. (11) ($\nu=1$) as

$$\bar{p} = \bar{p}\bar{A} + \bar{w} + \bar{p}\hat{G}\bar{F}, \; \hat{G}\bar{F} = \bar{K},$$

where

$$\hat{G} = \begin{bmatrix} g_1 & & & \\ & g_2 & & 0 \\ & & \cdot & \\ & & & \cdot \\ & 0 & & \cdot \\ & & & & g_n \end{bmatrix}$$

and g_i is the sector i's growth rate.

The "self-financing prices" system directly incorporates net investments, which are provided by the output equations. This price system may be associated with unbalanced growth, while the "production prices" system is associated with balanced growth. We have commented on the "self-financing prices" system from a theoretical view point. However, it should be noted that this price system can ensure realization of the self-financing principle in each sector, independent of the issues related to the determination of growth and accumulation.

Soviet mathematical economists further develop an input-output price system for determining sector price indexes by partially introducing the marginal pricing principle into the system. They apply either Eq. (10) or Eq. (11) to the sectors that do not supply primary, intermediate goods. On the other hand, they apply the marginal pricing principle to sectors producing primary, intermediate goods, including the iron ore, coal, gas, crude petroleum, lumber and agriculture sectors. Let us re-formulate the original Soviet price equations (Vavilov et al. (1986, p. 788)) more precisely as follows:

Redefine sector indexes

$i, j \in J$: sector indexes other than those for primary sectors ("tr" indicates the transportation and communication sector index) and their set;

$r, s \in R$: extraction sector indexes and their set.

Using sectoral data on static and dynamic rent coefficients, marginal input (cost) coefficients for the primary sectors are given as follows:

$$a_{hr} = D_r S_r^c \bar{a}_{hr} (h \neq tr), \ a_{tr,r} = D_r S_r^{tr} \bar{a}_{tr,r},$$

$$w_r = D_r S_r^c \bar{w}_r, \ k_{ir} = D_r S_r^k \bar{f}_{ir}, \quad h \in J \cup R,$$

where

S_r^c: the ratio of marginal to average "intermediate costs (*sebestoimosti*)";

S_r^{tr}: the ratio of marginal to average transportation costs;

S_r^k: the ratio of marginal to average capital intensity.

Sector marginal cost price indexes for primary sectors p_r are determined by

$$p_r = \sum_i \bar{p}_i a_{ir} + \sum_s p_s a_{sr} + w_r + E \sum_i \bar{p}_i k_{ir}, \quad r \in R, \tag{12}$$

where E is the time discount rate, or the investment efficiency normative. Corresponding to the above equation, sector average price indexes, in the case of the application of "self-financing prices," are determined by the following equations:

$$\bar{p}_j = \sum_i \bar{p}_i \bar{a}_{ij} + \sum_r p_r \bar{a}_{rj} + \bar{w}_j + \nu \sum_i \bar{p}_i \bar{k}_{ij}, \quad j \in J, \tag{13}$$

In the case of "production prices" the fourth term of the right-hand side of the above equations is replaced with $\mu \sum_i \bar{r}_i \bar{f}_{ij}$.

The system of price indexes consists of Eqs. (12) and (13).[11] We can refer to the system as a "hybrid" price system. This "hybrid" system yields a unique price index vector ($p, \bar{p}$) if the average input coefficients, the static and rent coefficients and (μ, ν, E) are given, and satisfy the

---

[11] The author's description of the Soviet input-output price system may be more convenient than the original rough description from the computational point of view. The terminology "hybrid price system" is the author's.

Table 3. Initial Data for Rent Coefficients, 1982

	S_r^c	S_r^k	S_r^{tr}	D_r	Z_r
Iron Ore	1.3	1.3	1.3	1	1.3
Coal (Asian region)	0.78	5.62	0.78	1	1.34
					[1.24]
Coal (European region)	1	1.38	1	1.23	1.44
				[1.31]	[1.52]
Crude Petroleum	1	1.27	1	2.15	2.74
				[2.74]	[3.43]
Lumber	1	5.64	2.4	1	1.82
					[1.75]
Grain	1.8	1.8	1.8	1	1.8
Livestock	1.2	1.2	1.2	1	1.2

Sources: Vavilov (1986, p. 75).
Notes: 1. [·] shows the initial data for $E=0.08$.
2. For one computation in the following section (case 2 in Table 4), the value of S and Z in the "Lumber" sector is 1.22 and in the "Grain" sector 1.3 (see Vavilov et al. (1986, p. 789)).

appropriate conditions.

Table 3 shows the initial data for sector-by-sector static rent co-efficients which determine the relationship between the average and (static) marginal cost structures. In Table 3 the data for coal in the European region and gas in the Asian region are not given. This is due to the Soviet assumption with regard to the substitute use of gas and coal. As has been mentioned, coal is considered to be the marginal energy source in the Asian region and gas is the marginal energy source in the European region. In each region the marginal cost of gas is assumed to be equal to that of coal. Namely,

$$P_{coal}=P_{gas}; \; p_{coal}P_{coal}^0=p_{gas}P_{gas}^0 .$$

P^0 is already given by Table 2. Therefore, if the price index for either coal or gas is given, the other is determined by the above equation. In the Asian region we subtract the price equation for the gas sector from Eq. (12) and insert $p_{gas}=\alpha p_{coal}(\alpha=P_{coal}^0/P_{gas}^0)$ into the price equations for the sectors using gas produced in the Asian region. Thus p_{coal} can be determined.[12] For the European region the position of gas and coal are reversed in the above computations. Accordingly, two price equations are redundant and are eliminated from the system of price indexes.

It is worth making some additional comments regarding the data compilation method employed by Soviet mathematical economists. As is known, the Soviet official input-output tables are compiled in terms of purchasers' prices, including the turnover tax with different rates. In calculating the system of price indexes, differentiated rates for the turnover tax for each commodity should be adjusted to a unique rate or set to zero.[13]

First, regarding the petroleum refinery (heavy fuel oil) sector, the turnover tax rate for intermediate use is also applied to final use. This causes a decrease in the intermediate uses of the product supplied by the petroleum refinery sector and thus a decrease in gross output of the sector. The turnover tax rate for electricity is regarded as being almost zero, which induces a decrease in the intermediate uses of power supplied by the electricity sector and causes a decrease in the gross output of the sector. Regarding the turnover tax for the food sector, two cases are considered. In one the turnover tax is set to zero (case 2 shown in Table 4 in the following section) and in the other no adjustment is made to the turnover tax, since the share of the turnover tax in the gross output of the sector is rather small, 0.5% (cases 1 and 4 shown in Table 4 in the following section). The turnover tax rate for the food industry is regarded as a unique rate, although, in effect it differs from user to user.

From the above observation it can be seen that the sector price index for heavy fuel oil is related to the current industrial wholesale price. The sector price index for electricity shows the ratio of the computed sector price to current tariffs, without turnover tax, in the material production sectors.

---

[12] Eq. (8) in Vavilov et al. (1986, p. 789) should be read as the above equation in the text. Also, the explanation in Vavilov (1986, p. 74) should be read as in the text.

[13] See Vavilov (1986, pp. 83–84) and Vavilov et al. (1986, pp. 792–793).

Table 4. Soviet Price Index System, Computed by TsEMI

Sector	case (1) $\nu=1.25$ $E=0.1$ [0.08]	case (2) $\nu=1.25$ $E=0.1$ [0.08]	case (3)	case (4) $\mu=0.072$ $E=0.1$	case (5) $\nu=1.25$ $E=0.1$
1. Iron ore	1.35 [1.39]	1.38 [1.4]	1.53	1.53	0.95
2. Other ferrous metallurgy	1.2 [1.22]	1.16 [1.18]	1.31	1.36	0.9
3. Nonferrous metallurgy	1.02 [1.06]	n.a.	n.a.	1.09	0.83
4. Coal (European region)	1.96 [2.0]	1.88 [1.93]	1.9	2.14	1.22
5. Coal (Asian region)	2.08 [1.98]	1.97 [1.8]	2.33	2.13	1.22
6. Crude Petroleum	3.08 [3.9]	2.96 [3.74]	4.34	3.35	1.98
7. Petroleum refinery	1.8 [2.21]	1.72 [2.11]	1.85	1.98	1.22
8. Gas (European region)	2.07 [2.11]	1.99 [2.04]	2.5	2.26	1.22
9. Gas (Asian region)	1.92 [1.82]	1.81 [1.66]	1.95	1.96	1.22
10. Oil fuel	1.36 [1.4]	1.3 [1.35]	1.66	1.69	1.16
11. Electricity (European region)	1.41 [1.52]	1.34 [1.44]	1.43	1.65	1.01
12. Electricity (Asian region)	1.41 [1.48]	1.33 [1.38]	1.42	1.62	1.01
13. MBMW	1.06 [1.08]	1.02 [1.05]	1.04	1.16	0.9
14. Chemicals	1.19 [1.23]	1.18 [1.16]	1.15	1.35	0.93
15. Lumber	2.06 [2.3]	1.4 [1.45]	1.51	2.35	1.03
16. Wood & Paper	1.26 [1.33]	1.07 [1.1]	1.1	1.4	0.89
17. Construction Materials	1.8 [1.23]	1.13 [1.18]	1.2	1.34	0.96
18. Light industry (Textiles)	0.92 [0.94]	0.8 [0.82]	1.08	0.95	0.67
19. Food industry	1.62 [1.63]	1.33 [1.35]	1.0	1.64	1.05
20. Industry n.e.c.	1.63 [1.67]	1.36 [1.39]	1.12	1.67	1.12
Industry, total	n.a.	n.a.	1.22	n.a.	n.a.
21. Grain	2.04 [2.05]	1.43 [1.46]	1.15	2.13	1.08
22. Livestock	1.75 [1.8]	1.49 [1.52]	1.12	1.81	1.08
23. Forestry	1.34 [1.36]	1.3 [1.32]	1.12	1.25	1.19
24. Construction	1.18 [1.22]	1.14 [1.17]	1.04	1.25	1.0

Table 4. (continued)

Sector	case (1) $\nu=1.25$ $E=0.1$ [0.08]	case (2) $\nu=1.25$ $E=0.1$ [0.08]	case (3)	case (4) $\mu=0.072$ $E=0.1$	case (5) $\nu=1.25$ $E=0.1$
25. Transport & Communication	1.28 [1.34]	1.24 [1.3]	1.23	1.43	1.07
26. Distribution	1.39 [1.41]	1.23 [1.25]	0.9	1.31	1.14
27. Other material production	1.05 [1.08]	0.98 [1.0]	1.03	1.11	0.88
National income	n.a.	1.2 [1.24]	1.052	n.a.	n.a.
Gross output	1.43 [1.5]	n.a.	1.172	1.53	1.02

Sources: Case 1: Vavilov (1986, p. 98);
    Case 2: Vavilov et al. (1986, p. 791);
    Case 3: Volkonsky et al. (1987, p. 16);
    Case 4: Vavilov (1986, p. 102).
    Case 5: Vavilov (1986, p. 109) and Vavilov et al.(1986, p. 792).

Notes: 1. Each price index in this table shows the ratio of normative prices to actual 1982 industrial wholesale prices except for the following sectors. The price indexes for "18. Light industry" and "19. Food industry" relate to retail prices. The price indexes for "21. Grain" and "22. Livestock" relate to 1983 procurement prices.
    2. [·] indicates the price indexes for $E=0.08$.
    3. The price index system in case 3 is computed by using estimated 1990 input-output data.

4. Computation Results of Sector Price Indexes and Reform of the Soviet Finance System

Table 4 describes five variants of the sector price index system computed by TsEMI, based on the "hybrid" input-output price system (Eqs. (12) and (13)), sectoral data (Table 3) and Soviet 1982 input-output table (not yet published). From this table we can first see that the prices of fuels and energy require a large increase due to the introduction of the marginal cost principle and rent. Considering cases 1 to 4 in Table 4, where $E=0.1$, we can state that the price of the crude petroleum sector product requires an approximately 300% to 434% increase, the price of the coal sector product requires a 188% to 233% increase and the price of the iron ore mining sector product requires a 35% to 53% increase. The price increase of crude petroleum induces a 72% to 98% increase in the price of petroleum refinery commodities, and the price increase of fuels, including coal, induces a 33% to 43% increase in the price of electricity.

Secondly, the remarkable increase in prices of fuel and energy requires only a slight increase in the prices of MBMW (machine building and metalworking) sector products. The relative price ratio of the crude petroleum price index to the MBMW price index is 2.88 [2.91] in case 1 [case 4], where the MBMW sector shows a 6% [16%] price increase. This computation result directly implies that the realization of "self-financing" is compatible with the radical reform of the relative price structures of fuels and machinery.

In a dynamic context, Soviet mathematical economists expect the Soviet economy to develop as follows:

An improvement in price proportions will induce a switch from inefficient energy usage to efficient energy usage, and this in turn will induce a decrease in the resource output growth rate. In addition, it will reduce the need for extracting energy resources from marginally productive sites and deposits. After these goals have been attained, the marginal cost prices of fuel and energy, which will initially be considerably higher than the average costs of these products, can be expected over the long term to decrease and approach the average costs.

The computation results in cases 1 to 5 in Table 4 can be classified from several points of view.

Classification I:

Based on the method of application of the price equation for sectors other than the extractive sectors, cases 1, 2, 3 and 5 employ "self-financing prices", while case 4 makes use of "production prices." However, we can see from Table 4 that the computed values of "self-financing prices" (case 1) are similar to those of "production prices"(case 4). This may be partly due to a similarity between the investment and capital stock structures in 1982. It may also be partly due to the method of application of the price equations, where the price equations for the extractive and agricultural sectors, in cases 1 and 2, are based on "production prices" principles, not on "self-financing prices."

Classification II:

The most important classification concerns the coverage of price formation based on marginal cost (MC), i.e., the extent to which the sectors apply the marginal cost prices. Cases 1, 2 and 4 apply the MC price to each basic extractive sector, including energy and agriculture. Case 3 applies the MC price to each basic extractive sector except agriculture. Case 5 applies the MC price only to the crude petroleum and gas sectors. Case 5 is the most passive policy proposal for the introduction of MC prices. Therefore, Soviet economists refers to this case as "first-stage pricing." Accordingly, we refer to case 3 as "second-stage pricing" and also to cases 1, 2 and 4 as "third-stage pricing."

The theoretical ideal of The Central Economic Mathematical Institute (TsEMI) is based on the concept that the optimal price system or MC prices should be applied to all commodities, including not only raw materials but also other products. In this ideal situation the "self-financing" system functions effectively in each intra-industry enterprise. In comparison with this ideal situation even "third-stage pricing" is an insufficient policy proposal. However, if "third-stage pricing" is applied we must deal with two problems; the general price level and the retail prices of agricultural products. If we regard the level of the retail price of agricultural products as constant, application of MC prices to the agriculture sector induces a remarkable increase in the State procurement prices for agricultural products, and in turn, a general increase in subsidies for agricultural products. This is an undesirable situation. On the other hand, application of MC prices to only the extraction and agriculture sectors requires an increase in the general price level in proportion to the extent of coverage of the price formation, based on marginal cost.

Case 1 [case 2] of "third-stage pricing" shows a 100% [43%] and a 75% [49%] increase in the prices of grain and meat, respectively. The high level of the MC price for agriculture induces a high level in the price of food industry output; in case 1 [case 2], 62% [33%] higher than the current retail price. This results in imbalances in food demand and household incomes; demand exceeds income. This imbalance cannot be eliminated by a general increase in the overall wage level since such an increase implies a corresponding rise in all values of the computed price indexes ($h\bar{p} = (I - \bar{A} - \mu \bar{F})^{-1} h \bar{w}$, where h is a proportional factor).

Setting the procurement and retail prices at the proposed price level leads to an increase in agricultural subsidies and retail food prices. If "third-stage pricing" is implemented, a radical review of both the retail price system and the household income structure is required. However, this problem is beyond the scope of the price computation provided by the Central Economic Mathematical Institute.[14]

If applied, "third-stage pricing" will result in a rather high increase in the general price index; 43% [20%] in case 1 [case 2] in terms of gross output [national income].

"First-stage pricing," case 5, seeks the attainment of two goals; elimination of income deficits in the coal industry through self-financing prices and acceleration of energy substitution from oil to coal. The procurement price for agriculture shows only a slight increase, 8%. The

---

[14] See Vavilov et al. (1986, p. 793). Increasing retail prices have a direct effect on people's lives and constitute a very delicate political problem.

general price level also shows a very slight increase, 2% in terms of gross outputs. However, limiting the application of the marginal pricing principle only to the crude petroleum and gas extraction industries may distort the inter-industry relation of price formation among the extractive industries. In this situation "second-stage pricing" appears to be the more appropriate proposal.

"Second-stage pricing," case 3, shows a 12% increase in the procurement prices. The retail price of food does not show any increase. The general price level in terms of national income shows a rather low increase, 5.2%. With "second-stage pricing," the share of rent in the national income is 12%, of which the fuel and energy sectors provide 92.5%. Dynamic rents make up 56% of the total amounts of rents for the extraction industries, of which 45% and 11% are generated by the crude petroleum and coal industries, respectively. An estimation of the total amount of rents for 1990 is expected to be 80 to 85 billion rubles. Total dynamic rent is estimated at 47 to 49 billion rubles, of which the crude petroleum sector provides 38 to 39 billion rubles and the gas sector 9 to 10 billion rubles. (Volkonsky et al. (1987, p. 9)).

It is worth making two additional comments regarding Soviet price computation methods.

First, regarding the effect of the time discount rate ("normative" of investment efficiency), E, on the price indexes, we can see from Table 4 that a lower value of the discount rate induces an increase in the dynamic rent coefficients (Table 1), and thus yields higher values of the MC price indexes for crude petroleum. It also induces a 1.9% increase in the coal price index in the European region of the Soviet Union and a 0.9% increase in the percentage that rents contribute to the national income.

Secondly, the absolute level of the MC price, p_r P_r^0, based on input-output calculation, shows a higher value in relation to the level which is based on sectoral optimal analysis (Table 5). In case 1 ($E=0.1$) this increase in the rates of the MC price level shows values in the range of 18% to 45%. The highest increase, 45%, is shown in the coal industry in the Asian region of the Soviet Union. Crude petroleum shows a 21% increase by the change of E; when $E=0.08$, this increase is 27%.

Table 5.   Soviet Marginal Cost Prices for Fuels, 1982
$E=0.1$ [$E=0.08$], $\nu=1.25$

(unit: rubles/s.f. 1 ton)

	Actual purchasers' prices	MC prices: sectoral analysis	MC prices input-output analysis (case 1 in Table 4)	Affects of IO relations (column 3/ column 2)
Coal (European region)	25.0	40.9	48.7	1.19
		[36.7]	[50.0]	[1.36]
Coal (Asian region)	12.72	20.0	28.9	1.45
		[18.1]	[25.1]	[1.39]
Gas (European region)	23.75	38.8	48.7	1.26
		[37.6]	[50.0]	[1.33]
Gas (Asian region)	13.82	22.6	28.9	1.28
		[21.9]	[25.1]	[1.15]
Crude petroleum	21.77	55.3	66.7	1.21
		[67.0]	[84.8]	[1.27]
Heavy fuel oil	26.4	44.6	52.8	1.18
		[56.0]	[70.0]	[1.25]

Sources: Vavilov (1986, pp. 103–104); Volkonsky and Vavilov (1986, p. 52).
Notes: [·] shows the values for $E=0.08$.

Let us next observe changes in the structure of budget revenues and expenditures associated with the aforementioned measures for reforming the Soviet price system.

Proposal (a) in Table 6 describes changes in the 1985 budget structure which will result from implementation of "second-stage pricing" (case 3 in Table 4). In regard to the revenue side, we can first see from Table 6 that the share of payments for resources (rents plus quasi-rents) in total revenue shows a remarkable increase from 17.6% to 39.4%, while the share of turnover tax conversely shows a considerable decrease from 25% to 13%. It should be noted that "rent" and "quasi-rent" indicate payments for natural resources and fixed capital, respectively. The share of rents is 15.9% in Proposal (a). The share of fixed (rent) payments for natural resources, which have been introduced since the 1965 reform, is 7.1%. The share of rents and fixed (rent) payments in total revenue

Table 6.   The State Budget Structure of the USSR, 1985
(in terms of percent of total)

		Practice in 1985	Proposal (a)	Proposal (b)
Revenues				
1.	Turnover tax	25.0	13.1	12.9
2.	Payments for productive capital	9.8	9.5	21.0
3.	Fixed (rent) payments	1.3	7.0	2.6
4.	Fees from the free residual of profits	12.1	—	—
5.	Rents on natural resources	—	15.9	—
6.	Progressive tax on profits	—	—	10.5
7.	Other deductions from profits and miscellaneous payments	7.4	—	—
8.	Income tax from cooperatives, collective farms, etc.	0.6	—	6.6
9.	State social security funds	6.5	6.9	10.5
10.	Other revenues	37.3	47.5	35.9
11.	Total	100.0	100.0	100.0
	Total payments for resources $(2+3+5+9)$	17.6	39.4	—
Expenditures				
1.	Investment finance	20.2	12.0	n.a.
2.	Subsidies for agricultural products	14.8	15.2	n.a.
3.	Social Cultural and Scientific expenditures	32.5	31.5	n.a.
4.	Defence	4.9	3.5	n.a.
5.	Administration	0.8	0.6	n.a.
6.	Other expenditures	26.8	37.2	n.a.
7.	Total	100.0	100.0	100.0

Notes: 1.   This table is based on Volkonsky et al. (1987, p. 31) and Petrakov (1987a, p. 53).
   2.   "—": not applicable; n.a.—not available.

constitute approximately one fourth the total revenue in Proposal (a). The decrease in turnover tax share and the increase in rent share are complementary. For example, the turnover tax on oil (gasoline and others) is transferred in part to the rent assessment of the crude petroleum industry. Further, it should be noted that an increase in the domestic price of petroleum causes a decrease in the foreign trade organization's procurement price for petroleum, and in turn, budget income from foreign trade decreases. However, this decrease is compensated for by revenues from rents. Incorporating rents in the petroleum price makes the evaluation of revenue, based solely on foreign trade activities, more accurate and increases the role of price incentives in the domestic extraction industries.

Turning to the expenditure side, we can first see from Table 6 that the share of state investment in terms of total expenditures decreases from 20.2% to 12% in Proposal (a). However, the share of subsidies for agricultural products increases from 14.8% to 15.2%. This increase is slight but shows the limitations of "second-stage pricing" since the enormous size of these subsidies casts a heavy burden on the Soviet budget.

According to Volkonsky et al. (1987, pp. 29–30), through a revision of prices the state investment share of the overall investment funds can be reduced from 48.3% to 33%. The remaining 67% investment can then be financed by profits reserved in the enterprises and through bank credits. In 1985, 56% of profits accrued by industry was collected and placed in the state budget under the category "deductions from profits." This share can also be reduced to 40%.

Proposal (b) in Table 6 was presented by Petrakov (1987a; 1987b). In place of rents in Proposal (a) a progressive tax is levied on profits in Proposal (b). The share of the progressive tax in terms of total revenue is a rather high 10.5%. The share of payments for fixed capital shows the largest value, 21%, which is double the value of the payments required in Proposal (a). As in the case of Proposal (a) the turnover tax share remarkably decreases from 25% to 12.9%. While the rent payments can be replaced by a progressive tax on profits, details regarding Proposal (b) have still not yet been published. Therefore, further research is required. During the author's interview, Professor Petrakov stated that the progressive tax on profits in his proposal includes the payments for capital, labor and natural resources. Also during another interview with Professor Volkonsky and Dr. Vavilov, both suggested that their proposal assumes the rate of payments for productive capital to be 3%, while Professor Petrakov's proposal assumes it to be 6%. As a result, the ratio of payments for productive capital in Proposal (b) is double that of Proposal (a). It should be noted that Professors Petrakov and Volkonsky have worked diligently and cooperatively for a reform of the Soviet price and finance system.

5. Conclusions: Toward Further Price Reform

This chapter has described the theoretical foundations of a sector price index system and a "hybrid" price system with rents developed by Soviet mathematical economists. The author would like to make the following comments regarding the price revision computation.

1. The practical proposals for Soviet price reforms put forward by Soviet mathematical economists imply, in effect, that the application of the recommended price increases at a single stroke will subject the Soviet Union to an enormous "energy shock," similar to that experienced by the rest of the world in the 1970's.

2. The price calculations for the extraction industries are primarily based on sectoral calculations which do not take into consideration interindustry relationships. It should be noted that in the Soviet Union over the past 20 years substantial sectoral experience in calculating marginal extraction costs has been accumulated and this has made possible the development of the "hybrid" input-output price system.

3. In a historical context it is ironic that the Soviet Government will henceforth rely on revenues from rents, since an original goal of the Soviet Union was land reform and the abolishment of the landlord system. However, the logic employed by economists on the staff of TsEMI has been successful in rationalizing the need for this policy.

4. While the "hybrid" price system is at present useful for reforming the Soviet economy, it suffers from some drawbacks. Specifically, in making use of the "hybrid" price system Soviet mathematical economists do not explicitly treat the "quasi-rents" for commodities supplied by the MBMW sector. When considering the quasi-rents (the concept of which is similar to that of the rents on natural resources), we may be able to obtain alternative price calculation results that may weaken the assertion regarding relative prices between machinery and fuels put forward by the

Soviet economists.

5.   Soviet mathematical economists have not yet reached a satisfactory solution for the comprehensive price revisions which should include an increase in the retail prices of food and light industry outputs and a radical reduction of subsidies to compensate for the difference between the procurement price and the retail price. This corresponds to the presently held attitudes of Soviet authorities, but limits the effectiveness of price reform.

Next, let us refer briefly to the recent controversy in the Soviet Union regarding the adoption of marginal cost pricing.

Deriabin (1987) proposed price formation oriented toward minimum enterprise cost of production without presenting any explicit quantitative formulation of his proposal, and criticized the marginal cost pricing by claiming that under the condition of the acceleration of scientific and technical progress and the increased efficiency of social production, marginal costs cannot exceed the level of average costs. However, as Borozdin (1987) pointed out, theoretically, the marginal cost of a product can exceed the average cost, and practically, the actual marginal cost of an extraction product is greater than the average cost in the present Soviet economy. When we consider only the aspect of inputs and costs as in Deriabin's paper, we cannot deal with the comparative calculation of costs and benefits, namely the efficiency of production. Further, the problem should be defined not in terms of "what prevails under the condition of the acceleration of technical progress?" but "what prevails under the present Soviet economy (in a system lacking the conditions required for the acceleration of technical progress)?" or "what should be done in order to create the conditions necessary for technical renovation and innovation?"

Danilov-Danil'ian, who attempted to describe a most complicated, hierarchical optimal system of models based on the "composition" method in the 1970's, criticized marginal cost pricing for extractive products (Danilov-Danil'ian (1987)) for the reasons; the impossibility of direct, precise, quantitative representation of the constraints on extraction, the possibility of price inflation and distorted extension of resources

227

caused by a positive correlation between increasing scarcity and increasing marginal cost and the uncertainty of future extraction conditions. As Albegov, Volkonsky and Gofman(1987) clarified, Danilov-Danil'ian placed the optimization approach to economic problems in general and economic management, applying a specific concrete optimal model, together in a single class, and as the result he adopted a form of economic "nihilism" where any kind of step-by-step approach to possible rationalization of the existing economy is rejected.

The author would like to conclude this chapter by considering some serious problems which bar the way to further price reforms in the Soviet Union.

The most important remaining issue is related to the possibilities for centralized and decentralized pricing. Energy prices may be effectively controlled by the pricing authorities, since the quality of the energy produced is uniform throughout the economy and the product mix of the energy enterprises is rather simple. However, this is not the case with other products, particularly MBMW products, which do vary widely in terms of quality from enterprise to enterprise.

Pricing of the MBMW products should be decentralized by using contract or free prices as Soviet economists insist (Volkonsky, et al. (1987, p. 2)). However, in order to implement demand-oriented and "anti-input" pricing, which reflects the relative scarcity of resources, the Soviet Union must establish a nationwide range of markets. This will require the abolishment of the "state commercial order (*goszakaz*)" system which the Gorbachev regime introduced in 1987 to replace the traditional system of centrally mandated targets for each enterprise.

The "state commercial order" system was originally developed more than twenty years ago in a paper by the late Academician V.S. Nemchinov, a founder of Soviet mathematical economics. (During the June 1987 Soviet Plenum, Gorbachev quoted a passage from this paper). Nemchinov wrote the following (Nemchinov (1964, pp. 77–78)):

"Profit-and-loss accounting relations should serve as the basis for ensuring that the economic potentialities of enterprises are in accordance with the requirements of the national economy as a whole. This can be attained only by radically changing the pattern of relationships between the planning bodies and the enterprises. This requires, in particular, that the planning bodies distribute, in an economically effective and rational way, sufficiently profitable orders—based on the national economic plan—among enterprises and construction sites through the network of economic agencies. Each enterprise should submit to the planning bodies preliminary proposals concerning the conditions under which it is prepared to fulfill one or another plan order (*planovyi zakaz*) for the delivery of goods, specifying the assortment, quality, time limits, and prices. The economic and planning bodies, for their part, should distribute their orders only among those enterprises whose terms for carrying out plan orders are most advantageous for the national economy as a whole.

The agreement of an enterprise to accept a definite plan assignment, being confirmed by a written document, converts the plan assignment into a plan order. As far as the planning bodies are concerned, this procedure is more complicated, but it is necessary as a filter against manifestations of pure voluntarism, and it is quite feasible. This system can be called a *profit-and-loss accounting system of planning* (*khozraschetnaia sistema planirovaniia*) because it effectively combines the planning and profit-and-loss accounting principles—the principles which should regulate any type of economic activity under conditions of socialism. What elements comprise this system and what conditions ensure its uninterrupted operation? The profit-and-loss accounting system of planning will operate smoothly only if it is based on the following principle: everything that is useful and advantageous for the national economy as a whole should also be advantageous for the enterprise carrying out the corresponding portion of the plan as an executive link. The operation of this principle can be guaranteed if the plan assignment is transformed into a plan order and if the basic conditions for fulfilling the order are established, in particular, if the price is acceptable both to the planning body and the enterprise."

Gorbachev has in effect adopted the suggestions put forward by Nemchinov, but has changed the name from "plan order" to "state commercial order."[15]

Of course, Nemchinov put forward positive suggestions, such as the abolishment of the administration assignment of resources, the introduction of "wholesale trade" (market) to eliminate the chronic shortage of commodities, and rationalization of the price system with implementation of a self-financing system. Gorbachev also adopted these suggestions. However, these positive policy measures are not compatible with the state commercial order system. So long as the Soviet authorities retain wide-ranging decision-making powers over enterprises, the state commercial order system is easily bypassed by the traditional centralized allocation system. Also, since all the input-output activities within each enterprise and among enterprises are closely related, the vertical relationship implied in the state commercial system for public and non-public goods contradicts the horizontal relationship expected to be found in wholesale trade.[16]

[15] In the documents of the June 1987 plenum of the CPSU Central Committee and the Law on the State Enterprise, two types of economic levers are posed which the Soviet authorities intend to use to replace the administrative-mandatory target figures of production: rules and economic parameters (normativy) and state commercial orders. Soviet authorities expect these levers to operate as follows:

Economic parameters lay out the general rules of economic activities. They are first determined by Gosplan and then adjusted by the ministries and territorial authorities. The parameters serve as the primary lever in developing long-term plans and as a kind of regulator of these plans, since they prevent the emergence of hare-brained schemes.

State commercial orders enable the central planning board (CPB) to attempt tasks which can be more effectively solved from the CPB, or which are in general harder to solve without the assistance of the CPB. A state commercial order will be profitable for the enterprise which fulfills the order. Further, the state commercial order will ensure that the enterprise is provided with the required materials and other resources.

[16] Popov, a noted radical Soviet economist issued the following two warnings in August 1987(Popov (1987)) while he positively appreciated the role of the state commercial orders:

"The state commercial order becomes mandatory not only in virtue of economic profitability, it also retains an element of administrative binding force. Moreover, there is a real danger of all current directive-based assignments being replaced by this state commercial order. I have already read about state commercial orders for flour. Therefore, the first line of the struggle for reconstruction means increasing the economic nature of the state commercial order."

"The price has a binding character, being fixed from above. And, given this price, both wholesale trade and the market may become a sphere of influence, not of the law of value, but of those ideas by which the authors of the prices were guided. The documents also mention contract prices, but their role has not yet been clearly legitimized. Therefore, the second line is the struggle for reconstruction and the development of such a price formation, in which the price would reflect the cost, instead of someone's opinion about the cost."

The "danger" that Popov warned of, in fact, appeared soon after the state commercial order system was implemented. On January 1988, Popov (1988) warned that the state commercial order system made a fiction of the autonomy of enterprises and the self-financing system.

The close relationships between the state commercial orders and the possibilities of centralization and decentralization of pricing are analyzed by Iashin (1987). We can confirm from this paper that the state commercial order system is associated with centralized pricing.

DERIVATION OF U.S. COMMODITY-BY-COMMODITY INPUT-OUTPUT TABLES FROM SNA USE AND MAKE TABLES

1. Introduction

This appendix presents the experimental results of aggregated input-output tables derived by merging the U.S. SNA use and make tables. The experimental results are based on the three alternative technology assumptions proposed by the United Nations and the Bureau of Economic Analysis (BEA) of the U.S. Department of Commerce.

Two of the assumptions, namely the commodity technology assumption and the industry technology assumption, are proposed in the SNA, and are well known. The modified industry technology assumption was first made by the BEA in the 1972 commodity-by-commodity Leontief inverse, which they refer to as the commodity-by-commodity total requirements. This modified industry technology assumption is referred to in this appendix as the BEA method.

The BEA published, in the 1972 and 1977 input-output accounts, the make and use tables, commodity-by-commodity input coefficient table, commodity-by-industry input coefficient table, commodity-by-commodity inverse table, and industry-by-commodity inverse table. The BEA has not published any commodity-by-commodity input-output table in complete form to-date. This appendix, therefore, presents a U.S. commodity-by-commodity input-output table in complete form, in order to extend the BEA method.

Further, this appendix makes a comparison of the input-output tables and technology coefficients derived from the alternative assumptions.

For the sake of brevity, this appendix is primarily confined to the U.S. 1977 input-output accounts, which are now the most up-to-date version available. The method employed in the appendix may also be applied for calculations based on the U.S. 1972 input-output accounts, since the BEA has used the same method in compiling the 1972 and 1977 input-output tables.

In section 2 of this appendix the U.S. 1977 aggregated 9-sector make and use tables, which reflect the main characteristics of the U.S. input-output experience, are compiled.

In section 3, the three alternative mathematical methods for deriving commodity-by-commodity input-output tables are briefly discussed. In this section it is made clear that the straight-forward extension of the BEA method for merging the use and make table results in an inconsistency. Namely, the row and column sums are not identical. Theoretically, this is an important consideration. On a practical level, however, this may be compensated for by assigning a fictitious row to the input-output table.

In section 4, the U.S. 1977 aggregated commodity-by-commodity input-output tables, based on the BEA and the SNA industry technology assumption, are presented and compared to verify the theoretical assertion mentioned above.

In this section, only the aggregated version of the U.S. 1977 input-output table is presented. However, in Kuboniwa et al. (1986), the 85-sector version of the U.S. 1977 commodity-by-commodity input-output table, based on the extended BEA method, is included for reference. As far as the author is aware, this is the first time the U.S. 1977 commodity-by-commodity input-output table has been presented for publication.

In section 5, commodity-by-commodity input coefficient tables, based on the SNA technology assumptions, are presented. Comparisons of input-output-related tables are also presented. These comparisons are confined only to the experimental results.

2. The U.S. 1977 Aggregated SNA Tables

In the SNA of the United Nations, there are two types of input-output tables which are classified both by commodity (goods and services) and industry (establishment). One type is the use or absorption table, and the other is the make table.

The use table shows commodity inputs by industry, and is variously referred to as the input table, U-table, input matrix, or U-matrix. The make matrix table shows commodity outputs by industry, and is often referred to as the output table, V-table, output matrix, or V-matrix, The output of the primary or characteristic product is shown on the principal diagonal of the make matrix, and the outputs of secondary products of the industry appear on the off-diagonal of the make matrix.

Combined in the U.S. use table are the so-called "use table," which shows only intermediate transactions, the final demand table by commodity, and the value-added table by industry. The U.S. make table is similar to the proto-type make matrix table proposed by the United Nations.

Definitions of notations are as follows:

j, k: commodity indexes ($j=1, 2, \ldots, n$; $k=1, 2, \ldots, n$);

h, i: industry indexes ($h=1, 2, \ldots, n$; $i=1, 2, \ldots, n$);

U: a use matrix, or an n by n commodity-by-industry matrix in which each column for an industry lists commodity inputs to produce that industry's total output and each element u_{ki} denotes the intermediate input of the k-th commodity used by the r-th industry;

V: a make matrix, or an n by n industry-by-commodity matrix in which each row for an industry lists commodity outputs produced by that industry and each element v_{ik} denotes the value of the k-th commodity produced by the i-th industry;

E: a final demand (by commodities) matrix;

e: a total final demand (by commodities) column n-vector;

Y: a value added (by industries) matrix;

y: a total value added (by industries) column n-vector;

q: a commodity output column n-vector;

235

Table 1. The SNA Input-Output Table

	Commodity	Industry	Final demand	Total final demand	Total
Commodity		U	E	e	q
Industry	V				g
Value-added		Y			
Total value-added		y'			
Total	q'	g'			

Table 2. Commodity-by-Commodity Input-Output Table

	Commodity	Final demand	Total final demand	Total
Commodity	X	E	e	q
Value-added	Z			
Total value-added	z'			
Total	q'			

g: an industry output column n-vector.

($'$) indicates the transpose of the corresponding vector.

In the SNA, use and make tables should be integrated into a system of national accounts, as shown in Table 1. In Table 1, there are three blank areas under the commodity column and one blank area under the industry column. The former are compensated for by constructing a commodity-by-commodity input-output table (see Table 2). The latter is compensated for by making an industry-by-industry intermediate transaction matrix. As the latter has only secondary importance in the input-output analysis, it is not treated in this appendix.

Table 3 shows the 1977 U.S. aggregated 9-order use table. Table 4 shows the 1977 U.S. 9-order make table. The correlation of 9-order sectoring with 85-order sectoring is also shown in Table 5. Since the aggregation level is very high, it may first appear that the importance of transferring inputs and outputs of secondary products is not an important consideration. However, as will later be shown, considering the

Table 3. The U. S. Aggregated 9-Sector Use Table, 1977

(1,000 millions of dollars at producers' prices)

Commodity \ Industry	Agriculture, forestry & fishery 1	Mining & manufacturing 2	Construction 3	Transporation & Communication 4	Trade 5	Services 6	Noncomparable imports 7	Scrap, used & secondhand goods 8	Others 9	Total intermediate use 10
1 Agriculture, forestry & fishery	32.	62.	1.	*	1.	5.	0.	0.	0.	100.
2 Mining & manufacturing	28.	685.	101.	19.	22.	97.	0.	0.	0.	953.
3 Construction	1.	15.	*	7.	3.	31.	0.	0.	0.	58.
4 Transporation & Communication	2.	39.	7.	19.	12.	19.	0.	0.	0.	99.
5 Trade	6.	60.	23.	3.	5.	16.	0.	0.	0.	113.
6 Services	12.	82.	20.	17.	67.	149.	0.	0.	0.	346.
7 Noncomparable imports	*	8.	*	4.	*	1.	0.	0.	0.	13.
8 Scrap, used & secondhand goods	0.	5.	*	*	0.	*	0.	0.	0.	5.
9 Others	0.	0.	0.	0.	0.	0.	0.	0.	0.	0.
10 Total intermediate inputs	81.	956.	153.	69.	109.	319.	0.	0.	0.	1688.
11 Compensation of employees	12.	343.	90.	71.	162.	278.	0.	0.	210.	1166.
12 Indirect business taxes	3.	34.	3.	10.	53.	63.	0.	0.	0.	166.
13 Property-type income	35.	205.	18.	38.	60.	285.	0.	0.	5.	645.
14 Total value added	49.	582.	112.	119.	275.	625.	0.	0.	215.	1977.
15 Total industry output	130.	1539.	264.	188.	384.	945.	0.	0.	215.	3664.

Sources: Survey of Current Business, May 1984.

Note: 1. (*) indicates figures less than $ 500 milion.

2. The 85-sector use table of the BEA was aggregated by the author.

237

Table 3. (continued)

Industry / Commodity	11 Personal consumption	12 Public consumption	13 Private fixed investment	14 Changes in business inventories	15 Exports	16 Imports	17 Total final demand	18 Total commodity output
1 Agriculture, forestry & fishery	11.	3.	0.	1.	13.	−3.	26.	126.
2 Mining & manufacturing	398.	70.	134.	36.	96.	−150.	583.	1536.
3 Construction	0.	56.	151.	0.	*	0.	207.	264.
4 Transportation & Communication	56.	10.	5.	1.	11.	*	83.	182.
5 Trade	223.	6.	25.	3.	12.	5.	273.	386.
6 Service	546.	42.	11.	*	9.	−1.	606.	953.
7 Noncomparable imports	9.	4.	*	*	0.	−27.	−13.	0.
8 Scrap, used & secondhand goods	6.	1.	−10.	*	2.	*	−3.	2.
9 Others	−1.	204.	0.	−19.	40.	−9.	215	215.
10 Total intermediate inputs	1246.	396.	315.	22.	182.	184.	1977.	3664.
11 Compensation of employees								
12 Indirect business taxes								
13 Property-type income								
14 Total value added								
15 Total industry output								

Table 4. The U.S. Aggregated 9-Sector Make Table, 1977
(1,000 millions of dollars at producers' prices)

Industry \ Commodity	1 Agriculture, forestry & fishery	2 Mining & manufacturing	3 Construction	4 Transportation & communication	5 Trade	6 Services	7 Noncomparable imports	8 Scrap, used & secondhand goods	9 Others	10 Total industry output
1 Agriculture, forestry & fishery	126.	4.	0.	*	0.	*	0.	0.	0.	130.
2 Mining & manufacturing	*	1518.	0.	0.	0.	19.	0.	2.	0.	1539.
3 Construction	0.	0.	264.	0.	0.	0.	0.	0.	0.	264.
4 Transportation & communication	*	1.	0.	178.	0.	8.	0.	*	0.	188.
5 Trade	0.	0.	0.	0.	384.	0.	0.	0.	0.	384.
6 Services	0.	14.	0.	3.	2.	926.	0.	0.	0.	945.
7 Noncomparable imports	0.	0.	0.	0.	0.	0.	0.	0.	0.	0.
8 Scrap, used & secondhand goods	0.	0.	0.	0.	0.	0.	0.	0.	0.	0.
9 Others	0.	0.	0.	0.	0.	0.	0.	0.	215.	215.
10 Total commodity output	126.	1536.	264.	182.	386.	953.	0.	2.	215.	3664.

Sources: Survey of Current Business, May 1984.
Note: See the footnotes in Table 3.

239

Table 5.   Correlation of 9-Sector Table with 85-Sector Table

Row and Column Code in 9-Order Tables	Corresponding Code in 85-Order Tables
1 Agriculture, forestry & fishery	1–4
2 Mining & manufacturing	5–10, 13–64, 68
3 Construction	11–12
4 Transportation & communication	65–67
5 Trade	69
6 Services	70–79
7 Noncomparable imports	80
8 Scrap, used & secondhand goods	81
9 Others	82–85

Row Code in 9-Order Tables	
10 Total intermediate inputs	86(I)
(Total commodity output in make table)	
11 Compensation of employees	88
12 Indirect business taxes	89
13 Property-type income	90
14 Total value added	87(VA)
15 Total industry/commodity output	91(T)

Column Code in 9-Order Tables	
10 Total intermediate use	86
(Total industry output in make table)	
11 Private consumption	91
12 Public consumption	90
13 Private fixed investment	91
14 Changes in business inventories	93
15 Exports	94
16 Imports	95
17 Total final demand	100
18 Total commodity output	101

different methods of transferring secondary products is quite necessary to ensure accurate calculation of the input-output tables.

The main characteristics of the U.S. SNA input-output tables are retained in the aggregated version: namely, the non-comparable import sector and the scrap, used and second-hand goods sector. The U.S. use table is primarily based on the competitive import method. However, it can be seen that the U.S. use table also partially employs the non-competitive import treatment. As this feature of the U.S. input-output table is common to all U.S. input-output tables since 1958, it is not necessary to fully discuss this feature in detail. A more important feature that should be addressed is the treatment of the scrap, used and second-hand goods sector.

In the U.S. SNA tables, the output of scrap, used and second-hand goods conforms to the SNA recommendation, even though it is included in the trade sectors. Transactions of scrap, used and second-hand goods are treated explicitly. According to the U.S. treatment, the value of scrap, used and second-hand goods is separated into a trade margin which includes dealers' margins, traditional transaction margins and the producers' values. In the use table, scrap, used and second-hand goods in producers' values are listed as inputs purchased by the intermediate users. However, in the final demand quadrant, in addition to purchases being entered as positive values, sales by final demand sectors are also entered as negative values. The net value of this row is therefore equal to the values of scrap, used and second-hand goods sold, or produced by the intermediate sectors, which are recorded separately in a column of the make table (UNSO (1985)). For the derivation of the tables by merging the use and make table, sales of scrap, used and second-hand goods are assumed to be proportional to industry outputs. This point is discussed in detail in the following section.

In regard to the make table, it should also be noted that the column for "construction" contains "0" elements for all the sectors other than the construction sector. Before merging the SNA tables, the BEA has redefined construction as a secondary product of all industries when compiling the SNA tables. Namely, construction as a secondary product is redefined; that is the secondary products and associated inputs are excluded from the industry that produced them, and are included in the industry where it was primary. This is based on the assumption that the input coefficients applicable to the re-defined product are similar to those of the industry to which the product is primary. This implies that the BEA partially applies the commodity technology assumption to the original data-source when compiling the SNA use and make tables (BEA (1984, p. 51)). In other countries, such as the Federal Republic of Germany, this type of transfer is performed when the SNA tables are merged, rather than when the SNA tables are compiled. Therefore, the ratio of the value of secondary products to the total industry output in the U.S. make table is rather low. For example, in the aggregated 9-sector table, the value is less than 1%.

3. SNA Technology Assumptions and the BEA Method

As previously mentioned, the SNA formulated two alternative assumptions to merge the SNA input-output tables:

(a). Commodity technology assumption: a commodity is assumed to have the same input structure, regardless of the industry in which it is produced. Namely, the inputs required to produce or make a given commodity are not affected by the industry in which the commodity is produced.

(b). Industry technology assumption: an industry is assumed to have the same input structure, regardless of its product mix. Namely, the composition of an industry's inputs is not affected by the composition of its output.

Basic input-output relations of the SNA input-output model are expressed by the following six equations (i denotes an aggregation vector $(1 \ldots 1)'$ and ($\hat{\ }$) for a vector denotes a diagonal matrix where the elements of the vector appear on the main diagonal):

Balance-equations:

$$q = Ui + e, \qquad (a.1)$$

$$q = V'i, \qquad (a.2)$$

$$g = Vi. \qquad (a.3)$$

Technology-equations:

$$U = B\hat{g}, \qquad (a.4)$$

$$V = C\hat{g}, \qquad (a.5)$$

$$V = D\hat{q}, \qquad (a.6)$$

where

B: a commodity-by-industry input coefficient matrix in which an element in each column denotes a commodity input absorbed by an industry to produce a unit of the industry output;

C: a commodity-by-industry output coefficient matrix in which elements in each column denote for a given industry the proportion of commodity outputs produced by that industry;

D: an industry-by-commodity output coefficient matrix, or a market share matrix, in which elements in each column denote for a given commodity the shares of that commodity produced by each industry to the total output of that commodity.

Eqs. (a. 4) and (a. 5) constitute the commodity technology assumption while Eqs. (a. 4) and (a. 6) constitute the industry technology assumption. Eq. (a. 6) implies that the market shares assumption is associated with the industry technology assumption.

If we employ the commodity technology assumption, commodity-by-commodity input coefficient matrix A is derived as follows:

Using Eqs. (a. 1), (a. 2), (a. 4) and (a. 5), we have

$$\begin{aligned} q &= Ui + e \\ &= Bg + e \\ &= BC^{-1}q + e. \end{aligned} \qquad (a.7)$$

In view of Eqs. (a. 4) and (a. 5), we can easily get

$$BC^{-1} = U(V')^{-1}.$$

Hence, the commodity-by-commodity input coefficient matrix A^{COM} is calculated by the following formulas:

$$A^{COM} = BC^{-1}, \text{ or } A^{COM} = U(V')^{-1} \qquad (a.8)$$

On the other hand, if we employ the industry technology assumption, matrix A is derived as follows:

$$q = Ui + e$$
$$= Bg + e$$
$$= BDq + e. \qquad (a.9)$$

Hence, the commodity-by-commodity input-output matrix A^{IND} is calculated by using the following formula:

$$A^{IND} = BD. \qquad (a.10)$$

Once the A matrix is derived, the first quadrant of the commodity-by-commodity input-output table X can be easily obtained through the following equation using the given total commodity output vector q:

$$X = A\hat{q}; \ X = A^{COM}\hat{q}, \ or \ X = A^{IND}\hat{q}. \qquad (a.11)$$

It follows from this equation that X can also be calculated as follows:

The commodity technology assumption:

$$X = A^{COM}\hat{q}$$
$$= U(V')^{-1}\hat{q}$$
$$= U(\hat{q}^{-1}D')^{-1}\hat{q}$$
$$= U(D')^{-1}. \qquad (a.12)$$

The industry technology assumption :

$$X = A^{IND}\hat{q}$$
$$= BD\hat{q}$$
$$= U\hat{g}^{-1}V\hat{q}^{-1}\hat{q}$$
$$= UC'. \qquad (a. 13)$$

The second quadrant of the commodity-by-commodity input-output table is the same as the second quadrant of the use table (E, e). The third quadrant of the commodity-by-commodity input-output table, that is, the *primary inputs* matrix or value-added matrix, is calculated by using the same method as the *intermediate inputs* matrix X:

The cost equation by industry is written as

$$g' = y' + i'B\hat{g}. \qquad (a.14)$$

The cost equation by commodity is written as

$$q' = z' + i'A\hat{q}. \qquad \text{(a.15)}$$

The commodity technology assumption:
Postmultiplying Eq. (a. 15) by D' and using Eq. (a. 5), we have

$$g' = z'D' + i'B\hat{g}. \qquad \text{(a.16)}$$

It follows from a comparison of Eqs. (a. 14) with (a. 15) that

$$y' = z'D'; \; z = y'(D')^{-1}. \qquad \text{(a.17)}$$

In a similar manner we have

$$Y = ZD'; \; Z = Y(D')^{-1}. \qquad \text{(a.18)}$$

The industry technology assumption:
Postmultiplying Eq. (a. 15) by $(C')^{-1}$ and employing the same method in the above, we have

$$y' = z'(C')^{-1}; \; z' = y'C', \qquad \text{(a.19)}$$

and

$$Y = Z(C')^{-1}; \; Z = YC'.$$

The BEA made a slight modification to the industry technology assumption. This modification is relevant only to the scrap, used and second-hand goods sector.

Let us now introduce the following notations:

V^{US}: a modified make matrix in which the column for scrap, used and secondhand goods has only zero elements;

D^{US}: a modified market share matrix in which the column for scrap, used and second-hand goods has only zero elements;

s: a scrap output column vector in which each element denotes each industry's total output of scrap, used and second-hand goods;

r: a scrap coefficients column vector in which each element denotes the ratio of the value of scrap produced by each industry to that industry's total output.

The relation between V and V^{US} is described as follows:

$$V=\begin{bmatrix} \cdots\cdots & & \cdots \\ \cdots\cdots & s & \cdots \\ \cdots\cdots & & \cdots \end{bmatrix} \overset{\text{scrap, used and second-hand goods}}{} \qquad \Rightarrow \qquad V^{US}=V-\begin{bmatrix} O & s & O \end{bmatrix}.$$

The input-output equations of the BEA input-output model are as follows:

Balance-equations:

$$q = Ui + e, \tag{a.20}$$

$$g = V^{US}i + s. \tag{a.21}$$

Equations for technology assumptions:

$$U = B\hat{g}, \tag{a.22}$$

$$V^{US} = D^{US}\hat{q}, \tag{a.23}$$

$$s = \hat{r}g. \tag{a.24}$$

Eq. (a. 23) implies that the industry technology assumption is not applicable to scrap, used and second-hand goods. Eq. (a. 24) implies that scrap output in each industry is proportional to that industry's output. The BEA treats scrap in such a way as to prevent its requirement as an input from generating output in the industries in which it originates. The BEA bases its treatment of scrap on the concept that scrap does not constitute an ordinary industry. Namely, in the commodity-by-commodity input-output framework, the scrap sector does not use any commodity as intermediate inputs to "produce" its product.

When we employ the BEA method, or the modified industry technology assumption, matrix A is derived as follows:

Using Eqs. (a. 20) and (a. 22), we have

$$q = Bg + e. \tag{a.25}$$

Postmultiplying Eq. (a. 23) by i and considering Eqs. (a. 21) and (a.

24), we have

$$D^{US}q = g - s$$
$$= g - \hat{r}g,$$

and thus

$$g = (I - \hat{r})^{-1} D^{US} q. \qquad (\text{a.26})$$

Define

$$\tilde{D} = (I - \hat{r})^{-1} D^{US}. \qquad (\text{a.27})$$

Substituting (a. 26) into (a. 25) and using (a. 27), we then have

$$q = B\tilde{D}q + e. \qquad (\text{a.28})$$

Hence, the commodity-by-commodity input-output matrix A is calculated by using the following formula:

$$A^{BEA} = B\tilde{D}. \qquad (\text{a.29})$$

Given that the A matrix is derived, the first quadrant of the commodity-by-commodity input-output table X can be easily obtained through the following equation, using the given total commodity output vector q:

$$X = A^{BEA} \hat{q}. \qquad (\text{a.30})$$

The BEA derived one of the fundamental equations of the conventional input-output model; the production equation. However, the BEA did not refer to the other fundamental equation; namely the cost equation, which is necessary to create a commodity-by-commodity input-output model. The straight-forward extension of the BEA method will provide us with primary input data by commodities.

It follows from Eq. (a. 30) that X can also be calculated as follows:

$$\begin{aligned} X &= A^{BEA} \hat{q} \\ &= B\tilde{D}\hat{q} \\ &= U\hat{g}^{-1}(I - \hat{r})^{-1} V^{US} \\ &= U\tilde{C}', \end{aligned} \qquad (\text{a.31})$$

where

$$\tilde{C} = [(I - \hat{r})^{-1} V^{US}]' \hat{g}^{-1} . \tag{a.32}$$

The third quadrant of the commodity-by-commodity input-output table, the primary inputs matrix, or value-added matrix, should be calculated by using the same method as the intermediate inputs matrix X:

$$z' = y' \tilde{C}; $$
$$Z = Y\tilde{C} . \tag{a.33}$$

However, this straight-forward extension results in an asymmetry. Namely, the duality of the production equation and the associated cost equation is lost:

Define

$$\tilde{q} = [(I - \hat{r})^{-1} V^{US}]' i . \tag{a.34}$$

The cost equation by industry is written as

$$g' = y' + i' B\hat{g} . \tag{a.35}$$

On the other hand, the cost equation by commodity is written as

$$\tilde{q}' = z' + i' A^{BEA} \hat{q} . \tag{a.36}$$

Postmultiplying Eq. (a. 36) by $(C')^{-1}$ and considering $g = C^{-1}q$ and $A^{BEA} = BD$, we have

$$\begin{aligned} g' &= z'(\tilde{C})^{-1} + i' B\tilde{D}\hat{q}(\tilde{C})^{-1} \\ &= z'(\tilde{C})^{-1} + i' B(I - \hat{r})^{-1}(V^{US})^{-1}V(I - \hat{r})\hat{g} \\ &= z'(\tilde{C})^{-1} + i' B\hat{g} . \end{aligned} \tag{a.37}$$

Comparing Eqs. (a. 35) and (a. 37), we have

$$y' = z'(\tilde{C})^{-1}; \ Y = \tilde{C}^{-1}Z .$$

Thus Eq. (a. 33) can be derived. However, the cost equation by commodity is now different from Eq. (a. 15). q is not identical to $\tilde{q}$ if some element of scrap coefficients vector r is positive. This problem may be eliminated if we assign a row vector to compensate for the difference between q and $\tilde{q}$ in the commodity-by-commodity input-output table.

Let a column vector for the adjustment of computational discrepancy be

$$h = q - \tilde{q}. \tag{a.38}$$

Then Eq, (a. 36) can be rewritten as

$$q' = h' + z' + i' A^{BEA} \hat{q}. \tag{a.39}$$

4. The U.S. 1977 Commodity-by-Commodity Input-Output Table

Employing the extended BEA method, we merged the U.S. 1977 SNA tables. The aggregated 9–sector version of the merged commodity-by-commodity input-output table is shown in Table 6.

It can be seen in Table 6 that:

(1) The BEA method does not include a column for the scrap sector, but does include a row; i.e., 2 billion dollars.

(2) The l6th row (for statistical adjustment) contains negative elements. Column 2, row 16 (mining and manufacturing) contains a negative element; i.e., minus 2.

On the other hand, in a commodity-by-commodity input-output table based on the 'pure' industry technology assumption (Table 7), the scrap sector is treated in a manner similar to other industry/commodity sectors. The adjustment row contains only zero elements, therefore, no further adjustment is required.

These facts verify the theoretical considerations developed in the previous section. It follows then that the scrap sector should not be assigned as an ordinary industry/commodity, since the scrap industry produces a positive output with no inputs; the primary characteristic of the scrap, used and second-hand sector. We can therefore conclude that in the case of the U.S. SNA accounts, the extended BEA method is more suitable than the 'pure' industry technology assumption from an economic point of view, although the latter appears to be more sophisticated in its approach.

Table 8 shows the relative deviation of the input-output table, based on the extended BEA method and the table based on the 'pure' industry

Table 6. The U.S. Aggregated Commodity-by-Commodity Input-Output Table, 1977: The BEA Method
(1,000 millions of dollars at producers' prices)

Commodity	1 Agriculture, forestry & fishery	2 Mining & manufacturing	3 Construction	4 Transportation & Communication	5 Trade	6 Services	7 Noncomparable imports	8 Scrap, used & secondhand goods	9 Others	10 Total intermediate use	17 Total final demand	18 Gross domestic output
1 Agriculture, forestry & fishery	31.	63.	1.	*.	1.	5.	0.	0.	0.	100.	26.	126.
2 Mining & manufacturing	27.	679.	101.	19.	22.	105.	0.	0.	0.	953.	583.	1536.
3 Construction	1.	16.	*.	6.	3.	31.	0.	0.	0.	58.	207.	264.
4 Transportation & Communication	2.	39.	7.	18.	12.	20.	0.	0.	0.	99.	83.	182.
5 Trade	5.	59.	23.	3.	3.	17.	0.	0.	0.	113.	273.	386.
6 Services	11.	84.	20.	17.	67.	148.	0.	0.	0.	347.	606.	953.
7 Noncomparable imports	*.	8.	*.	4.	*.	1.	0.	0.	0.	13.	−13.	0.
8 Scrap, used & secondhand goods	0.	5.	*.	*.	0.	*.	0.	0.	0.	5.	−3.	2.
9 Others	0.	0.	0.	0.	0.	0.	0.	0.	0.	0.	215.	215.
10 Total intermediate inputs	78.	952.	153.	67.	110.	328.	0.	0.	0.	1688.	1977.	3664.
11 Compensation of employees	11.	344.	90.	68.	163.	280.			210.	1166.		
12 Indirect business taxes	3.	35.	3.	10.	53.	62.			0.	166.		
13 Property-type income	34.	207.	18.	37.	60.	283.			5.	645.		
14 Total value added	48.	586.	112.	115.	276.	625.			215.	1977.		
15 Total commodity output	126.	1538.	264.	182.	386.	953.			215.	3666.		
16 Adjustment	0.	−2.	0.	*.	0.	*.		2.	0.	−2.		
17 Total commodity output (15+16)	126.	1536.	264.	182.	386.	953.	0.	2.	215.	3664.		

Notes: 1. (*) indicates figures less than $ 500 million.
2. The final demand quadrant of this input-output table is similar to that of the use table (Table 3), and was therefore omitted.

250

THE U.S. 1977 COMMODITY-BY-COMMODITY INPUT-OUTPUT TABLE

Table 7. The U.S. Aggregated Commodity-by-Commodity Input-Output Table, 1977: The Industry Technology Assumption (1,000 millions of dollars at producers' prices)

Commodity	1 Agriculture, forestry & fishery	2 Mining & manufacturing	3 Construction	4 Transportation & communication	5 Trade	6 Services	7 Noncomparable imports	8 Scrap, used & secondhand goods	9 Others	10 Total intermediate use	17 Total final demand	18 Gross domestic output
1 Agriculture, forestry & fishery	31.	62.	1.	0.	1.	5.	0.	*	0.	100.	26.	126.
2 Mining & manufacturing	27.	678.	101.	19.	22.	105.	0.	1.	0.	953.	583.	1536.
3 Construction	1.	16.	*	6.	3.	31.	0.	*	0.	58.	207.	264.
4 Transportation & communication	2.	39.	7.	18.	12.	20.	0.	*	0.	99.	83.	182.
5 Trade	5.	59.	23.	3.	5.	17.	0.	*	0.	113.	273.	386.
6 Services	11.	84.	20.	17.	67.	148.	0.	*	0.	347.	606.	953.
7 Noncomparable imports	*	8.	*	4.	*	1.	0.	*	0.	13.	−13.	0.
8 Scrap, used & secondhand goods	0.	5.	*	*	0.	*	0.	0.	0.	5.	−3.	2.
9 Others	0.	0.	0.	0.	0.	0.	0.	0.	0.	0.	215.	215.
10 Total intermediate inputs	78.	951.	153.	67.	110.	328.	0.	1.	0.	1688.	1977.	3664.
11 Compensation of employees	11.	343.	90.	68.	163.	280.	0.	1.	210.	1166.		
12 Indirect business taxes	3.	35.	3.	10.	53.	62.	0.	0.	0.	166.		
13 Property-type income	34.	207.	18.	37.	60.	283.	0.	0.	5.	645.		
14 Total value added	48.	585.	112.	115.	276.	625.	0.	1.	215.	1977.		
15 Total commodity output	126.	1536.	264.	182.	386.	953.	0.	2.	215.	3664.		
16 Adjustment	0.	0.	0.	0.	0.	0.	0.	0.	0.	0.		
17 Total commodity output (15+16)	126.	1536.	264.	182.	386.	953.	0.	2.	215.	3664.		

Notes: See the footnote in Table 6.

251

Table 8. Relative Deviation of the I-O Table Based on the Extended BEA Method and the I-O Table Based on the Industry Technology Assumption (unit: %)

	1	2	3	4	5	6	7	8	9
1	0.0	0.14	0.0	0.0	0.0	0.02	0.0	−100.00	0.0
2	0.0	0.14	0.0	0.03	0.0	0.01	0.0	−100.00	0.0
3	0.0	0.13	0.0	0.03	0.0	0.0	0.0	−100.00	0.0
4	0.0	0.14	0.0	0.04	0.0	0.00	0.0	−100.00	0.0
5	0.0	0.14	0.0	0.04	0.0	0.01	0.0	−100.00	0.0
6	0.0	0.14	0.0	0.03	0.0	0.00	0.0	−100.00	0.0
7	0.0	0.14	0.0	0.03	0.0	0.0	0.0	−100.00	0.0
8	0.0	0.13	0.0	0.0	0.0	0.0	0.0	−100.00	0.0
9	0.0	0.0	0.0	0.0	0.0	0.0	0.0	0.0	0.0
10	0.0	0.14	0.0	0.04	0.0	0.01	0.0	−100.00	0.0
11	0.0	0.14	0.0	0.04	0.0	−0.03	0.0	−100.00	0.0
12	0.0	0.13	0.0	0.03	0.0	−0.00	0.0	−100.00	0.0
13	0.0	0.12	0.0	0.04	0.0	0.00	0.0	−100.00	0.0
14	0.0	0.13	0.0	0.04	0.0	−0.01	0.0	−100.00	0.0
15	0.0	0.14	0.0	0.04	0.0	−0.01	0.0	−100.00	0.0
16	0.0	****	0.0	****	0.0	****	0.0	****	0.0

Notes: 1. (****) indicates 'overflow'.
2. The sectoring of the Table corresponds to that of Table 6 or 7.

technology assumptions.[1] As can easily be seen, the respective intermediate transactions of the 2nd, 4th and 6th sectors in Table 6 are inflated, as compared with Table 7. The primary inputs of the 2nd and 4th sectors are also inflated. These inflation ratios by each column sector are uniform. The 8th sector, (the scrap sector), has a value of -100% to compensate for this inflation.

In this section, only the aggregated commodity-by-commodity input-output table is presented. In Kuboniwa et al. (1986), the 85-sector version of the U.S. 1977 input-output table, based on the extended BEA method, is included. With regard to this table, it should be noted that the

[1] The relative deviation between the matrixes $A^{(1)} = (a_{ij}^{(1)})$ and $A^{(2)} = (a_{ij}^{(2)})$ is defined as
$$r_{ij} = (a_{ij}^{(2)} - a_{ij}^{(1)})/a_{ij}^{(1)}.$$
If $a_{ij}^{(1)}$ and $a_{ij}^{(2)}$ are equal to zero, we define $r_{ij} = 0$. If $a_{ij}^{(1)}$ is zero but $a_{ij}^{(2)}$ not zero, we denote r_{ij} as ****.

Table 9.   Exclusion of the Inputs of the CCC from Federal Government
Enterprises; Column Code 78(1977)

(millions of dollars at producers' prices)

Industry Commodity	(1) Inputs of the FGE Column 78	(2) Imputs of the CCC	(1)−(2) Revised Inputs of the FGE
2 Other agricultutal products	124	108.4	15.6
14 Food & kindred products	490	− 29.6	519.6
27 Chemicals & selected chemical products	2166	.1	2165.9
65 Transportation & warehousing	1360	129.0	1231.0
69 Wholesale & retail trade	253	.8	252.2
78 Federal government enterprises	289	81.3	207.7
90 Property-type income	− 673	− 290.0	− 383.0
Total	—	0.0	—

Sourcs: BEA *IED 84-001, p. 5*
Notes: FGE: = Federal Government Enterprises
CCC: = Commodity Credit Corporation

inputs of the commodity credit corporation are excluded from the federal
government enterprise column. This corresponds to the method used by
the BEA in deriving the commodity-by-industry input coefficient matrix
B, to eliminate instability. This exclusion is shown in Table 9.

5. A Comparison of the SNA Technology Assumptions

When we compare the input-output-related matrixes, based on the
"pure" SNA technology assumptions, using the U.S. use and make tables,
we must omit "special" industries or commodities, such as non-comparable imports, scrap, used and second-hand goods, and the "others"
sector. In performing the calculations for the 9– sector table, it should be
noted that the three sectors listed above have been omitted, and not
aggregated into 6 sectors. This procedure has been taken since the make
matrix, which includes the three omitted sectors, does not have an
inverse matrix. It can be seen then, that when the commodity technology
assumption is employed, it is assumed that the matrix has an inverse.

Table 10 shows the commodity-by-commodity input coefficient ma-

Table 10.　Commodity-by-Commodity Input Coefficient Matrix, 1977
Commodity Technology Assumption: A^{COM}

	1	2	3	4	5	6
1	0.2520	0.0410	0.0025	−0.0005	0.0017	0.0044
2	0.2084	0.4503	0.3838	0.1011	0.0570	0.0982
3	0.0107	0.0097	0.0011	0.0353	0.0067	0.0336
4	0.0171	0.0255	0.0262	0.1057	0.0322	0.0201
5	0.0432	0.0392	0.0884	0.0150	0.0129	0.0167
6	0.0909	0.0521	0.0756	0.0892	0.1733	0.1594

Industry Technology Assumption: A^{IND}

	1	2	3	4	5	6
1	0.2457	0.0406	0.0025	0.0002	0.0017	0.0056
2	0.2153	0.4415	0.3838	0.1034	0.0572	0.1100
3	0.0107	0.0102	0.0011	0.0350	0.0068	0.0327
4	0.0174	0.0254	0.0262	0.0999	0.0322	0.0213
5	0.0431	0.0387	0.0884	0.0153	0.0130	0.0175
6	0.0899	0.0544	0.0756	0.0932	0.1732	0.1550

Notes: 1.　Sectoring corresponds to the 9-order tables.
　　　　2.　These matrixes were derived from Table 3 and 4 by omitting sectors 7, 8 and 9.

trixes derived from the aggregated U.S. SNA tables, based on the "pure" commodity technology assumption and the "pure" industry technology assumption.

It can be seen that the input coefficient matrix, based on the commodity technology assumption has a well-known defect;the input coefficient matrix has a negative element.

In this aggregated version, only one element has a negative value. However, in the 85–order version, more than 100 elements have a negative value. Therefore, it is not possible to derive meaningful results by mechanical use of the commodity technology assumption.

Table 11 shows the relative deviation between the two input coefficient matrixes, based on the commodity technology assumption and the industry technology assumption. It should be noted that the figure in row 1, column 4 of Table 11 contains a significant negative value. This is due to

Table 11.   Relative Deviation between A^{COM} and A^{IND} (unit: %)

	1	2	3	4	5	6
1	2.56	.99	.00	−350.00	.00	−21.43
2	−3.20	1.99	.00	−2.22	−.35	−10.73
3	.00	−4.90	.00	.86	−1.47	2.75
4	−1.72	.39	.00	5.81	.00	−5.63
5	.23	1.29	.00	−1.96	−.77	−4.57
6	1.11	−4.23	.00	−4.29	.06	2.84
	1.47	2.30	.00	60.86	.44	7.99

Notes: 1.   See the footnotes in Table 10.
    2.   Each Entry of the last row shows an 'average' of each absolute column sum.

Table 12.   Relative Development of the Commodity-by-Commodity Input-Output Tables Based on the Commodity Technology Assumption and the Industry Technology Assumption   (unit: %)

	1	2	3	4	5	6
1	2.59	.88	.00	−403.45	−.93	−21.41
2	−3.17	2.00	.00	−2.15	−.37	−10.77
3	.07	−5.01	.00	.85	−1.76	2.56
4	−1.60	.40	.00	5.75	.16	−5.56
5	.33	1.37	.00	−1.80	−.14	−4.20
6	1.18	−4.23	.00	−4.21	.04	2.84
7	.00	.00	.00	.00	.00	.00
8	.00	.00	.00	.00	.00	.00
9	.00	.00	.00	.00	.00	.00
10	.08	1.13	.00	−.27	−.08	−2.83
11	−4.69	−.46	.00	1.74	.14	−.42
12	−.26	−4.12	.00	−1.05	.23	2.37
13	1.50	−2.86	.00	−2.91	−.42	2.48
14	−.07	−1.53	.00	.01	.03	1.55
15	.02	.12	.00	−.09	.00	.04
	1.04	1.61	.00	28.29	.29	3.80

Notes: 1.   Sectoring corresponds to the 9-order tables.
    2.   Each Entry of the last row shows an 'average' of each absolute column sum.

255

the negative value of the figure contained in row 1, column 4 in Table 10. In addition, the "services" sector also shows significant deviations. Namely, the input structure of the "services" sector has a significant deviation between the commodity technology assumption and the industry technology assumption. However, the difference is not significant, when compared to the tables of other countries, such as West Germany. This is due to the characteristics of the U.S. use and make tables. In these tables, some subsidiary products, such as construction, have already been transferred.

Table 12 shows the relative deviation between the commodity-by-commodity input-output tables based on the two assumptions. It can be seen from this table that the trends and results obtained by the comparison are similar.

REFERENCES

Åberg, M. and Persson, H. (1981), "A Note on a Closed Input-Output Model with Finite Life-Times and Gestation Lags," *Journal of Economic Theory*, 24, 446–452.

Abouchar, A. ed. (1977), *The Socialist Price Mechanism*, North Carolina.

Aganbegian, A. G. (1987), *Perestroika ekonomiki v SSSR* (forthcoming), Moscow. (The Japanese version was published in 1988, prior to the Russian version.)

Aganbegian, A. G. ed. (1987), *Reforma upravleniia ekonomikoi*, Moscow.

Aganbegian, A. G. and Bagrinovsky, K. A. (1968), "Teoremy o vzaimnykh zadachakh matematicheskogo programmirovaniia," Bagrinovsky, K. A. ed., *Matematicheskie metody v ekonomike*, Novosibirsk.

Aganbegian, A. G. and Bagrinovsky, K. A. (1972a), "The System of Optimal Intersectoral Models," in Brody and Carter (1972), 435–448.

Aganbegian, A. G., Bagrinovsky, K. A. and Granberg, A. G. (1972b), *Sistema modelei norodnokhoziaistvennogo planirovaniia*, Moscow.

Al'-Ashkar, A. (1974), *Analiz dinamiki proizvodstva v optimizatsionnykh mezhotraslevykh modeliakh* (Dis. na soisk. uchen. step. kand. ekon. nauk), Moscow.

Albegov, M. M., Volkonsky, V. A. and Gofman, K. G. (1987), "Optimizatsionnyi realizm ili ekonomichesky nigilizm ?," *Ekonomika i matematicheskie metody*, No. 4.

Allen, R. I. G. (1974), "Experiments with the RAS Method of Updating Input-Output Coefficients," *Oxford Bulletin of Economics and Statistics*, 36(3), 215–228.

Alton, T. (1977), "Comparative Structure and Growth of Economic Activity in Eastern Europe," in JEC, *East European Economies Post-Helsinki*.

Anchishkin, A. I. (1973), *Prognozirovanie rosta sotsialisticheskoi ekonomiki*, Moscow.

Anchishkin, A. I. (1986), "Novoe kachestvo ekonomicheskogo rosta," *Voprocy*

REFERENCES

ekonomiki, No. 9.

Arrow, K. J. and Hurwicz, L. (1960), "Decentralization and Computation in Resource Allocation," in Pfouts, R. W. ed., *Essays in Economics and Econometrics*, North Carolina.

Arrow, K. J. and Hurwicz, L. (1977), *Studies in Resource Allocation Processes*, London.

Baranov, E. F. and Matlin, I. S. (1976), "Ob eksperimental'noi realizatsii sistemy modelei optimal'nogo perspektivnogo planirovaniia," *Ekonomika i matematicheskie metody*, No. 4.

Barengol'ts, M. (1928), "Emkost' promyshlennogo rynka SSSR," *Planovoe khoziaistvo*, No. 7.

Bazarov, V. (1927), *Kapitalisticheskie tsikly i vostanovitelnyi khoziaistva USRR*, Moscow-Leningrad.

BEA; Interindustry Economics Division of Bureau of Economic Analysis, U. S. Department of Çommerce (1979), "The Input-Output Structure of the U. S. Economy, 1972," *Survey of Current Business*, Feb.

BEA; Interindustry Economics Division of Bureau of Economic Analysis, U. S. Department of Commerce (1984), "The Input-Output Structure of the U. S. Economy, 1977," *Survey of Current Business*, May.

BEA; Staff Paper (1979), "Mathematical Derivation of the Total Requirements Tables for the 1972 Input-Output Study."

Belen'ky, V. Z. and Volkonsky, V. A. ed. (1974), *Iterativnye metody v teorii igr i programmirovanii*, Moscow.

Belkin, V. D. (1963), *Tseny edinogo urovnia i ekonomicheskie izmereniia na ikh osnove*, Moscow.

Belkin, V. D. (1972), *Ekonomicheskie izmereniia i planirovanie*, Moscow.

Belkin, V. D. (1988), "Mify i pravda o sotsialisticheskom tsenoobrazovanii," *Kommunist*, No. 1.

Belkin, V. D. et al. (1965), "Ischislenie ratsional'nykh tsen na osnove covremennoi ekonomicheskoi informatsii," *Ekonomika i matematicheskie metody*, No. 5, 1965.

Belkin, V. D. and Ivanter, V. V. (1983), *Planovaia sbalansirovannost'*, Moscow.

REFERENCES

Belkin, V. D., Medvedev, P. A. and Nit, I. V. (1986), "Perekhod k optovoi torgovle produktsiei proizvodstvenno-tekhnicheskogo naznacheniia: sostavliaiushchaia ekonomicheskoi reformy," *Ekonomika i matematicheskie metody*, No. 6.

Berezneva, T. D. (1976), "Nekotorye asimptoticheskie cvoistva optimal'nykh traektorii dinamicheskoi mezhtraslevoi modeli," *Ekonomika i matematicheskie metody*, No. 4.

Berman, A. and Plemmons R. J. (1979), *Nonnegative Matrices in the Mathematical Sciences*, New York.

Boiarsky A. G. (1957), "Sebestoimost' i stoimost'," *Voprosy ekonomiki, planirovaniia i ctatistiki*, Moscow.

Bornstein, M. (1987), "Soviet Price Policies," *Soviet Economy*, 3(2), 96–134.

Borozdin, Iu (1987), "Zakon stoimosti i tsena v sotsialisticheskom khoziaistve," *Voprosy ekonomiki*, No. 12.

Brody, A. (1970), *Proportions, Prices and Planning*, Amsterdam.

Brody, A. and Carter, A. P. ed. (1972), *Input-Output Techniques*, Amsterdam.

Brus, W. (1967), *The Market in the Socialist Economy*, Warsaw.

Cave, M. (1980), *Computers and Economic Planning: the Soviet Experience*, London.

Cave, M., McAuley, A. and Thornton, J. ed. (1982), *New Trends in Soviet Economics*, New York.

Chenery, H. B. and Watanabe, T. (1958), "International Comparisons of the Structure of Production," *Econometrica*, Oct., 487–521.

Cheremnykh, Ia. N. (1982), *Analiz povedeniia traektrii dinamiki narodnokhoziaistvennykh modelei*, Moscow.

Cheremnykh, Ia. N. (1986), *Matematicheskie modeli razvitiia narodnogo koziaistva*, Moscow.

Dadaian, V. S. (1970), *Ekonomicheskie zakony sotsializma i optimal'nye resheniia*, Moscow. [German edition: *Oekonomische Gesetze des Sozialismus und Optimale Entsheidungen*, Berlin, 1973.]

Dadaian, V. S. ed. (1973), *Modelirovanie narodnokhoziaistvennykh protsessov*, Moscow.

259

REFERENCES

Danilov-Danil'ian, V. I. (1987), "Metodologicheskie aspekty ischisleniia i ispol'zovaniia zamykaiushchikh zatrat," *Ekonomika i matematicheskie metody*, No. 3. [English version: *Matekon*, 24(2), 3–25.]

Dantzig, G. (1963), *Linear Programming and Extensions*, Princeton.

Dantzig, G. and Wolfe, P. (1961), "The decomposition Algorithm for Linear Programs," *Econometrica*, 767–778.

Dement'ev, N. P. (1982), "Obobshchennye magistrali v modeliakh Leontieva s peremennoi tekhnologiei," *Izvestiia sibirskogo otdeleniia AN SSSR*, No.6.

Dement'ev, N. P. (1986), *Generalized Turnpikes in Models with Slowly Changing Technology*, (preprint), Novosibirsk.

Deriabin, A. A. (1987), "Osnovy perestroiki tsenoobrazovaniia," *Voprosy ekonomiki*, No. 1. [English version: *Problems of Economics*, July 1987, 54–69.]

Dmitriev, V. K. (1904), *Ekonomicheskie Ocherki*, Moscow. [English version: Nuti, D.M. ed. *V. K. Dmitriev Economic Essays on Value, Competition and Utility*, London, 1974.]

Domar, E. D. (1957), *Essays in the Theory of Economic Growth*, New York.

Dorfman, R., Samuelson, P. A. and Solow, R. M. (DOSSO) (1958), *Linear Programming and Economic Analysis*, New York.

Dudkin, L. M. ed. (1979), *Iterativnoe agregirovanie i ego primenenie v planirovanii*, Moscow.

Dudkin, L. M. and Ershov, E. B. (1965), "Maxhotraslevoi balans i material'nye balansy otdel'nykh produktov," *Planovoe khoziastvo*, No. 5.

Dudkin, L., Rabinovich, I. and Vakhutinsky, I. (1987), *Iterative Aggregation Theory*, New York.

ECE (1972); Conference of European Statisticians, Statistical Standards and Studies, No. 25; *Standardized Input-Output Tables of ECE Countries for Years around 1959*, United Nations, New York.

ECE (1977); Conference of European Statisticians, Statistical Standards and Studies, No. 30; *Standardized Input-Output Tables of ECE Countries for Years around 1965*, united nations, New York.

ECE (1982a); Conference of European Statisticians, Statistical Standards and Studies, No. 33; *Standardized Input-Output Tables of ECE Countries for Years around 1970*, United Nations, New York.

REFERENCES

ECE (1982b); Conference of European Statisticians, Statistical Standards and Studies, No. 34; *Standardized Input-Output Tables of ECE Countries for Years around 1975*, United Nations, New York.

Efimov, M. N. and Movshovich, S. M. (1971), "Model' sbalansirovannogo rosta. Ravnovesnye narodnokhoziaistvennye proportsii i tseny," *Pervaia konferentsiia po optimal'nomu planirovaniiu i upravleniiu narodnym kkoziaistvom, Vyp. 1*, Moscow.

Efimov, M. N. and Movshovich, S. M. (1973), "Model' sbalansirovannogo rosta v dinamicheskoi modeli narodnovo khoziaistva," *Ekonomika i matematicheskie metody*, No. 1. English version: *Matekon*, 10(4), 40–59.]

Ekonomicheskaia entsiklopediia. Politicheskaia ekonomiia., Moscow, 1972–1980.

"Ekonomicheskaia teoriia i praktika perestroiki. Na voprosy *Kommunista* otvechaiut uchenye," *Kommunist*, 1987. No. 9. [English version: *Problems of Economics*, Dec. 1987, 22–37.]

Ekonomika i matematicheskie metody. Vyp. 1. Narodnokhoziaistvennye modeli. Teoreticheskie problemy potrebleniia, Moscow.

Ellman, M. (1971), *Soviet Planning Today*, Cambridge.

Ellman, M. (1973), *Planning Problems in the USSR*, London.

Ellman, M. (1979), *Socialist Planning*, Cambridge.

Fedorenko, N. P. ed. (1972), *Problemy optimal'nogo funktsionirovaniia sotsialisticheskoi ekonomiki*, Moscow.

Fedorenko, N. P., Baranov, E. F., Danilov-Danilian, V. I. and Zavelsky, M. G. (1972), "Optimization of Intersectoral Input-Output Relations: Its theoretical Aspects," in Brody and Carter (1972), 421–434.

Feinstein, C. H. ed. (1969), *Socialism, Capitalism and Economic Growth*, London.

Fel'dman, G. A. (1928), "K teorii tempov narodnogo dokhoda," *Planovoe Khoziaistvo*, 1928, No. 11, No. 12.

Gallik, D. M. et al. (1979), "The 1972 Input-Output Table and the Changing Structure of the Soviet Economy," U. S. Congress Joint Economic Committee, *Soviet Economy in a Time of Change*, Washington, D. C.

Gallik, D. M. et al. (1983), "Input-Output Structure of the Soviet Economy: 1972," U. S. Dept. of Commerce, *Foreign Economic Report*, No. 18.

REFERENCES

Gallik, D. M. et al. (1984), "Construction of a 1977 Soviet Input-Output Table," U. S. Dept. of Commerce, CIR Staff Paper, January.

Goskomstat SSSR i Gosplan SSSR (1988), *Metodika ischisleniia valovogo natsional 'nogo produkta SSSR*, Moscow.

Granberg, A. G. (1969), "Issledovanie svoistv prostykh modelei optimizatsii mezhotraslevykh sviazei," Aganbegian, A. G. et al. ed., *Problemy narodnokhoziaistvennogo optimuma*, Moscow.

GUS (the Polish Statistical Office) (1974), *Rocznik Statyczny 1974 (Polish Statistiacl Yearbook 1974)*, Warsow.

Gustafsson, B. ed. (1979), *Post-Industrial Society*, London.

Hare, P. G. (1981), "Aggregate Planning by Means of Input-output and Material Balances Systems", *Journal of Comparative Economics* 5, 272–291.

Hare, P. (1981), "The Organization of Information Flows in Systems of Economic Planning," *Economics of Planning*. No. 1, 1–19.

Heal, G. M. (1973), *The Theory of Economic Planning*, Amsterdam and London.

Howard, R. A. (1960), *Dynamic Programming and Markov Processes*, New York.

Iahin, E. G. (1987), "Perestroika planirovaniia proizvodstva i khoziaistvennykh sviazei," *Voprosy ekonomiki*, No. 10.

Isaev, B. L. (1972), "Material-Financial Balance of a Union Republic," in Brody and Carter (1972), 277–300.

Iushkov, L. P. (1928), "Osnovnoi vopros planovoi metodologii," *Vestnik Finansov*, No. 10.

Johansen, L. (1966), "Soviet Mathematical Economics," *The Economic Journal*, Sept., 593–601.

Johansen, L. (1976), "L. V. Kantorovich's Contribution to Economics," *Scandinavian Journal of Economics*, 78(1), 61–80.

Johansen, L. (1978), *Lectures on Macroeconomic Planning* (Part 2), Amsterdam.

Johansen, L. (1978), "On the Theory of Dynamic Input-Output Models with Different Time Profiles of Capital Construction and Finite Life-Time of Capital Equipment," *Journal of Economic Theory*, 16, 513–533.

Johansen, L. (1979), "Comment [on Nove (1979)]," in Gustafsson (1979), 142–

152.

Kantorovich, L. V. (1959), "Dal'neishee razvitie matematichskikh metodov i perspektivy ikh primeneiia v planirovanii i ekonomike," in V.S. Nemchinov ed. (1959), 310–353.

Kantorovich, L. V. (1959), *Ekonomichesky raschet nailuchshego ispol'zovaniia resursov*, Moscow.

Kantorovich, L. V. (1987), "Moi put' v nauke," *Uspekhi matematicheskikh nauk*, No. 2.

Kantorovich, L. V. and Makarov, V. L. (1976), "Growth Models and Their Application to Long-Term Planning and Forecasting," in Khachaturov, T. S. ed., *Methods of Long-Term Planning and Forecasting*, London.

Katsenelinboigen, A. (1978), *Studies in Soviet Economic Planning*, New York.

Khobarova, T. (1988), "O sotsialisticheskoi modifikatsii stoimosti," *Kommunist*, No. 1.

KHS (the Hungarian Statistical Office) (1981), *Agazati Kapcsolatok Merlege 1970–1979 (1970–1979 Input-Output Tables)*, Budapest.

KHS (1987), The Hungarian Input-Output Tables, Import Matrixes and Fixed Capital Matrixes, 1970–1979, (unpublished computer printout).

Konius, A. A. (1924), "Problema istinnogo indeksa stoimosti zhizni," *Ekonomichesky biulleten' kon'iunkturnogo instituta*, No. 9–10. [English version: *Econometrica*, Jan., 1939, 10–29.]

Koopmans, T. C. (1951), "Analysis of Production as an efficient Combination of Activities," in Koopmans T. C. ed., *Activity Analysis of Production and Allocation*, New York.

Kornai, J. (1959), *Overcentralisation in Economic Administration*, London. (Original Hungarian edition was published in 1957.)

Kornai, J. (1969), "Man-Machine Planning," *Economics of Planning*, No. 3, 209–234.

Kornai, J. (1972), *Rush versus Harmonic Growth*, Amsterdam.

Kornai, J. (1981), *Economics of Shortage*, Vols. A, B, Amsterdam.

Kornai, J. (1982), *Growth, Shortage and Efficiency*, Oxford.

Kornai, J. (1986), *Contradictions and Dilemmas*, Cambridge.

REFERENCES

Kornai, J. and Liptak, T. (1965), "Two-Level Planning," *Econometrica*, 141–169.

Kostinsky, B. L. (1974), "Description and Analysis of Soviet Foreign Trade Statistics," *Foreign Economic Report*, No. 5.

Kostinsky, B. L. (1976), "The Reconstructed 1966 Soviet Input-Output Table; Revised Purchasers' and Producers' Prices Tables," *Foreign Economic report*, No. 13.

Kostinsky, B. L. (1985), "The 1982 Soviet Input-Output Table," the table presented at the 3rd World Congress for Soviet and East European Studies, Washington D. C., November 1st.

Kostinsky, B. L. and Treml, V. G. (1976), "Foreign Trade Pricing in the Soviet Union: Exports and Imports in the 1966 Input-Output Table," *Foreign Economic Report*, No. 8

Kuboniwa, M. (1982), "Survey: Dynamic Multi-Sectoral Models of Socialist Reproduction," *Keizai Kenkyu(The Economic Review)*, 33(1), 61–82 (in Japanese).

Kuboniwa, M. (1983), "A Comparison of Convergence Speed of Old and New Iterative Processes for an Input-Output System, *Discussion Paper* , No. 79 (The Institute of Economic Research, Hitotsubashi University, Kunitachi, Tokyo).

Kuboniwa, M. ed. (1984), *Economics by Micro-computer(Miconomics)*, Tokyo, (in Japanese). (The Russian version: forthcoming.)

Kuboniwa, M. (1984), "Stepwise Aggregation for Material Balances," *Journal of Comparative Economics*, 8(1), 41–53.

Kuboniwa, M. (1985), "Input-Output Structure of Soviet and East European Economies", *Keizai Kenkyu* (The Economic Review), 36(4) (in Japanese).

Kuboniwa, M. (1987), *Interv'iu s D-rom Makarovym V.L. (May 15, 1987)*, Tokyo. (Available from the author.)

Kuboniwa, M. (1988), "Iterativnoe agregirovanie v optimal'nom planirovanii," *Ekonomika i matematicheskie metody*, No. 1.

Kuboniwa, M. et al. (1985), "Soviet and East European Input-Output Tables," *Discussion Paper*, No. 131 (The Institute of Economic Research, Hitotsubashi University, (in Japanese).

Kuboniwa, M. et al. (1986), "Derivation of U. S. Commodity-by-Commodity

REFERENCES

Input-Output Tables from SNA Use and Make Tables," *Hitotsubashi Journal of Economics*, 27(1), June, 49–75.

Kuboniwa, M. and Arita, F. (1986), *ACCESS* (*Computer Programs for Input-Output Analysis: IBM-PC and Mainframe version*), Tokyo. (Available from the author.)

Kuboniwa, M. et al. (1987), *Computer Programs for Turnpike Computations: PC and Mainframe version*, Tokyo. (Available from the author.)

Kurabayashi, Y. (1977), *Studies on National Economic Accounting*, Tokyo.

Lakhman, I. L., Levin, M. I. and Polterovich, V. M. (1986), *Mekhanizm dogovornykh tsen i problemy ego sovershenstvovaniia* (Preprint), Moscow.

Latsis, O. R. (1987), *Ekonomicheskaia tsentralizatsiia i tsentralizm upravleniia*, Moscow.

Leontief, W. W. (1963), "The Structure of Development," in Leontief, W. W. *Input-Output Economics*, New York, 1966.

Levine, H. S. (1959), "The Centralized Planning of Supply in Soviet Industry." *In Comparisons of the United States and Soviet Economies*, Comp. of Papers, Joint Econ. Comm., U. S. Congress. Washington, D. C.

Lubny-Gertsyk, L. I. (1922), *O perevode kapitala v trudovye ekvivalenty*, Moscow.

Luenberger, D. G. and Arbel, A. (1977), "Singular Dynamic Leontief Systems," *Econometrica*, May.

Lur'e, A. P. (1957), "Izmerenie dinamiki proizvoditel'nosti truda pri pomoshchi tsennostnykh indeksov", *Uchenye zapiski po statistike*, Vol. III.

Makarov, V. (1987), "O razvitii ekonomiko-matematicheskogo instrumentariia na sovremennom etape," *Ekonomika i matematicheskie metody*, No. 3.

Makarov, V. L. and Rubinov, A. M. (1973), *Matematicheskaia teoriia ekonomicheskoi dinamiki i ravnovesia, Moscow*. [English Version: *Mathematical Theory of Economic Dynamics and Equilibria*, New York, 1977.]

Malinvaud, E. (1967), "Decentralized Procedures for Planning," in E. Malinvaud ed., *Activity Analysis in the Theory of Growth and Planning*, London, 170–208.

Manove, M. (1976), "Soviet Pricing, Profits and Technological Choice," *The Review of Economic Studies*, October, 413–421.

REFERENCES

Manove, M. and Weitzman, M. L. (1978), "Aggregation for Material Balances," *Journal of Comparative Economics* 2(1), March, 1–11.

Matematika i kibernetika v ekonomike: Slovar'-spravochnik, Moscow, 1975.

Matlin, I. S. and Bardina A. A. ed. (1986), *Kompleks modelei perspektivnogo planirovaniia*, Moscow.

McKenzie, L. (1963), "Turnpike Theorems for a Generalized Leontief Model," *Econometrica*, Jan.-April, 165–180.

Meier, R. and Schilar, H. (1967), "Objektiv bedingte Bewertungen (Schatten-preise) und Volkswirtschafts Modelle," *Wirtschaftswissenschaft*, No. 8.

Melent'ev, L. A., and Makarov, A. A. ed.(1983), *Energetichesky kompleks SSSR*, Moscow 1983.

Meyer, U. (1982), "Why Singularity of Dynamic Leontief Systems Doesn't Matter," in *Input-Output Techniques*, Budapest.

Miyanabe, N. (1988), "Retrospect and Prospect of the Gorbachev Economic Reform," *NIRA Seisaku Kenkyu*, 1(3), 4–8 (in Japanese).

Montias, J. M. (1959), "Planning with Material Balances in Soviet-Type Economies," *American Economic Review* 49, Dec., 963–985.

Morishima, M. (1961), "Proof of a Turnpike Theorem: the "No Joint Production Case"," *Review of Economic Studies*, Feb., 89–97.

Morishima, M. (1973), *Marx's economics*, Cambrige.

Morishima, M. (1976), *The Economic Theory of Modern Society*, London. (The original Japanese version was published in 1973.)

Morishima, M. (1978), *Value, Exploitation and Growth*, London.

Movshovich, S. M. (1972), "Magistpal'nyi rost v dinamicheskikh narodnokhzi-aistvennykh Modeliakh," *Ekonomika i matematicheskie metody*, No. 2.

Movshovich, S. M. (1983), "Tsenoobrazovanie po zamykaiushchim zatratam i effekty v usloviiakh tsentralizovannogo planirovaniia," *Ekonomika i matematicheskie metody*, No. 4.

Mstislavsky, P. (1961), "O kolichestvennom vyrazhenii ekonomicheskikh sviazei i protsessov," *Voprocy ekonomiki*, No. 2.

Nemchinov, V. S. (1956), "Primenenie normativnoi statistiki pri izuchenii proizvoditel'nosti truda v sel'skom khoziaictve," *Uchenye zapiski po statistike*,

REFERENCES

Vol. II.

Nemchinov, V. S. ed. (1959), *Primenenie matemakiki v ekonomicheskikh issledovaniiakh*, Moscow. (the English version: Nove, A. ed., *The Use of Mathematics in Economics*, Edinburgh, 1964.)

Nemchinov, V. S. (1964), "Sotsialisticheskoe khoziaistvovanie i planirovanie proizvodstva," *Kommunist*, No. 5. [English edition: Scharpe, M. E. (1966, pp. 173–192)].

Nemchinov, V. S. (1970), *Obshchestvennaia stoimost' i planovaia tsena*, Moscow.

Nikaido, H. (1968), *Convex Structures and Economic Theory*, New York.

NIRA (Sato, T. ed.) (1987), *Medium-and-Long Term Forecasting of the Soviet Economy*, Tokyo (in Japanese).

Nove, A. (1979), "Recent Developments in East European Economies," in Gustafsson (1979), 119–142.

Novozhilov, V. V. (1926), "Nedostatok tovarov," *Vestnik Finansov*, No. 2.

Novozhilov, V. V. (1959) "Izmerenie zatrat i ikh rezul'tatov v sotsialisticheskom khoziaistve, in Nemchinov ed., (1959, 42–213).

Novozhilov, V. V. (1967), "Novyi etap razvitiia sistemy upravleniia sovetsko ekonomikoi," *Ekonomika i matematicheskie metody*, No. 5.

Novozhilov, V. V. (1972), *Problemy izmereniia zatrat i rezul'tatov pri optimal'nom planirovanii*, Moscow.

Obshchie voprocy primeneniia matematiki v ekonomike i planirovanii, Moscow 1961.

Oka, M. (1963), *Essays on the Theory of planned Economy*, Tokyo (in Japanese).

Okishio, N. (1957), *The Theory of Reproduction*, Tokyo, (in Japanese).

O korennoi perestroike upravleniia ekonomikoi, Moscow, 1987.

Oldak, P. (1988), "Politicheskaia ekonomiia sotsializma na novom rubedze," *EKO*, No. 4.

"Osnovnye polozheniia korennoi perestroiki upravleniia ekonomikoi," *Pravda*, 27 June, 1987.

Pavlov, V. S. (1987), "Radikal'naia reforma tsenoobrazovaniia," *Pravda*, 25 Aug.

REFERENCES

Petrakov, N. (1970), "Upravlenie ekonomikoi i ekonomicheskie interesy," *Novyi mir*, No. 8.

Petrakov, N. Ia. (1983), "Ob otrazhenii planovykh material'no-veshcestvennykh proportsii v sisteme tsen," *Ekonomika i matematicheskie metody*, No. 2.

Petrakov, N. Ia. (1987a), "Planovaia tsena v sisteme upravleniia narodnym khoziaistvom," *Voprosy ekonomiki*, No. 1.

Petrakov, N. Ia. (1987b), "Prospects for Change in the Systems of Price Formation, Finance and Credit in the USSR," *Soviet Economy*, 3(2), 135–144.

Petrakov, N. Ia. (1987c), "Management Processes in a Planned Economy," *Economic Analysis and Interdisciplinarity*, 113, 377–385.

Petrakov, N. Ia., Volkonsky, V. A., and Vavilov, A. P. (1987), "Tsena: Nuzhny krutye izmereniia," *Sotsialisticheskaia industriia*, 3 April.

Polterovich, V. M. (1969), "Blochnye metody vognutogo programmirovaniia i ikh ekonomicheskaia interpretatsiia," *Ekonomika i matematicheskie metody*, No. 6.

Polterovich, V. M. (1978), "Ravnovesnye traektorii ekonomicheskogo rosta," Efimov,B.A. ed., *Metody funktsional'nogo analyza v matematicheskoi ekonomike*, Moscow. [English version: *Econometrica*, May 1983, 693–729.]

Polterovich, V. M. (1986), "Optimal'noe raspredelenie resursov po stabil'nym i dogovornym tsenam (model' sinteza mekhanizmov)", *Ekonomika i matematicheskie metody*, No. 5.

Popov, P. I. (1926), *Balans narodnogo khoziaistva Soiuza SSR 1923–24 goda*, Moscow.

Popov, G. Kh. (1987), "Ekonomichesky realizm: izmenenie otnosheniia k kontrol'nym tsifram (Economic Realism: Changed Attitude Towards Target Figures)," *Moskovskie novosti (Moscow News)*, No. 31, 2 Aug.

Popov, G. Kh. (1988), "Konservatory i avangardity," *Sovetskaia kul'tura*, 5 Jan.

Rabinovich, I. N. (1980), "O dostatochnykh usloviiakh skhodimosti algoritmov iterativnogo agregirovaniia", *Matematicheskie metody resheniia ekonomicheskikh zadach*, Sbornik 9, Moscow.

Rakitsky, B. (1987), "Problemy perestroiki politicheskoi ekonomii sotsializma," *Voprosy ekonomiki*, No. 10. [English version: *Problems of Economics*, Aug., 1988, 24–41.]

REFERENCES

Rasmussen, P. N. (1956), *Studies in Inter-Sectoral Relations*, Amsterdam.

Schroeder, G. E. (1969), "The 1966–67 Soviet Industrial Price Reform: A Study of Complications," *Soviet Studies*, 20(4), April, 462–477.

Seliunin, B. (1988), "Tempy rosta na vesakh potrebleniia," *Sotsialisticheskaia industriia*, 5 Jan.

Seliunin, V. and Khanin, G. (1987), "Lukavaia tsifra," *Novyi mir*, No. 2.

Seneta, E. (1981), *Non-negative Matrices and Markov Chains*, 2nd ed., New York.

Seneta, E. (1984), "Iterative Aggregation: Convergence Rate," *Economics Letters, 14, 357–361.*

Seton, F. (1981), "A Quasi-Competitive Price Basis for Intersystem Comparisons of Economic Structure and Performance," *Journal of Comparative Economics*, 5(5) December, 367–391.

Seton, F. (1985), *Cost, Use, and Value*, Oxford.

Sharpe, M. E., ed. (1966), *Planning, Profit and Incentives in the USSR (Vol. I: The Liberman Discussion)*, New York.

Shchevelev, Ia. v. (1984), "Primenenie diskontirovannykh zatrat dlia otsenki effektivnosti khoziaisvennykh meropriiatii v iadevnoi energetike," *Ekonomika i matematicheskie metody*, No. 6.

Shemelev, N. (1987), "Avansy i dolgi," *Novyi mir*, No. 6. [English version: *Problems of Economics*, Feb. 1988, 1–43.]

Shemetov, P. V. (1983), *Ekonomicheskaia issledovaniia v Sibiri*, Novosibirsk.

Shubkin, V. (1987), "Biurokratiia," *Znamia*, April.

Shukov, N. S. (1987), "Matematicheskaia ekonomiia v Rossii (1867–1917)," *Ekonomika i matematicheskie metody*, No. 4. [English version: *Matekon*, 24 (3), 3–31.]

Slutsky, E. E. (1927), "Zur Kritik des Bohm-Bawerkschen Wertbegriffs und seiner Lehre von der Messbarkeit des Wertes," *Schmoller's Jahrbuch fur Gesetzgebung, Verwaltung und Volkswirtshaft*, No. 4.

Smekhov, B. (1987), *Logika planirovaniia*, Moscow.

Spulber, N. ed. (1964), *Foundations of Soviet strategy for economic growth*, Bloomington.

REFERENCES

Stahmer, C. (1985), "Transformation Matrices in Input-Output Compilation," the paper presented at IIASA Task Force Meeting on Input-Output Modeling.

Starovsky, V. (1957), "XX s"ezd KPSS i zadachi sovetskoi statistiki," *Vestnik statistiki*, No. 2.

Sverdlik, Sh. B. (1981), *Obshchestvennyi produkt i denezhnei oborot*, Novosibirsk.

Stone, R. (1961), *Input-Output and National Accounts*, Paris.

ten Raa, Th. (1986), "Dynamic Input-Output Analysis with Distributed Activities," the paper presented at the 8th International Conference on Input-Output Techniques in Sapporo, Japan.

Tochilin, V. A. (1979), *Tseny i optimizatziia mezhotraslevykh sviazei*, Kiev.

Treml, V. G. (1964), "Economic Interrelations in the Soviet Union," U. S. Congress Joint Economic Committee, *Annual Economic Indicators for the U. S. S. R.*, Washington, D. C.

Treml, V. G. (1966), "The 1959 Soviet Input-Output Table (As Reconstructed)," U. S. Congress Joint Economic Committee, *New Directions in the Soviet Economy*, Part-A Washington, D. C.

Treml, V. G. et al. (1972), *The Structure of the Soviet Economy*, New York.

Treml, V. G. et al. (1973), "Interindustry Structure of the Soviet Economy: 1959 and 1966," U.S.Congress Joint Economic Committee, *Soviet Economic Prospects for the Seventies*, Washington, D. C.

Treml, V. G. et al. (1973), "Conversion of Soviet Input-Output Tables to Producers' Prices: The 1966 Reconstructed Tables," U. S. Dept. of Commerce, *Foreign Economic Report*, No. 1.

Treml, V. G. et al. (1976), "The Soviet 1966 and 1972 Input-Output Tables," U. S. Congress Joint Economic Committee, *Soviet Economy in a New Perspective*, Washington, D. C.

Treml, V. G. ed. (1977), *Studies in Soviet Input-Output Analysis*, New York.

Tretyakova, A. and Birman, I. (1976), "Input-Output Analysis in the USSR," *Soviet Studies*, April 1976, 157–186.

Tsukui, J. and Murakami, Y. (1979), *Turnpike Optimality in Input-Output System*, Amsterdam.

UN; SNA (1968), *A Sysrem of National Accounts*, New York.

REFERENCES

UN (1977), *Structure and Change in European Industry*, New York.

UNSO; United Nations Statistical Office (1985), "Study of Country Practices in Implementing the SNA Input-Output Framework in the 70 's,', A Draft for Meeting for the ECE Working Party on National Accounts and Balances, Geneva, 1986.

Vakhutinsky, I. Ia., Dudkin, L. M. and Ryvkin, A. A. (1979), "Iterative Aggregation: A New Approach to the Solution of Large Scale Problems," *Econometrica*, 47(4), 821–841.

Vakhutinsky, I. Ia. (1979), "Odin protsess iterativnogo agregirovaniia dlia resheniia zadachii vypuklogo chastichno separabil'nogo programmirovaniia," *Doklady Akademii Nauk SSSR*, 195, No. 6.

Vavilov, A. P. (1986), *Metody opredelenia urovnei normativov prirostnykh zatrat* (Dis. na soisk. uchen. step. kand. ekon. nauk), Moscow.

Vavilov, A. P., Volkonsky, V. A., Kuzovkin, A. I., Pavlov, N. V., Petrakov, N. Ia., Solov'ev, Iu. P. and Iasin, E. G. (1986), "Metody ucheta renty v tsenakh i planovykh raschetakh," *Ekonomika i matematicheskie metody*, No. 5. [English version: Matekon, 23(3), 3–27.]

Ven, V. L. and Babadzhanian, M. N. ed. (1986), *Teoriia i praktika ispol'zovaniia metodov agregirovaniia v planirovanii i upravlenii*, Erevan.

Volkonsky, V. A. (1965), "Optimal'noe planirovanie v usloviiakh bol'shoi razmernosti. Iterativnye metody i printsip dekompozitsii," *Ekonomika i matematicheskie metody*, No. 2.

Volkonsky, V. A. (1967), *Model' optimal'nogo planirovaniia i vzaimosviazi ekonomicheskikh pokazatelei*, Moscow.

Volkonsky, V. A. (1973), *Printsipy optimal'nogo planirovaniia*, Moscow.

Volkonsky, V. A. (1981), *Problemy sovershenstvovaniia khoziaistvennogo mekhanizma*, Moscow.

Volkonsky, V. A. and Vavilov, A. P. (1987), "Tseny i prirostnye zatraty," *Eko*, No. 4.

Volkonsky, V. A., Arushaniia I. I., Vavilov, A. P. and Povlov, N. V. (1987), *Peresmotr tsen i igo finansovye aspekty*, (mimeo.), Moscow.

Zauberman, A. (1967), *Aspects of Planometrics*, London.

Zauberman, A. (1976), *Mathematical Theory in Soviet Planning*, London.

REFERENCES

Zhuravlev, S. N. (1981), O resheniiakh dinamicheskoi mezhotraslevoi modeli s kriteriem maksimuma fonda potrebleniia, *Ekonomika i matematicheskie metody*, No. 2. [English version: *Matekon*, 18(3), 50–64.]

KEY WORD INDEX